Multicultural Girlhood

In the series *Global Youth,*
edited by Craig Jeffrey and Jane Dyson

Also in this series:

Daniel Mains, *Hope Is Cut: Youth, Unemployment, and the
Future in Urban Ethiopia*

Multicultural Girlhood

Racism, Sexuality, and the Conflicted Spaces of American Education

Mary E. Thomas

TEMPLE UNIVERSITY PRESS
Philadelphia

TEMPLE UNIVERSITY PRESS
Philadelphia, Pennsylvania 19122
www.temple.edu/tempress

Library of Congress Cataloging-in-Publication Data

Thomas, Mary E. (Mary Elizabeth), 1970–
   Multicultural girlhood : racism, sexuality, and the conflicted spaces of American education /
Mary E. Thomas.
      p. cm. — (Global youth)
   Includes bibliographical references and index.
   ISBN 978-1-4399-0731-3 (cloth : alk. paper) — ISBN 978-1-4399-0732-0 (pbk. : alk. paper) —
ISBN 978-1-4399-0733-7 (e-book)   1. Teenage girls—United States.   2. Minority teenagers—
'United States.   3. Multiculturalism—United States.   4. Racism—United States.   5. Social
interaction in adolescence—United States.   I. Title.
   HQ798.T46 2011
   305.800973—dc22

                                                                                    2011015414

∞ The paper used in this publication meets the requirements of the American National
Standard for Information Sciences—Permanence of Paper for Printed Library Materials,
ANSI Z39.48-1992

Printed in the United States of America

2 4 6 8 9 7 5 3 1

Contents

Acknowledgments

Anyone who has written a book will know exactly what I mean when I say I am so happy to be finished. Part of the pleasure of being done is that I can finally give credit, where it is due, to those many friends and colleagues who have carried me through this book's completion. Most importantly, I thank the girls. I owe my entire career to the young women who were courageous enough to pick up the phone and call a stranger's number from a flier. Their openness and interest propels my thinking always, even though many may disagree with my final arguments. Thank you all for being a part of my life so briefly in person and so lastingly in effect. Thanks must also go to the girls' parents, almost exclusively mothers, for allowing their daughters to meet with me.

This research project owes its existence to Ed Jackiewicz and his San Fernando Valley network. In some ways, the project was an accident that Ed facilitated. Although I cannot thank the teachers or the principal of the high school by name, their help and their approval of the project were

Note: A portion of Chapter 2 was previously published as Mary Thomas, "The Paradoxes of Personhood: Banal Multiculturalism and Racial-Ethnic Identification among Latina and Armenian Girls at a Los Angeles High School," *Environment and Planning A* 40, no. 12 (2008): 2864–2878. Used with permission of Pion Limited, London. A portion of Chapter 4 was previously published as Mary Thomas, "The Identity Politics of School Life: Territoriality and the Racial Subjectivity of Teenage Girls in LA," *Children's Geographies* 7, no. 1 (2009): 7–19. I gratefully acknowledge Taylor and Francis for affording me the right to reuse this material.

generous, and I am greatly indebted to them. The research project was conducted while I was a faculty member in the Department of Geography at the University of California–Los Angeles and was funded by a UCLA Faculty Senate Grant. I thank my treasured and greatly missed colleagues at UCLA, who were always wonderfully supportive.

At Ohio State University, I benefited from a Coca-Cola Critical Difference for Women Faculty Research Grant, a Social and Behavioral Sciences Small Grant, and research support from the Department of Women's, Gender, and Sexuality Studies (WGSS). I especially thank my WGSS chair, Jill Bystydzienski, for her unfailing support, as well as my feminist comrades and friends in the department. I also thank my colleagues in the Department of Geography at OSU for their support of the project. My WGSS colleagues Cricket Keating and Shannon Winnubst are due special recognition for reading chapters and pushing my thinking. My research assistant at OSU, Katie Linder, did a superb job with the interview transcriptions. A special note of appreciation goes to Tanya Erzen, who read more versions of the Introduction than any friend should have to read. Her sharp intellect and supreme editorial eye are represented throughout this book. I also thank my dear Columbus friends, especially Janel, Marc, Susan, Steve, Shannon, Jenny, Tanya, and Bill, for reminding me of the joys beyond work during the time of this book's writing.

For advice and help with sections of the book, I thank Ishan Ashutosh, Bruce Braun, Adriane Brown, Caitlin Cahill, Mathew Coleman, Rachel Colls, Kathrin Hörschelmann, Cindi Katz, Gerry Kearns, Megan Kough, Natalie Oswin, Karen Till, and Joel Wainwright. The editors of the Temple University Press series *Global Youth*, Craig Jeffrey and Jane Dyson, provided keen input and carefully shepherded the book through the manuscript stage. Craig's collegiality and kindness were the important first steps of our collaboration, and I owe him hearty thanks for making academic work less lonely. My Temple University Press editor, Mick Gusinde-Duffy, is simply a gem; I thank him for everything he does. The anonymous reviewers for Temple University Press provided a strong push that aided my thinking and guided the book toward more substantial arguments.

Finally, I end by thanking my family. My parents, Patricia Thomas and Edward Thomas, and my sister, Carrie Thomas, have provided me with over forty years of unfailing support and love. I probably would not have become an academic if my sister hadn't forged the path first. I am fortunate to count the Colemans as family and to have their humor and goodwill in my world. Finally, and most of all, I thank my husband, Mathew Coleman, and our son, Thomas Cosmo Coleman. Thomas's sweet nature and lovely laugh—and insistence that I share his ice cream—make each day so delicious. Boys may outnumber me at home, but Mathew's feminist passion and commitment sometimes rival even my own. He brings everything together for me.

Multicultural Girlhood

1

Introduction

Why Can't We Just Get Along?

One spring morning in 2005, I contacted a high school principal in the San Fernando Valley of Los Angeles about the possibility of doing research with teen girls at her school. By coincidence, a large fight broke out at noon that day on the school campus. Over the lunchtime break, hundreds of Armenian and Latino students, almost exclusively boys, battled each other in the center of campus, where their segregated turfs met. The LA Police Department was summoned, the school was locked down, and the students were allowed to leave only under police escort in groups of two or three after the police finished a weapons sweep several hours later. Thrown trash cans, scattered litter, and the mess of hurled food—from milk to chicken patties to bananas—left the school campus in complete disarray. Fearing retaliatory fighting—a false fear as it turned out—hundreds of students stayed away from school the next day, and a mostly regular routine then quickly reestablished itself.

This fight was not the first racial brawl in this school's history, and the city of Los Angeles had witnessed several highly publicized race riots that year, from South Los Angeles to the San Fernando Valley. That same spring, the Los Angeles Unified School District (LAUSD) released data showing that campus hate crimes had surged in the previous decade by over 300 percent; most were race related. School officials claimed that better reporting contributed to the growth in hate crime numbers, but they also conceded that racial tension and violence were major problems in the nation's second largest school district. José Huizar, then the president of the Board of Education (and now a city council member), suggested that a new era of heightened racial tensions in LA schools had begun, and he tied these tensions to the city's welfare: "The bigger question is, is this a prelude to what the city of Los Angeles will be facing in the next five to ten years— these same types of issues on the city streets? We need to help them deal with the issues at schools or the city has to prepare itself" (quoted in Boghossian and Sodders 2005). That warning, of course, recalls the memorable 1992 LA Riots and 1965 Watts Riots, which were both sparked by racial tensions with police. The city's history and urban geography are intimately entwined with racial violence. Huizar's urgent warning brings that context to the schools. To him, fixing school racial violence is the frontline struggle for ensuring peaceful urban futures. I came to see that youth make similar connections between school fights and the prospects for race relations in both the city and the nation.

The high school principal returned my e-mail inquiry that same day. Surprisingly, she made no mention of the riot; she merely consented to the project, which set me loose on campus to recruit interviewees. After I received final approval from my university's Institutional Review Board, I arranged to visit the school; the front office staff gave me a campus map and pointed me in the direction of a classroom where I had been offered a pulpit to explain my research goals to the students. There were no security precautions, and I met with no administrators. The administration at that time was not overly anxious, although that situation may have since changed. Since that violent spring, LAUSD has allocated over $4 million for new security officers for its secondary schools.

Part of my pitch to the students was a brief—and, I hoped, enticing— lesson on social geography. I talked about place, identity, and migration—topics that the vast majority of them could easily relate to since, overwhelmingly, they were first- or second-generation Americans. The students were relieved to have a change in routine for the day and quickly engaged with me about the importance of geography for a person's sense of her or his place in the world. My presentation was brief, however, and I had only a short conversation with them before I distributed the fliers and left.

The real lessons came after I spoke to twenty-six girls over the next two months about what became known as simply "the riot," and about school life and race relations, geography, identity, and migration. The riot predictably took center stage in these interviews. Each girl, across all racial identities, denounced the outbreak of racist violence at the school and adamantly called for multicultural understanding and peaceful coexistence at school. In 1992, Rodney King, the famous victim of LA police brutality, implored Angelinos in the bloody aftermath of his aggressors' acquittals, "Can we get along?" But the girls reinterpreted this refrain and struggled instead with the issues, feelings, and other people who stood in the way of racial harmony. This book attempts to answer the question "Why can't we just get along?"

The Effects of Banal Multiculturalism on American Girlhood

My aim is to interrogate the subjectivity of girls by exploring the themes of multiculturalism, school segregation, sexuality, race and ethnicity, family life, migration, and girls' struggles with an urban educational system that they think has abandoned them. As a feminist geographer, I draw particular attention to the spaces of girls' identities and daily practices. Like many schools in multiracial U.S. cities, this particular high school's campus is dramatically marked by racial segregation. There are few liminal spaces for integrated socializing. The spaces of segregated urban education are no mere backdrops to youth violence, however, and I show the importance of accounting for the active production and maintenance of such contexts. Racism and sexism are defined through everyday spatial interactions and contexts, and space contours the possible responses to segregative tendencies of girls. The most important spaces to the girls I interviewed are school niches and territories (including those shaped by multicultural education), public urban consumption spaces, families, and homes.

Many of the girls are first- or second-generation Americans, and their global and national space making mark significance beyond their immediate contexts; the space of school violence extends far beyond their school campus (see Holloway et al. 2010). Geography can offer vital insight for educators seeking an end to racial violence in urban schools. Perhaps understanding the spaces of youth subjectivity will help to interrogate consumerist multiculturalism as the "fix" to local urban segregation. To youth, the school is as much a global and familial space as it is a local place to meet friends and get an education. Simplistic prescriptions that are focused merely at the local—or on the body of a girl or a boy—fail to address challenges that require a much wider geographic lens (see Holloway et al. 2010; Ansell 2009a; Evans 2008; Holt and Holloway 2006; Jeffrey and McDowell 2004; Katz 2004; Nayak 2003a; Aitken 2001a, 2001b; Holloway and Valentine 2000). Focusing on schools as the frontline struggle of peaceful urban futures neglects that spatial complexity and places even more responsibility on youth to overcome their intimate, emotional, and material geographies. The girls' family stories about place and national belonging, their struggles with generational change through migration, and their self-evaluations within the constraints of American white hegemony illustrate how these teens acculturate to idealized girlhood, even though they do not nearly approximate its white, feminine, middle-class embodiment.

The girls themselves did not understand racial and school conflicts within this complex geography. Instead, they vociferously pointed to boys' fighting as the cause of the riot, repeatedly calling it "stupid." Yet I argue in this book that this reproach and the girls' desire to get along mask their own investments in racial, class, and gender-sexual differences and hierarchy. As they pleaded for racial harmony, sometimes in the very next breath, the girls also overwhelmingly articulated racist resentment and detailed their markedly segregated social practices at home, at school, and in the city. With few exceptions, the Armenian, Latina, Filipina, and African American girls I met did not have close friendships with girls outside their own race or ethnicity. Those who did have friends of other races or ethnicities did not visit each other's home or get together in the city beyond the school campus. Out of the twenty-six girls I met, I encountered only two exceptions.

The girls detailed their racism by describing others in terms of their body odor, unpropitious femininity and sexuality, scary masculinity, below-the-belt fighting tactics, unfair government aid and preference, and easier national belonging after immigration. In turn, the girls depicted the poor treatment they felt that they constantly received from others. "Getting along" was an easy and persistent fantasy, but it became harder and harder for me to see it as a practical motivation for easing the ills of racial tension at the school. Racial epithets, misogyny, distrust, and emotional-economic resentment were more common themes from the girls' daily lives. Throughout my interviews, despite what I heard as loud and pervasive racism in their narratives, the girls insisted that they were always the victims of racism, never the perpetrators. They were largely unaware of the racist and misogynist beliefs often embedded in their own stories because they time and again repeated this heartfelt question: "Why can't we just get along?" Yet oblique racism is deeply instructive. The mutual commitment to postracial space, where everyone is equal and happily coexists, and racist differentiation, where no one admits culpability and feels deep resentment to others while also feeling deeply wounded by others, illustrates something important about the range of possible selves in contemporary times (see Brown 1996, 2006). These American selves are intimately framed through banal multiculturalism and the fantasy that America is a postracial society.

I use the word *banal* as a qualifier to indicate that multicultural programming has become rote in many public high schools, while its purposes are unexplained and uncontextualized to students. While Maria Lugones and Joshua Price (1995: 103) suggest that such forms of multiculturalism result in an appreciation of diversity without an *effect* on other cultures, I suggest, to the contrary, that the effects of everyday saturation of uncritical banal multiculturalism are palpable (see also Ahmed 2010; Fortier 2008). Multiculturalism shapes contemporary forms of racialization and racial identifications; it racializes subjects within a narrow definition of cultural expression. Some even argue that banal multiculturalism actually exacerbates conflicts by stoking the fires of racial-ethnic resentment (Lustig 1997). Rarely do public urban high schools, either through curricular or extracurricular programs, approach the difficult issues of ongoing social, racial, and economic inequality and questions of privilege in the United States (Gillborn 2005; see also Roberts, Bell, and Murphy 2008). Public schools do not systematically teach students about the trenchant racism and the economic disparity that fuel racial-ethnic differences and segregation (Fordham 1996). Such a focus would indicate a radical shift in U.S. education policy and practice that currently emphasizes standardization and neoliberal school accountability—not to mention status quo social, political, and capitalist systems, which are reflected in part by the tracking of students (Stearns 2004; Perry 2002). Critical multiculturalism—that is, multiculturalism that contends that only profound social, economic, and political change will bring about the achievement of diversity and equality—has had only limited impact in urban U.S. high schools.

Compounding the banal multiculturalism of American education is a dominant consumer economy that teaches today's young women to celebrate (and purchase) their femininity and gender strength (Deutsch and Theodorou 2010; Zaslow 2009). Postfeminism emphasizes individualized gendered agency, yet its facile investment in girl power leaves young women responsible for fixing the same disempowering structures of difference that also give them their identities (Charlton 2007; Gonick 2006; Currie 1999). As "girls with power," they are told that they can be feminine *and* fight misogyny, even though femininity is thoroughly defined through misogynist foundations. Postfeminism also implies that girls and young women can redirect cultural forms and products away from the inequities of capitalism or the imprint of sexism and misogyny (McRobbie 2009). Girl power itself is largely framed around middle-class consumption and white hegemonic ideals of the primacy of a gendered agency not marked by color (Aapola, Gonick, and Harris 2005). Thus, both dominant and banal forms of multiculturalism and postfeminism insist that girls have pride in their gender-sexualities, race, and ethnicities. Yet both insist that youth assimilate to white hegemonic standards of success, comportment, and citizenship, especially in educational spaces. Both emphasize the responsibility of the individual girl, and both fail to situate the girl within multiple structures of exploitation and status quo education (Hey 2009; Lee 2005). These conflicting messages help to explain how the girls call for racial belonging with a strong feminine voice: "Boys are stupid; why can't we just get along?"

On the other hand, a simple rebuttal of these messages risks placing responsibility for fixing racism on youth. Accusing girls, especially girls who are racial-ethnic minorities in the United States, of racism is a difficult indict-ment for me to make—both personally and politically. As a feminist and anti-racist scholar, I do not want to produce a project that insinuates a "blame the victim" bottom line. Unfortunately, the existing scholarship on American girl-hood offers little advice on how to examine racism, segregation, classism, and misogyny among nonwhite girls. The tendency instead is to concentrate on the agency of girls and young women—their ability to "build identities" (Deutsch 2008) and resist negative racialization given white hegemony, poverty, sexism, and heteronormativity (e.g., Sears 2010; Sharma 2010). From this vantage point, girl power's weighty assumptions suggest that all girls can design new subjectivities for themselves, enjoy their youthful individuality, celebrate mul-ticulturalism, and control the contours of their sexuality—in sum, an agency for self-creation and pleasure however they choose to define these concepts. This tone implies that girls not only have the capacity but also want to choose girlhoods that are racially and sexually progressive, feminist, and optimistic (Gonick et al. 2009). However, clearly not all girls share the sexual politics and antiracism of the feminist scholars who examine their practices.

Saba Mahmood (2005: 7) points out that this sort of predominant feminist notion "locates agency in the political and moral autonomy of the subject." Agency, she argues, must be delinked from liberal feminist assumptions that all subjects are inclined toward progressive politics. Such assumptions are deeply problematic because women and girls do not necessarily desire "to be free from relations of subordination" (10); nor do they necessarily have the capacity for freedom beyond social norms and subordinating structures. Rather, Mahmood asserts, agency is also found "in the multiple ways in which one *inhabits* norms" (15). Her critique is instructive as a counterlogic to girlhood studies of the at-risk, minority girl. When agency is a gendered and racialized potential in the body of a girl, subjectivity is decoupled from subordination. To fit the feminist profile of human agency that Mahmood criticizes, a girl must be able to exert her agency against not only the social forces oppressing her but also the very legibility of her own body.

It is therefore vital that the range of beliefs and practices of girls be consid-ered as much as their resistant accomplishments and possibilities for "future girls" (Harris 2004). Focusing on girls' agential voices closes down a possible reading of their conservative practices. Both are important, obviously, but situating agency as the organizing analysis in yet another text (i.e., providing another story about girl power) would be an injustice to understanding the lives of these girls, a misreading of their subjectivities, and an illusion that girl power articulated by individual girls can undo oppression. That these girls are not white poses another challenge: how to theorize girls as racist and segregationist while also unburdening them of the individualized "choice" to undo violent American racism and hegemonic whiteness simply through their own volition. Indeed, personal, social, and spatial constraints mean that the girls' promises of getting along are difficult, if not impossible. Instead, we need a better theory for how girls contend with the powerful mixed messages with which they are barraged in a supposedly postracial and postfeminist but trenchantly extremely racist and sexist America.

The Subjects of Girlhood

Girlhood is burdened by both the responsibility posed by multicultural girl power and the problems and risks of young femininity—of indelible bodies and personalities. The girlhoods of self-harm, alleged growing meanness and delinquency, violently entrenched racial segregation, and sexuality run amok are girlhoods that do not live up to the celebratory promises of girl power, postfeminism, and postracial American diversity. Anita Harris classifies these kinds of girlhoods as "can-do" and "at-risk," arguing that the intense scrutiny of girls in Western, late modernity indicates an intense anxiety about normalization and its failures. The effects are all too real for girls themselves. The can-do girls get mainstream status with its attendant privileges, while those girls who fail to live up to the promises of a neoliberal economy and a multicultural society must shoulder the blame for succumbing to their risks (2004: 16).

Let's be clear about who these at-risk girls are, particularly in the United States: they are certainly not suburban whites, the middle class, or the upwardly mobile. Moral panic about inner-city and migrant girl gangs, juvenile delinquency, teen pregnancy and parenting, or even soulless consumption illustrates the social stakes placed on urban, at-risk girlhood and the pressures that police girls' bodies and punish their transgressions and crimes (see also N. Jones 2010; Miller 2008; Chesney-Lind and Irwin 2004; Alder and Worrall 2004; Aitken 2001b). The overwhelming focus on risk by scholars studying nonwhite girls leads to a narrow examination of the individual, with an intensely local lens and a resulting call to arms to empower girls. Individual psychology displaces an analysis of the constraints of identity and relations of power (Walkerdine, Lucey, and Melody 2001: 32; Hey 2009: 22; compare Gagen 2006). Again, this is true of both banal multiculturalism and postfeminism. Fostering positive and prideful racial-gender-sexual identities for girls often becomes the fix for risk.

Unfortunately such a widespread investment in the individual reflects only a victim-hero dichotomy for girls of color. Strong girls are those who can harness a racialized agency to meet their daily hardships. (This agency might even be the ability to "fight back" by learning to counter violence with violence; see N. Jones [2010].) Victimized girls, on the other hand, simply cannot harness racialized agency. The hero-victim dichotomy burdens girls to fix the conditions of their lives, despite the conditions often being far beyond their control.

Scores of studies rightly document the overwhelming odds against urban, poor, nonwhite, and migrant girls in the United States, yet reinscribing agency as a formula for addressing these odds dilutes the importance of spatial and institutional disempowerment over the life course. Girls might know that the cards are stacked against them in many ways (see, e.g., Miller 2008), but a loud message embedded in many programs for girls is that they must make do as independent players by relying on themselves and their own strength to make their lives livable (Alonso et al. 2009). This fact becomes especially true as they become older adolescents and young women.

Scholars often emphasize that institutional settings for youth can offer supporting roles in the development of agency. The institution, in other words, is meant to bring out the best prospects of youth by providing a helping hand on the road to individual development (e.g., afterschool programs; see Deutsch 2008). Schools are an obvious example. However, self-help remains paramount. Institutions provide contexts for youth to develop an ability to make good and moral decisions—that is, graduate, remain childless, avoid violence, obey the law, and respect one another (compare Alonso et al. 2009). This ability ensures that girls can remain strong once they exit the institutional space—such as the school—that marks a particular time of life. The psychological development of girls with respect to agency, then, is not seen to be contingent on the institutional spaces where a girl is supposed to learn to be independent. Obviously, her mobility over time and space ensures that she will exit these institutions, but hope is placed on her ability to maintain her good sense and the capacity for good decisions once she grows out of the spatial context of the institution. She is expected to carry the lessons of her strong agency and capability to forge positive futures from one space to another, despite extreme variation in levels of support in different contexts and spaces (familial, financial, emotional, or other).

The Conflicting Geographies of Girlhood

Throughout this book, the girls' stories paint a picture of their school that shows a stark contrast. While they often insisted that personally they could "get along" with everyone, they also identified the strict segregation on campus. The way they identified themselves—as postracial, peace-loving girls—in fact hit the wall of geography. Their ideal selves did not match the spaces they created and adapted themselves to; simply put, the strict segregation on campus did not accommodate the images they gave me of their best selves. Consider, for instance, the following note from Mayra, a fifteen-year-old, self-described Hispanic girl (all names are pseudonyms that the girls chose for themselves). She wrote the note to accompany some photographs of her school's territories that she took for me. Mayra's depictions succinctly

Figure 1.1 The Armenian "forest." *(Photo by Mayra; used with permission and parental consent.)*

illustrate the spatial, racial logic of her urban school, that wall of geography that youth hit every day on campus:

My school is shaped like a rectangle. There is a big piece of grass in the middle and surrounding the piece of lawn are four sides lined up with buildings. The Punks, Goths, and Rockers hang out on one side of the school. Most of them are Whites and Asians. They hang out on the lawn or on the left side of school. One of my best friends [who is white] hangs out there and although she's my best friend, we don't hang out [there] together. On the opposite side of the punks, there's the place where the gangsters hang out. That building is where their main spot is. You will not see Armenians there because mainly Hispanics hang out there. On the up side of school is where the preps, "pretty people," and populars hang out. The lower side of school, "the forest," is where the Armenians hang out [Figure 1.1]. You won't see Hispanics there because this is their [Armenian] territory. The gangster spot and the Armenian spot are divided and the picture shows you the "border line" that divides these two [Figure 1.2]. Where there are fights between the two, they meet up here and that's where it happens. And finally there's the picture which explains all four major hang out spots and where they are located [Figure 1.3].

Figure 1.2 The 300s building marks the "border line" between Latinos and Armenians. *(Photo by Mayra; used with permission and parental consent.)*

Figure 1.3 Central campus and its cliques. *(Photo by Mayra; used with permission and parental consent.)*

The campus is divided into student cliques that self-congregate into clear turfs, demarcating territories of belonging and exclusion. These might be social groups that come together around a style (e.g., punk rock, hip-hop), a practice (e.g., sports, academic clubs, or gangs), or class (e.g., the preps are rarely the smokers; see Bettie 2003), but it is clear from Mayra's note that they are also segregated by race and ethnicity. In this school, many are new immigrants, so language is also important. Mostly, as Mayra's description tells us, the spaces of school segregation combine all three groupings: social activities, race, and class provide the contours of youth groupings and interactions. The strict segregation of the groups stands out in Mayra's note about territory and racial exclusion, in contrast to racial mobility and openness on campus. The school's segregated territories, which I discuss throughout this book, are commonly communicated and deeply enforced spaces of racial boundaries, class divisions, heterosexual normativity, and personal styles looking for a peer community. To disregard the complicated interarticulation of all these spaces would be to reduce the impact of the school's spatiality on youth and their understandings of who they are and where they fit in (Jeffrey 2010). The configuration of school space offers a lifelong lesson to youth about social and racial hierarchy (Lewis 2003; Lopez 2003; Hyams 2000; Fordham 1996; hooks 1994; Thorne 1993).

In many ways, youth naturalize the divisions between them at school (Thomas 2005a), assuming that peer groups organically come together because of similar tastes, personalities, and identities. David Delaney (1998: 6) emphatically offers another view: "Complex territorial configurations—and the codes of access, exclusion, and inclusion of which these configurations are the physical expression—are inseparable from the workings of large-scale power orders," which have a long history. He writes:

> [Racial] relations are what they are because of how they are spatialized. The long struggle against racial segregation demonstrates that the spatiality of racism was a central component of the social structure of racial hierarchy, that efforts to transform or maintain these relations entailed the reconfigurations or reinforcing of these geographies, *and* that participants were very much aware of this. Space and power are so tightly bound that changing one necessarily entails changing the other. (7)

While social and legal movements against racial exclusion in U.S. immigration, Jim Crow segregation, and even abolition, to name just a few examples, raised racial consciousness and relied on participants' awareness of injustice and exclusion, the everyday segregation of school space does not always raise the ire of its participants (compare Pollock 2004). In fact, that it does not straightforwardly and consistently do so, despite the struggles of many in the United States to counter racist segregation, calls into question the possibilities of desegregation in contemporary spaces. The struggle for desegregation must not only focus on the large-scale policies of education per se but also work to decenter individual agency and personal responsibility embedded in banal multiculturalism. This struggle requires a new understanding of racial identification and segregation in the American high school as a spatial practice not fully conscious or easily territorialized.

A new color-blind racism, Eduardo Bonilla-Silva (2003) suggests, is at work in the contemporary American framing of race identities, relations, hierarchy, and exclusion. "Overt" racism tends to be relegated to the Jim Crow era (and before), which "explained blacks' social standing as the result of their biological and moral inferiority" (2). Yet in the supposed postracial American meritocracy, it is presumed that everyone enjoys equal status and the freedom to choose the conditions of her or his life. The ideologies of race, framed by white privilege, and the impediments to equality are "opaque, indirect, subtle, and full of apparent ambivalence and even flat-out contradictions" (163–164; see also Lewis 2003). Individualized agency and choice were repeated themes in the girls' narratives about racial segregation in their lives, where a "live and let live" ideal came to represent an explanation for segregation, yet this explanation does not contend with the forces of white supremacy and privilege that form its contours. This explanation also does not account for the legacies of American immigration policy and the subsequent shifts in U.S. demographics that result from it. The everyday understandings of racism in the United States have yet to catch up with these demographic shifts, and the reliance on "overt" racism against African Americans fails to consider new multicultural identities and segregations.

Although segregation was often framed by the girls as a "choice" to self-protect against others' hostility, this view skirts the issue that segregation is always painful, exclusionary, and spatially productive of the material differentiation of bodies. While high school social segregation can be a strategy to self-protect against racism (per Tatum 1997) by emphasizing racial identity, it is problematic to assume that self-segregation is productive at only countering racism. In other words, while self-segregation might be a personal or collective decision to shelter oneself from harmful and hurtful racism, it is simultaneously segregative and a process of spatial differentiation (Thomas 2005a). It relies on a fantasy of neutrality in space, rather than contending with the ways that whiteness enforces racial differentiation (Bonilla-Silva 2003; DiPiero 2002). Also, many examples of what might be so-called protective or positive self-segregation work to reaffirm other prejudices and uphold masculinism, heteronormativity, and classism (something I illustrate throughout this book).

No matter *where* a practice occurs, it is shaped by psychic and spatial processes that may not be evident and are contingent on social and spatial formations and idiosyncratic personalities. Whatever the example—school, street, consumption spaces, homes, hideouts, work—the contingency of spatial propriety, relationality, and interconnectedness imparts normative lessons about identification and practice and the inherent geography of social relationships, conscious or not. (For the variances of space and subjectivity in geography, see Pile 2008.) Through the act of joining her segregated clique on campus, for example, a girl "chooses" her social allegiances. In many of today's urban schools, these are highly gendered, classed, sexualized, and raced (see, e.g., Maira 2009; Bettie 2003; Lewis 2003; Perry 2002). But she encounters a school campus that is *already* shaped by these allegiances, so she clearly has a limited range of choice in the matter.

At the same time, however, the normative spaces of segregation are extremely fragile (compare Butler 2004b; on the precarity of identity and difference, see Butler 2004a). The school yard depicted by Mayra's photographs is defined through the possible spatial transgressions that might tear its logic. She identifies the area where Hispanic "gangsters" gather by stating, "You will not see Armenians there because mainly Hispanics hang out there." In reference to the Armenian "forest," she says, "You won't see Hispanics there because this is their [Armenian] territory." The borderline between these territories marks the zone where transgressions of the racial segregation might turn into fights: "Where there are fights between the two, they meet up here, and that's where it happens." Mayra's account succinctly illustrates the fragile nature of spatial segregation. The border is a site of anxiety because of the ever-present possibility of transgression. There is nothing natural about such divisions; they are highly regulated and policed, while at the same time they are highly precarious—both socially and psychically. Students must actually work very hard day in and day out to maintain the spatial codes on campus, since transgressors could potentially disrupt its logic by simply failing to obey it. This is an emotionally taxing process that is rife with painful exclusions. That girls understand the pain of racial exclusion as primarily individualized further stymies possible collective efforts to undo violent segregation (Brown 1995, 2006).

I make this point not to reinstate racial conciliation as a responsibility of girls through a new conscientiousness but to argue that identity is always painful, conflicted, and multispatial. The young person facing a segregated high school campus does not employ social and psychoanalytic theory when she encounters and feels the terror of social and spatial stratification (or when she does not feel pressure in the least). Youth do not necessarily have the conscious ability to think through all the reasons why they so thoroughly police spatial segregation by excluding those unlike themselves (Ahmed 2000,

2002). Certainly the current state of urban education in the United States does not provide many—or, in some cases, any—critical tools for addressing these arguments, and I return to this point many times in the pages that follow. Girls and all subjects act out everyday lives without fully or consciously knowing why they have acted in one way but not another. The visceral terror, disgust, or anger at spatial transgression also indicates the psychic attachments, the struggle and pain of belonging and being outcast—or perhaps the fear of being seen as just mediocre—and the process of disidentification ("I am not a racist") that is also part of such scenes. Both the conscious and the unconscious are at play when a subject, through everyday practice, takes on social and spatial configurations as aspects of the self and, importantly, when a subject rejects or is precluded from taking on other configurations (Sibley 1995). Segregation, to be sure, is a spatial practice of both group identification *and* exclusion; identification and disidentification are part and parcel of the same act. This book seeks to illuminate the geographies of that ambivalence and conflict.

Putting the Psychoanalytic in Girlhood Subjectivity

I use the term *subjectivity* to denote the ways that a girl comes to think of herself through fundamentally social terms and spaces. The identification processes of becoming an "I" (i.e., "I am an Armenian girl") point to the social differences that are taken up as personal attributes through often unacknowledged or unknown psychic processes: subjects enter into a conditioning and contingent sociality. Tim Dean outlines psychoanalysis as a project less about "'blurring the boundaries' between inner and outer [than] it is [about] revealing how the outside—an alien alterity—inhabits the subject's most intimate inwardness" (2000: 53). Internalizing social meanings is not mechanistic, and different subjects do not place equal value on the objects that they desire and invest in; what is universal is that every subject must take on objects of difference through the processes of subjectivity (Leledakis 1995).

My particular interest in employing psychoanalysis lies in exploring the moments in the girls' narratives that belie the logic of a self-evident and fully descriptive subject. Given the immediacy of racial violence at their school, these moments often arose through the themes of racial identities, conflict, racist segregation, and resentment. Therefore, my tactic is to consider the girls' words and narratives as not only personal reflections but also social, psychic, and spatial phenomena (see Kingsbury 2007, 2010). This enables an analysis beyond girls' spoken intent to "get along." Remaining just at those words forecloses an examination of racism and lets hegemonic whiteness off the hook, when in fact the effects of whiteness tinge all racial identities in the United States. The narratives are not just present through a social exchange, and they do not merely reflect social reality. Rather, narratives also result from other—unconscious—processes. As Christopher Lane writes in *The Psychoanalysis of Race*, the "social" problematically implies a chartable map of interaction, and in these terms racism then "derives largely from ignorance and false consciousness" (1998: 4). The normative assumption that follows is that enhanced knowledge of the other would reduce conflicts. Lane emphatically questions the basis of this assumption, since it presumes that "individuals voluntarily would place the needs of others on par with their own. . . . To this perspective, psychoanalysis adds a difficult truth: When people and groups are locked in conflict, they are—beyond their immediate interest in securing sovereignty over another land or people—already experiencing tangible gains" (5). In short, prejudice and inequality can be psychically pleasurable (and as Skeggs [1997] puts it, gender, class, and sexual inequalities are both pleasurable and painful for the subject). Enmity, Sigmund Freud (1961a) tells us in *Civilization and Its Discontents*, is intensely satisfying (see also Lane 1998: 9).

Identification holds something of this conflict too. The investment in any identity is laden with psychic longing and loss, narcissistic requirements for social existence and visibility, anxiety, and love; to Freud, identification is ambivalent (1959: 47). It is a symptom of both love *and* hate, of attachment *and* loss (see also Freud 1957). The similarities and differences that identities imply falsely indicate cohesion, since identities are not merely an affinity or a rejection of a category. They are fantasies that one can ever fully be the way that one describes oneself. Identities are based on social fantasies of group affiliation (e.g., girlhood, racial identification), fueled contradictorily by the desire for social self-inclusion and by the desire to exclude others. Thus, David Eng suggests a distinction between identities and desire—in other words, between political or social forms of identity and the psychic process that determines how a subject will take these identities as aspects of the self: "To understand this distinction—to understand that identification is the mechanism through which dominant histories and memories often become internalized as our own—is to understand that we are all borrowers and thus not pure" (2001: 26).

This view represents the problem with taking a racial identity as an indication of the inner truth of the self, or as an indication of an inherent ability to act based on the fact of identity. In fact, multicultural, postfeminist girl power does just that; these social discourses of power, identity, and self indicate that the agent can self-determine her identities and cast away the "dominant histories and memories" that contour identities like "girl" or "Latina," for example. Eng claims, "As the subject can never be aligned with the agent, so, too, identity and identification never quite meet" (2001: 26). Identification always is *less* than the subject, since every subject exceeds the identities that she attempts; her unconscious and the psychic process that frame identification are vastly expansive in comparison with an identity. The unconscious attachments, for example, indicate the scope of any identity: it cannot be described simply by the identity itself but rather must be theorized by "its ample scale" (Freud 1959: 51). In this book, I also consider the ample *space* of the subject: the subject beyond an immediate proximity that includes her personal, familial, urban, and national geographies. These multiple spaces inform and shape identities, and they must be considered when thinking about any story or practice of segregation at school and peer relationships.

Identification is therefore always *more* than the individual subject, since it is a broader social, psychic, and spatial phenomenon than that of an "individual." Indeed, identities are failures of personal translation and coherency. No subject can be held accountable for the histories and memories that compose group social categories, such as gender or race. The girl subject is therefore not equivalent to her gender or racial identity or the empowered agency that scholars and advocates have posited to follow identity, since the subject is always a process of unconscious attachments, resistances, wishes, loss, and affect. (For a detailed and excellent introduction to psychoanalytically informed girlhood subjectivity, see Gonick [2003].) In other words, the girls' narratives about their racial, class, and gender agencies (like "getting along") are not to be taken for granted and must be interrogated for the psychic and social fantasies and deceptions that cover up—or rather constitute—gender, sexual, spatial, and racial attachment and resentment. The narratives offer glimpses of the ample space and time of identification when contextualized by the dominant histories and memories they rely on.

In the context of American girlhood, the feminine is idealized through the priorities of capitalism and whiteness and not least of all heteronormativity. Those who are "racialized" as minorities and as others to the white ideal must deal constantly with the devaluations that frame their social visibility and contextualize their daily practices. This racialization is also a psychic dealing, since the subject must take up the devalued racial qualities of difference through identification. And there is both psychic pleasure and injury in doing so. As Anne Anlin Cheng (2001: 24) writes, "The next generation of race scholars has to address the fundamental paradox at the heart of minority discourse: how to proceed once we acknowledge, as we must, that 'identity' is the very ground upon which both progress and discrimination are made." Cheng insists that the strength racial minorities gain from their identities also contains injury; she calls this race's "haunting negativity" (25). The contradictory nature of identification thus points to the range of payoffs and pains associated with racial identification (see Eng 2001: 22).

This argument is not always popular, especially for scholars whose work promises an emphasis on social change, progressive politics, and antiracism. It is time, Cheng insists, to question the following: "What constitutes ideas of progress, change, and social health? Before we can entertain the hopes of cure, especially in arenas of power where the psychic life of power not only lives on but also lives within us, we have to acknowledge—a difficult enough task— the profound and enduring melancholia that the legacies of imperialism, colonialism, patriarchy, and other forms of discrimination have bequeathed" (2009: 91; see also Walkerdine, Lucey, and Melody 2001, especially chap. 4). Oppression, Cheng says, is not simply a top-down suppression; oppression "has both compromised and conditioned the very possibility of subjecthood" (92). As scholars we must "remain in the gift of discomfort" (93–95); discrimination cannot be overcome merely through recognition (as much of multiculturalism would have it) or agency, particularly that of those at-risk girls (see also McNay 2008). The "gift" is Cheng's way of articulating the contemporary fixation on reassurance, or what Sara Ahmed (2010) has recently called, simply, the happiness turn (see also Ehrenreich 2009). In particular, Cheng is wary of the ideal that subjects can recognize each other—"that 'I' recognize 'you' as a separate, individual and equal subject and vice versa" (2009: 96). This implies a neoliberal subject in charge of her destiny, able to take agency to forge a new world as a crusader of change (see also Winnubst 2006).

Girl power and "strong minority" girlhood each try to fit girls into an autonomous, neutral subjectivity, but surely no subject can actually contour to this mold (see Skeggs 1997). By seeking to employ the assumptions of powerful agents and autonomous subjects, girlhood studies, despite great intentions, undermine the struggles of real girls who cannot possibly embody girl power's exclamations and images. Scholars provide little critical education about how social change could proceed, thus failing to help girls situate—and possibility develop through alternative politics—those aspects of themselves that do desire to get along. This desire is not a banal one, however, that signals simple intention and consistency. The messages of self-help and choice (Salecl 2009; Gill 2008) have been extraordinarily effective in molding girls' narratives around the possibilities of getting along, as I demonstrate throughout this book. They are affective, heartfelt, and deeply problematic when placed in a psychoanalytic subjectivity that insists that recognition and a racial "coming together" are fantasies and that identities can be facile, spatially coherent, fully addressed, and fully communicated.

Psychoanalysis thus provides a method to understand girls' "identification with the master" (Salecl 2009: 171) but does not hold them personally responsible for the conditions of their subjectivities. The fact that minoritized identity categories have been objectified and vilified through the legacies of racism, sexism, and nationalism does appear in the girls' narratives about their lives and beliefs. The girls both reflect and resist these legacies in their stories about themselves and others; the point, I believe, is to consider both and not concentrate solely on the resistance. To concentrate solely on the resistance would imply that a girl could also pick the agential and progressive self and disregard her racism and segregation. Therefore, in what follows, I focus very narrowly on the speaker and her words, thinking through how each girl presents herself. But I theorize these words as products of the social and spatial complexity of subjectivity. Narratives and subjectivity exist in a complex spatiality of the psychic life of power (Butler 1997b); to neglect this psychic life would be to rely instead on a notion of the individual who has autonomy over the conditions of social life. One who is thought to have an ability to pick and choose identities in a social-power vacuum indicates a self whose agency is omnipresent. Racial or gendered conflict, internal or with others, is cast aside as fixable by means of better communication about the self, a misguided lens that forgets the unconscious attachments to the objects that are as oppressive and aggressive as they are hopeful and loving. It is important to think carefully about girls' words but to take care not to assume that they tell the whole story of the subject.

Locating the Research Project

I met with twenty-six girls, alone or in friendship groups (and in two cases, sisters were interviewed together), for seventy-five- to ninety-minute interviews about two months after the school riot between Latinos and Armenians. The girls heard about the research from me directly when I visited their classes or from a flier that I had provided, which had been passed among the students; those who elected to participate in the research called me to arrange a time to meet. The girls identified racially in the following ways: twelve Hispanic or Latina (Hispanic was the most common self-identifier, and most of these twelve girls were Mexican American), seven Armenian, three Filipina, two African American, and two Anglo or white. They ranged from fourteen to eighteen years old, with most of the girls (twenty-one of the twenty-six) either fifteen or sixteen years old. All girls under age eighteen obtained parental consent to participate in the research. The girls chose their own pseudonyms. (See Table 1.1.) On the basis of my evaluation of their parents' occupations and family housing, I determined that the girls' families were working or lower middle class. Additionally, at my suggestion, two of the girls took photographs to document their social lives and spaces, but because of time constraints, I did not undertake a systematic auto-photography project. I obtained parental consent and participant assent to reproduce all photographs.

When the girls called me to arrange a meeting time, I told them to look for a white woman with glasses and short curly brown hair. I was easy to spot at the coffee shop across the street from campus as I waited by the door of the building with an expectant look. The room was otherwise packed with students, and I was clearly not one of them. I bought the girls snacks and frothy, sugary drinks, and we sat with a tape recorder between us. Later, when I

TABLE 1.1   RESEARCH PARTICIPANTS

NAME OF PARTICIPANT	AGE	RACE-ETHNICITY (SELF-IDENTIFIED)
Alexis	16	Armenian
Alison	16	Hispanic
Amy	15	Armenian
Anne	16	Armenian
Blindy	14	Hispanic
Britney	16	Anglo
Chibi-Kim	15	Filipina
Daija	15	African American
Denise	16	Latina
Elizabeth	18	Anglo
Gaby	16	Hispanic
Grisselle	15	Armenian
Jackie	16	Armenian
Jane	14	Armenian
Julie	18	Hispanic
Keshia	15	African American
Lola	15	Hispanic
Mayra	15	Latina
Nane	14	Hispanic
Rachelle	16	Hispanic
Sammie	16	Armenian
Sarah	15	Hispanic
Sephi	15	Filipina
Susie	15	Hispanic
Violet	15	Latina
Zelda	15	Filipina

listened to the tapes, they often returned the loud sounds of steaming milk and espresso machines, drowning out voices for several minutes, but it was more convenient, and surprisingly private, to meet the girls at the coffee shop than at their homes. Almost all of the girls lived in apartments where they shared bedrooms with siblings. I lived across town, too far for them to come to me. None of the girls had easy access to a car.

Feminists have long struggled with how to deal with their own subjectivity in the research process and how to think through its importance to the research encounter. Many agree, however, that a facile listing of social identifiers—such as adult, white, and middle class—does little more than reemphasize the fantasy of self-evident social differences. Agreeing to a certain logic of positionality, in which I could predict my own self and its impact on the girls, also works against the conceptual arguments in this book. Since I argue against the socially chartable subject, one who can be known by her identities or fully known to herself (see also Thomas 2007, 2010, 2011), it would be incongruous to represent myself in those terms. Researchers also, obviously, have complex and opaque subjectivities. Audrey Kobayashi (2003: 348) rightly warns against what she calls an "indulgence" in reflexivity because it "is ironi-cally the very act that sets us apart" from research subjects. Reflexivity assumes that researchers can engage in full self-reflection in research contexts but that research subjects cannot.

Valerie Walkerdine, Helen Lucey, and June Melody (2001) include an excellent chapter in *Growing Up Girl* that delves into how unconscious pro-cesses affect researchers and the research process; we should not assume that the unconscious is always a "problem" of the researched (see also Pile 2010; Proudfoot 2010). We should not presume that thinking about the unconscious leads to the "truth" of the subject (see Kingsbury 2007: 237). "We maintain that no matter how many methodological guarantees we try to put into place in an attempt to produce objectivity in research, the subjective always intrudes" (Walkerdine, Lucey, and Melody 2001: 84; see also Bondi 2005). The research-ers considered this intrusion by examining the moments in their interviews when, for example, the questioner shifted topics abruptly (and thus away from areas that prompted discomforting personal reactions); the interviewee made demands on the interviewer (attempting to shift power differentials and thus control the terms of the interview); and the three researchers' analysis of the interview manuscripts resulted in very different conclusions about the mean-ings of interview narratives. Walkerdine and coauthors offer a vital corrective to assumptions about the transparency of researcher reflexivity, confirming that it cannot accommodate subjectivity.

Following their advice, I discuss my whiteness, class, language, and age and how they might have affected my conversations with the girls only when I had a sense that they did so—a sense that came from reading and rereading transcripts and noting moments, for example, of pause or confusion or an abrupt rerouting. In longer interview excerpts, I have included my own ques-tions and statements so that readers can consider my own guiding language and reactions. These can sometimes be jarring, and certainly anyone who has conducted an interview may later wonder about a strange or curt reaction or even a failure to hear certain messages that come through loudly and clearly on the tape or in the transcript itself. I cannot determine the "truth" of these moments in hindsight. In group interviews, considering why I followed one girl's comment rather than another's is also important, but it is not always possible to determine since I do not always know what occurred at that exact moment to influence my decision. In groups, the majority often silences the sole voice of disagreement. Sometimes the din of the group and the shriek of steaming milk in the background simply make that voice hard to hear.

Of course, any conversation or storytelling is also a contextual telling: a specific rendition of lives and exchange, conscious and not, given the moment of the interview. Another day the girls might have told me different stories, I might have asked different questions, a cell phone might not have interrupted to shift our flow of talk, or a friend at the next table might have altered the mood of the interview. Interviews are very much particular to the space and time of the moment (Elwood and Martin 2000; Pratt 2000). The girls' interactions with one another also shaped their stories in group settings.

Perhaps more than reflexivity, it is important to focus on "how [researcher] identities intersect with institutional, geopolitical, and material aspects of their positionality" (Nagar and Geiger 2007: 268; see also Pratt 2002; Rose 1997). The research encounter in the case of these interviews started from the $20 payment I offered each girl per interview. The funds, which were provided by a faculty grant from the University of California–Los Angeles (UCLA), made the project possible; the girls were aware that I was not paying them from my personal funds because they were required to sign a UCLA receipt. These institutional resources thus became a key term of meeting with the girls. The money was meaningful to them since most did not have jobs or any consistent means of income; the $20 indicates the material terms of our coming together for the interviews. I can only assume that the girls would not have volunteered without the offer of payment, an offer posted on the fliers distributed in their classes. Perhaps having access to institutional funds, in white adultist America, seemed usual to them.

As the interviews wound down, I told the girls that they could ask me anything they wanted, since I had asked them intimate details about their lives. During the interviews, I should note, I often told stories of my own and offered my opinions so that they would know something about me before our time together ended. Most did not have questions, perhaps because of the many exchanges we'd had on a variety of topics during the interviews, but when they did, for the most part the girls wanted to know my age. A few also asked if I was married or had children. Those who guessed my age thought I was twenty to twenty-two years old; I made them guess before I revealed the answer—perhaps an indication of my egoistic investments in trying to look younger than I am (I was thirty-five at the time). One girl asked about my faculty position at UCLA, since she was interested in going to college there. No one else asked about my job or about the larger purpose of the research beyond the brief introductions I gave at the start of the interview. Because most of the girls would not attend college and had little contact with people who did so, I think they had no clear sense of what my job was or meant; perhaps some felt intimidated by a topic with which they were not familiar. I do not want to assume that they found this aspect of my life unimportant or even uninteresting, but it is possible that their general lack of questioning in this area indicates just that. Those who asked me personal questions were interested in my assumed heterosexuality and where I fell into normative gender roles, such as mother or wife.

I started the interviews by asking about the riot, and I made sure to ask the girls what they thought about the school's response to it; otherwise, I asked questions according to the flow of conversation, about the particular stories the girls were telling me. Enmity and the aftermath of the fight at school gave the girls plenty to talk about, and their explanations for the source of racialized fighting then prompted stories about migration, family life, ethnicity, and urban geographies. I asked many of the girls whether they liked living in Los Angeles. In many ways, the girls' idealism about their own postracial subjectivities mirrored their views about life in Los Angeles more generally. Virtually all of the girls *loved* the city—emphatically. Time and again the girls cited diversity as a core reason for their love for the city. They thought they lived in the center of the universe, and in their social worlds framed by pop culture, consumption, and the currency of the entertainment industry, I suppose they did. The city offered them mobility, entertainment, a plethora of shopping venues, and lots of other youth to watch. Its racial tensions; extreme class segregation; obsession with thinness, fame, and beauty; and exclusionary service economy might not have much to offer these girls in economic benefits, but its sex appeal and glamour sure did. They were proud to travel outside the city, embodying the chic of Los Angeles to families in Mexico, Armenia, or rural California and showing off their relative wealth and suave.

Relative is an important qualifier to the girls' wealth. By U.S. standards, most of these girls were from working-class and working-poor families. But by Filipino or Armenian standards, they were rich. (The girls who were born in Armenia or the Philippines and those who traveled to Mexico to visit extended family also scoffed at the stereotypes of Los Angeles as polluted or crowded.) They did not have their own bedrooms, and some of the older girls even contributed rent money from afterschool and summer jobs. For the most part, they lived in apartment complexes, as do the majority of people in this area of the San Fernando Valley. The median income[1] for the area where the girls lived was $37,000 in 2005, which was 20 percent lower than that of the city overall. One-fourth of the adult population consisted of school dropouts, and 16 percent lived below the poverty line; 21.5 percent of the children under eighteen lived in poverty. The LAUSD gives "racial ethnic history" data for each school, and Hispanics and whites (many of whom are first- and second-generation Armenians) are the two largest racial groups at the school, although Hispanics outnumber non-Hispanic whites two to one. Confidentiality requirements prohibit me from identifying the school or giving detailed descriptions of its demography, but I can say that this high school has between two thousand and three thousand students, and a significant majority of them qualify for the

---

1. I took an average of two U.S. Census Bureau public use microdata areas (PUMAs) in the San Fernando Valley to obtain these data; one PUMA contained the school's address, and the other was a neighboring PUMA where many of the girls lived. To protect the identity of the school, I do not identify the PUMA numbers. The data come from the 2005 American Community Survey.

free federal lunch program. Other minority groups, which represent a small percentage of the high school's total population, include American Indian, Asian, Pacific Island, Filipino, and African American students. Of these, Asians, Filipinos, and African Americans constitute the vast majority of the small group of "other minority" categories. Thus, the school is multiethnic and multiracial but dominated by Latinos, with Armenians as the second most populous group.

The common practice among the high school's students is to refer to Hispanics and Armenians as different "races" of people. Also, the girls referred to their ethnicity as their "race" (e.g., Mexican race, Armenian race, white race [which in Los Angeles is commonly referred to as Anglo]). I largely follow their use of *race* here, rather than insist that they use the term *ethnicity* (see also Pulido's use of *racial* or *ethnic* to indicate that racial groups can also "function" as ethnic groups [2006: 17]). Little is gained by rejecting the girls' reference to race in discussions of national, linguistic, or ethnic differences. Very rarely did an interviewee use the words *ethnic* or *ethnicity*. In my view, racial identification relies on a quotidian lexicon of difference that rarely cuts a fine distinction between ethnicity and race in contemporary U.S. social life, including in urban schools. Therefore, the racial identifiers that I use to label the girls are those that the girls themselves used. There is a range of identifiers for "Hispanic" girls, from Mexican American to Latina. Not all of the girls are a single "race," but I use their overarching self-labels when it seems unimportant to draw out their multiethnicities. For example, in a case where a girl's mother was American Indian and her father was Mexican and the girl chose to self-label as Hispanic, I did not theorize the girl's "racial" mix.

Language data provide a view of the racial-ethnic diversity of Los Angeles and contextualize the city's geography of recent migration.[2] Of a total population of 3.5 million in 2004, 70,203 Angelinos (city dwellers living in households and over five years of age) spoke Armenian at home, the third most common foreign language spoken at home after Spanish (1.57 million) and Korean (89,349). Tagalog was fourth at 68,076. English was spoken in 38.6 percent of the city's households (i.e., it was spoken by 1.34 million people). Note that these data are for the city, not the county, of Los Angeles. The number of Armenians would increase if I included the Valley cities of Glendale and Burbank, areas with predominantly Armenian populations.

---

2. Language data serve here as a proxy for race since the U.S. Census Bureau does not include "Armenian" as a race category. Individuals had the option of specifying "some other race" on the 2000 Census long and short forms, but 97 percent of the respondents who did so wrote in Latino or Hispanic.

The urban and neighborhood context immediately surrounding the school reflects the ethnic and racial diversity of Los Angeles, and many of the students at the school are first- or second-generation migrants. Almost half of the population in the San Fernando Valley where the school and its students are located are foreign born (44 percent); 63.5 percent of people over the age of five speak a language other than English at home (mostly Spanish), and half of them do not speak English well.[3] Mexico, Armenia, the Philippines, and El Salvador are the most common national origins of students at the school. Most of the first-generation girls who participated in the research were Armenians and Filipinas who had moved to the United States when they were young children. All of the participants spoke English very well, and most were also fluent in the language spoken at home (Spanish, Armenian, or Tagalog). In 2005, the school had a sizable English Learners (EL) program, constituting about one-third of its total student body (EL participants represented a wide range of ability, however). Of these, 70 percent were Spanish speakers, and just over 20 percent were Armenians.

Content of the Book

My goal in analyzing girls' narratives about the fight is not to seek a multicultural solution to conflict; I do not in any way attempt to solve the problem of racial violence in urban U.S. schools. Indeed, my goal is quite the contrary: to critique simplistic solutions to youth violence and racial segregation. I aim to draw out the ways that racism, sexism, and resentment permeate the girls' narratives, just as do ideals for humanism, harmony, and dreams of peaceful coexistence. I show how the girls situate the fight in their narratives as not only psychically and sexually pleasurable but also personally abhorrent. Chapters 2 and 3 discuss the girls' responses to the fight. Chapter 2 evaluates their insistent prescriptions for multicultural understanding alongside their racialized resentments of other-raced girls. Racial and gender-sexual conflict, at the end of the day, may not be re/solvable, especially, as I argue in this chapter, not by strengthening racial identities through multiculturalism. I argue that racial harmony is an illusion that disregards the pleasures of group conflict and is itself founded on the fantasy that identity is immutable and foundational. The chapter asks, "On what basis can we assume that racial harmony is a realistic hope?"

Chapter 3 examines narratives that point to the gendered instigation that started the riot: an Armenian boy hit a Hispanic girl. Or was it the other way around? Whatever the true equation, this violent act, which gained mythic status in the weeks after the fight, fueled hundreds of mostly male students to

---

3. Data are from U.S. Census Bureau PUMA data.

come together at the line that separated Latino and Armenian spaces on campus. In their discussion about boys' fighting, the girls articulated a frustration about masculine displays of "stupid" violence, yet they also valorized boys' strength and considered their protective response to the alleged blow against "a girl" to be sexy. The chapter considers the slippery interarticulation of heterosexuality, racism, and gender difference and shows how the attachment to boys' strong-armed racism presents intractable challenges to multicultural programs intent on easing racial tensions at the school.

The line marking the site of the fight's beginning is a spatial division marking the inflexibility of racial mobility at this school, and its everyday regulation is a method of racialized grouping and identification. Chapter 4 explores the processes through which the girls contend with racial territories and segregation on campus. They express discomfort and pain when their racialized bodies enter into the "wrong" segregated territory, where they are met with stares, racial epithets, or silence. I argue that the girls' pain indicates the power of social categories to mark their bodies, but the girls' subjectivities exceed their bodies of difference. Rather, their narratives point to the ways their racial identifications are fundamentally social and intersubjective (that is, made in relation to other bodies and subjects) and spatial, (that is, articulated through struggles over territory and space at school). The chapter also provides a psychoanalytic reading of their social and racialized practices of suspicion, surveillance, and antagonism. Many of the girls aggrandize their own racial identities as based on respect and love, but intense distrust and suspicion surround their dealings with girls in other racial groups. Paranoia, anxiety, and narcissism frame the girls' racial practices at school and in the city.

Chapter 5 situates the girls' subjectivities and racializations beyond the space of the high school and explores the migration stories the girls tell about their families. The ways the girls distinguish themselves as "more American" than their parents show interesting modes of self-articulation yet simultaneously situate these immigrant girls as nonideal, non-Anglo Americans. I also consider the ways the girls present the United States as a land of opportunity offering more promise than the poor countries from which their families came. A few of the Mexican American girls in particular, however, question fairness in America and suggest that Armenians prosper without having to struggle as hard as Mexican Americans. Resentment of the status symbols of others—expressed primarily through such possessions as name-brand clothing and cars—indicates that economic and social disparity become interwoven with racial differences in the urban United States.

To emphasize only this consumption and resentment would overshadow the girls' other concerns about their teenage lives. What the girls say they want, as I show in Chapter 6, is a nurturing education and a safe school. However, their call for controlled campuses and classrooms and caring teachers also indicates their investment in normative school spaces. The girls ask for more surveillance tactics on campus, to address their safety concerns. They also request feminine teaching and administrative styles, which normalizes a gendered, nurturing stereotype for education. Therefore, I suggest that stereotypes about gender and race steer girls' ideals about school life and space. Rather than calling for revamping or democratizing urban educational access and practice, they call for conservative, surveilled educational spaces.

In the final chapter, I consider girlhood as a time of subjectivity and question what assumptions gird the idea that girls hold a special potential as agents of change. By emphasizing the futures of girlhoods, feminist scholars neglect the spatial and psychic contingency of their subjectivities and identities, and end up placing incredible, and unviable, responsibility onto girls themselves to undo the oppressions that concurrently shape their social and spatial worlds. Instead, I argue in favor of an opaque politics of girlhood subjectivity so that conflict is not normalized as a blockade to social change but an affect on which to consider new social and spatial formations.

2

Banal Multiculturalism and Its Opaque Racisms

New Racial Ideals and the Limits of "Getting Along"

W hen I first sat down with the girls, I asked them for their thoughts about what happened on the day of the riot. Their hearty stories, emotional descriptions, and passionate pleas for peace all illustrate the force that the day exerted on them. As I make clear in this book, however, the emotive force of these events does not indicate a direct or self-evident process, and their replies to the riot do not represent a fully conscious experience for the girls themselves. In this chapter, I examine their articulated commitments to countering racial tension at school, but I juxtapose the narratives pleading for racial harmony with those illustrating a contradictory investment in racism by the same girls. The following two excerpts indicate their commitment to "getting along," and I suggest in what follows that these are buttressed by girls' investments in what I call "banal multiculturalism."

The first dialogue is excerpted from a group interview with three Armenian girls (Alexis, Anne, and Grisselle) and one Anglo (Britney). Throughout this book, ellipses in the dialogues denote deleted text.[1]

---

1. By *deleted text*, I mean insignificant words, including repetition, my own clarification, more of the same kinds of words, side remarks, comments that do not change the meaning of the narrative, telephone calls that briefly interrupt the flow of conversation, and the like.

Alexis: We had nothing to do with it [the riot].

Britney: It was very racial.

Anne: It was a normal thing for us, something we're used to. . . .

Grisselle: There shouldn't be fights against race because we're all people; we all have feelings; we all [share] stuff. It's just stupid.

Mary: So why does it happen then? What do you think?

Grisselle: I guess the people who are in the fight are not understanding.

Anne: They just think it's cool, oh, "We're, like, fighting," you know, "in a riot."

Alexis: So it's just sad how closed-minded they are.

The second dialogue is excerpted from a group interview with three Filipina girls (one girl did not speak in this exchange).

Chibi-Kim: We're all the same. . . . I think it's very stupid.

Zelda: Why can't they, like, set their animosities aside and just, like, harmonize.

Chibi-Kim: Peace.

"We're all the same" is a repeated claim from most of the girls in this study. Overwhelmingly, the girls insist that racial conflicts are a "stupid" and misinformed outcome of "not understanding." As I show in this chapter, the girls' prescription for opening the minds of violent fighters is a heartfelt plea to respect cultural difference. Respect for difference, they think, would lead to a harmonious coming together around the similarity that humanity provides. They have few specific ideas about how such respect could be fostered, but "talking" through problems to recognize commonalities—despite racial-ethnic difference—portends their primary assumption about how to address racial violence. Their appeals for open-mindedness and harmony present their surficial pledges to a multiculturalism that remains, unfortunately, undeveloped and uncritical in their own educational and social-spatial experiences. This argument is compounded in the following chapters.

Multiculturalism is a predominant tenor within American urban educational spaces that saturates girls' conscious ideals of behavior and, indeed, outlines for them the very merits of identity itself. However, the ways that multicultural ideals function for the girls' senses of identity and personhood are sharply limited (Dolby 2000: 16). Even as they espouse multiculturalism and the hopes of humanism, they vividly detail their own racist resentments, fears, and suspicions (see Mac an Ghaill 1999). What do these confounding and contradictory narratives indicate for the hopes of girls like Chibi-Kim and Zelda, who call for peace and harmony at school?

Despite the state's clear retreat from multiculturalism (compare Katharyne Mitchell 2004: 641), multiculturalism remains an important ideal in educational and social spaces in the United States. Proponents of multicultural education recognize that racial and ethnic diversity is a lasting fixture of U.S. society and suggest that citizens should harness such diversity as a valuable attribute of American life (Ladson-Billings 2003; Torres 1998). These values have deeply informed high school curricula nationwide, affecting the books that students read, the histories that students learn, the pedagogy that teachers use, and the programs that schools offer. However, as Katharyne Mitchell suggests, successful multiculturalism properly entails *achieving* diversity, not merely *accepting* the fact of differences (2004: 642; see also Giroux 1992). As it stands, celebratory, "boutique" (Fish 1997) pluralism and a quest for a common (i.e., assimilated [see Katharyne Mitchell 2003]) society more often gird the multicultural projects in many urban U.S. high schools, restricting discussions of social, racial, and economic difference and replacing them with consumer ideals of diversity. For example, multicultural programs at schools often involve purchasing foods or crafts made by diverse (i.e., non-Anglo) students. (Lugones and Price [1995] call such programs "ornamental multiculturalism.") Nationwide, public urban high schools also contend with racial conflict by attempting to create spaces of "respectful" cultural difference via multicultural programming. In underfunded, overcrowded schools with few extracurricular offerings, these programs are banal, intermittent, and superficial, yet they are highly visible and symbolic. They serve to reinscribe whiteness as the national normative in education by (1) excluding multiculturalism from the curriculum and the classroom, (2) asserting color-blind ideologies, and (3) maintaining racial assimilation in knowledge attainment and campus embodiment (Riley and Ettlinger 2011; Hurd 2008; Lewis 2003).

Because Latinos and Armenians constitute the vast majority of the student body of the high school where I did my research, the school's multicultural activities largely represent this population. Two examples include a moment of silence to honor the victims of Armenian genocide and a presentation on Cinco de Mayo with dancing and singing. The school also has smaller populations of other nationalities and races, and it holds an annual student-run food fair, where students can purchase ethnic foods from extracurricular (particularly Filipino, Mexican, Salvadorian, and Armenian) groups. Neither the moment of silence for Armenian genocide nor the Cinco de Mayo celebration is accompanied by any educational content that details the historical or geographical significance of the events. The school's teachers and administrators do not address issues of racial-ethnic pride, competition, or pain that these programs may evoke in students.

This school's multiculturalism (which is not atypical) thus merely represents ethnic, national, and racial diversity by emphasizing the "fun" of difference or, less frequently, the respect students should have for others' painful histories—through dancing, eating, colors, costumes, and honoring the victims of racism and ethnocentrism. Throughout the United States, the standardization of education and the emphasis on "teaching to the test" mean that schools cannot afford to devote too much class time to specific topics that are tailored to a school's unique populations (Alonso et al. 2009). In addition, there is no funding—or even the political will—to train teachers in such histories. The multicultural banalities that American public urban high schools offer thus fail to provide a critical or specific education that considers—or even a language with which to understand—students' daily experiences of racial-ethnic conflict, racism, and poverty. The racial riot on this campus overwhelmed any multicultural attempts to encourage respect for difference.

The failure to educate students about difference, however, does not indicate that youth are unaffected by the multiculturalism evident in school programming. The articulation of racialized identities and subjectivities for youth and the way that they come to understand, experience, and reproduce racial and ethnic difference themselves, I argue, are deeply informed by multicultural norms of celebratory diversity. This chapter's content shows this reproduction very clearly (racial fighting is "stupid" or Chibi-Kim's ideal statement, "We're all the same"). However, because this multiculturalism is overwhelmingly devoid of any analysis of racism and racist identification, its impact on youth constricts their ability to deal with racial-ethnic conflict. The students reiterate multicultural phrasing to shrug away racial conflict as created by "stupid" boys. (See Chapter 3 for more on the gendered meanings of the riot.)

Therefore, I suggest that the possibilities for successful, critical multiculturalism in most urban U.S. schools are extremely constrained. No matter how heartfelt some youth are about commitments to a peaceful coexistence, most poor, urban school systems lack the educational content needed to contextualize racialized and ethnic conflict and the economic, social, and geographic disparities that fuel such conflict. Indeed, as Stuart Aitken and Randi Marchant (2003) show, attention placed on school violence in the United States generates a huge range of reaction and masks the racist undertones of the differences between investments in white, middle-class students and investments in those falling outside normative whiteness. More to the point, they argue that the spatial contexts of school violence are rarely extended beyond the local body of the boy or boys who perpetrate the violence (162).

The effects of multicultural education in urban schools are spatially broader and more complicated than just youthful fantasies of diversity, "getting along," or bad behavior by individuals. As Katharyne Mitchell, Sallie Marston, and Cindi Katz (2004: 4) explain, accepted norms such as neoliberal education—and here I specify banal multiculturalism—become commonsensical over time and through space and produce certain subject positions and subjectivities (compare Ruddick 2003). Only when multiculturalism can disrupt the commonsensical—or in many cases stereotypical—ideas about difference can it propel new discourses on race and conflict. I thus stand with Elizabeth Povinelli, who writes the following about Australian multiculturalism:

> I propose that we only approach a true understanding of liberal forms of multiculturalism by inching ever nearer to the good intentions that subjects have, hold, and cherish and to the role these intentions play in solidifying the self-evident good of liberal institutions and procedures. Many Australians . . . truly desire a form of society in which all people can have exactly what they want . . . if they deserve it. They do not feel good when they feel responsible for social conflict, pain, or trauma. This is, after all, a fantasy of liberal capitalist society too simply put: convulsive competition purged of real conflict, social difference without social consequences. (2002: 16)

My purpose in this chapter is to ask how banal multiculturalism in U.S. urban education spaces produces and perpetuates a commonsensical norm that youth associate as the logic of the social and the self. The issue, in my mind, is therefore not whether banal multiculturalism can work but what work it does on limiting possible racialized identities. Racialization within banal multiculturalism maintains identity within liberal humanism's forceful reliance on whiteness and color-blind ideologies and on the abjection of conflict (again, see the excellent Povinelli 2002).

In this chapter, I explore how a constrained but normalized multicultural commitment to appreciating and celebrating diversity seeps into narratives by teenage Latina and Armenian American girls about racial conflict at their school and informs their own racial-ethnic identifications and practices. I emphasize *constrained* commitment, given that social-racial segregation and racialized violence are competing practices within the high school, the homes, and the urban geographies of the girls. The girls may articulate commitment, but it is limited in practice. At the heart of this chapter is thus the issue of how these contradictory messages and practices frame subjectivity. How do the girls justify—seemingly unconsciously—their commitments to multicultural norms *and* everyday segregation and resentment? The articulation of multicultural hopes in the girls' narratives marks a depoliticized racial stance. In a way, multiculturalism becomes a placeholder for the girls and allows them to avoid their own trenchant commitments to racial difference and the racist evaluation of others. Thus, multicultural hopes, I argue, must consider that girls' constitution as subjects is also reliant on the devaluation of other racial-ethnic youth as a part of their own racial identification processes. This argument begs the question of whether banal multiculturalism can ever have a progressive effect on the violence in schools or even everyday interpersonal relationships among youth.

Of course, schools are not the only spaces in the lives of youth. Certainly, families, urban spaces, and other social contexts bombard subjects with normative discourses that affect and shape their practices of identification. As this book indicates, the examples in each chapter must all be taken together as proof of the spatial complexity of subjectivity, not as containers of social struggles. Most important, all of these spaces work in and through one another so that family lessons about racial history, for example (the topic of Chapter 5), are conceptualized as active at school as well as in homes.

Multicultural Ethnic Identity: An Oxymoron?

The following narratives illustrate the girls' overwhelming beliefs in an underlying humanism that highlights people's similarities within the logic of multicultural diversity. I use humanism to denote the girls' unwavering belief in an essential human nature (i.e., that people are the "same" underneath their skin). This sameness is insinuated to be good, moral, and often based on the commonality of emotions and feelings (i.e., being sensate). The ideal of "we are similar because we are people" arose in almost every conversation, and the remarkable repetition of the wording in the narratives illustrates the girls' beliefs in fundamental humanism. Coupled with this humanism is a corresponding multiculturalism, or the simultaneous acknowledgment that people have a diversity of personal histories, cultures, and geographies that need to be respected. These narratives, I argue, show that the girls' central organizing belief is that understanding humanism will ensure peaceful multiculturalism. Stupidity, which is often masculine in the girls' minds, restricts successful multiculturalism.

I have grouped the interview excerpts in this chapter to show the commonalities across the girls' narratives about racial differences. Jane, the speaker in the following excerpt, is Armenian.

> Because, okay, back in Armenia [in school], you would be with Armenians, and here, there's, like, people of different ethnicities and backgrounds. So, this [riot] is the result, which I really don't like. When people fuse, this is what happens. I guess they just try to keep—the reason there's riots and stuff is that they're trying to keep who they are. They don't want to fuse and become like one. [*Two minutes later*] I think everyone should get along. . . . If people realize that they have more in common [that would make it better] because I think that people are more alike than they think, you know? Because it's not all race that matters. Okay, they might have a different culture,

they might have a different lifestyle, you know, but we think almost the same.

Amy, who is Armenian, was interviewed with her sister, Jackie (who is not represented in this excerpt).

Amy: They [the fighters] didn't understand each other, obviously. Both Latinos and Armenians are from different areas; they're not from the United States. And, I think, it's not worth fighting for because we're both from other places; we should try to be friends instead of fighting. We have more similarities. We think we have more differences. . . . We think we have more differences, but we don't know our similarities. . . .

Mary: What are the similarities?

Amy: Like, one I just named: we're not from the United States. And we're both, like, different in color. We don't speak English; our native language isn't English. And it's just, that's it, you know. . . . But there's other people who, just, they're not about school; they're not about life; they don't think this. They're just, like, oh, "You're Latino, I'm Armenian, okay, we're different, oh, let's fight now."

The following dialogue involves Nane and Blindy, who both identify as Hispanic.

Nane: I mean, I respect religions; I don't know what the hell I am, but still it's, like, oh, if they would be doing, like, parties and stuff based on their religion, I'm going to respect them. I'm not going to say, oh, like, screw you, don't do that stuff. . . . If you have a religion, good for you; you have something that you want to follow. But if you do, don't go running around saying things, you know, [like you'll go to hell if you're different].

Blindy: Yeah, [ironically] because I always hear that God loves all his children.

Nane: I know. And the gay stuff. The gay and lesbian things—

Blindy: The gay stuff, yeah, that's gotten to me. . . . I think it's really stupid that they won't let gays or lesbians marry or something. It's like, they're same as us. Just, it's just [that they] loved somebody else; it's not their—from their sex.

Nane: I know. They say, oh, we're all children, God's children or something. . . . Then why can't they accept his other children, too, that have a different way of living? They're actually very—I love them. They're, like, very interesting; they have great opinions about everything. You can ask them something, and they'll have very interesting opinions.

Blindy: It's like, they're not even different from us. It's like, they're the same as us.

The predominant assertion in these narratives (and the two excerpts at the beginning of this chapter) is the girls' common idealization that people are naturally and universally aligned, via humanity, and are fundamentally "alike" despite their social-cultural or natal differences. That is, the common claim is that *humanism trumps racial-ethnic difference and its conflicts and can aid in multicultural understanding.*

This premise is represented in the following paraphrases: we're all people, we're all the same, people experience common things in life, we have more similarities than differences, and we're all God's children and deserve respect. The interview excerpts indicate that the girls believe in—indeed, consciously advocate for—the ethic of multiculturalism that emphasizes respect and peaceful coexistence and that is justified in a belief in universal humanism. They insist that people fundamentally share lived experiences. Less directly, they insinuate that all people are moral and good on the inside. A seemingly typical youthful response ensues: stupidity keeps people (i.e., mostly boys) from practicing this peaceful coexistence at school. The girls insist that if people could only understand that they naturally share a deep human connection, then violent divisions would end, and the result would be a harmonious coming together. Thus, multicultural ideals of peace with diversity find easy reflection in the girls' narratives. They use phrases such as "cultural difference" and "respect for religions" without hesitation and with affective heartfelt sincerity.

Of course, we must surpass this simple story. A second theme embedded in these girls' insistences that people are people despite racial-ethnic difference (and the coterminous fantasy that people are good) is the paradoxical evidence that the girls are vested by difference, not similarity. Paraphrases that represent this second theme include that racial conflict is normal and common, that the fusing of different ethnicities results in riots, that dark-haired and dark-skinned immigrants are different from Anglos, and that homosexuals are extraordinarily interesting despite their queerness.

The girls rely on a humanist trope of universality that blunts their engagement with difference in its particularity at school and with their peers. Thus, their arguments that we are all alike serve to elide the very types of antiracist politics that more radical—and, I would suggest, more effective—multicultural education and programming would insinuate. They end up displacing blame for racial conflict on those who do not subscribe to the universal humanism that they themselves repeat. Amy, for example, insists that those who fought on the day of the riot "didn't understand each other, obviously." The "obviously" marks her own commitment to the normative multiculturalism that situates "understanding" as the process through which peaceful coexistence proceeds. She immediately suggests that this lack of understanding comes from the immigrant status of Latinos and Armenians, which implies their lack of an ideal American multicultural position. At the same time, Amy defines immigrants as a similar class of people, in this case based on their common darkness. "We're both different in color"—that is, with dark hair and dark skin. (Note that for Amy, this connective phenotype excludes African Americans in addition to Anglos.) Her example of language is another signifier of the "new American," given the tendency of her high school peers to speak a language other than English in social spaces and at home.

After these two examples, however, Amy realizes that she cannot quickly identify any other similarities; she says hesitatingly, "And it's just, that's it, you know." She disavows racial difference by placing the blame for racial fighting on other people: "But there's other people who, just, they're not about school, they're not about life." Education's ideal social space, according to Amy, is a positive and idealized multicultural mixing pot. For her, racial difference and racism are quite literally deathlike ("they're not about life"), so for Amy and the others, racism and difference must be disavowed. In Amy's words, multiculturalism, which is signified through knowing our similarities despite our differences, comes to represent happiness at school, good school relationships, friendship, and living a proper American life. Her optimism is embedded in a normative belief that getting along would be better (i.e., it would be more moral and ethical, since it is based on being "about life") and would more accurately reflect student subjectivities as similar. The agency she advocates around paying close attention to sameness thus implies a moral, progressive self (compare Mahmood 2005) and intimately abjects conflict and difference. Amy seems to cling to a psychology of positive thinking, a danger Sara Ahmed (2010: 14) warns against. The "promise of happiness," Ahmed argues, means that subjects bring objects that feel good closer, "affecting how the world gathers around us." Only those who share Amy's view of sameness deserve a spatialized legitimacy to exist. This sameness is both a personal spatiality—in that Amy's own identities function to gather the world around her—and a material spatiality of moral indictment for those not properly embodying American multiculturalism.

Nane and Blindy similarly hint at the possibilities that respect would offer, but in their exchange, they focus on religious difference. Nane even suggests that parties could offer a way to illustrate difference—a clear reference to the kind of multicultural programming at schools that emphasizes the fun and celebrations of difference, rather than a critical engagement with the scope of the difference itself. That a group simply offers "parties and stuff" indicates to Nane that the group is worthy of respect, since group members are using the party platform as a vehicle to communicate their openness to dialogue about their group identity. Nane juxtaposes this example with the opposite, a stereotype about a religious position that condemns those who fall outside the normative sexual subject (i.e., homosexuals).

Nane and Blindy's exchange about religious diversity points to their skepticism that the Christian injunction to "love all God's children" is possible within a cultural context of severe homophobia. Nane asks, "Then why can't they accept his other children, too, that have a different way of living?" The unspecified "they"—her foils—in her mind unjustly condemn the homosexual's right to love and life. Yet Nane immediately segues into her estimation of homosexual *extraordinariness*. Rather than being just among God's many children, gays and lesbians hold a special and different status, according to her. She remarks that "they have great opinions about everything. You can ask them something, and they'll have very interesting opinions."

These examples share common messages. While the girls' disdain for violence was clearly spoken and animated, the discourse they use to convey this contempt relies on an acceptance of diversity that did not play out in the rest of our conversations (more on this later). Although they seem to epitomize multicultural subjects, given their spoken commitment to respect for difference, the context of these sound bytes—that is, the second embedded theme of racialization and difference—belies the ideal. Multiculturalism itself is articulated through differences—as different from Anglos and therefore as other to white and heteronormative. A gulf thus opens in the narratives between a voice that normalizes multiculturalism and the unspoken, perhaps unconscious, embedded theme of fundamental investments in racial difference. Taking the girls' stories of multicultural connection for granted therefore constricts our view on the speaking subject while neglecting a theory of how subjects are made only through an intense commitment to a symbolizing chain of difference, not similarity (Sedinger 2002). In other words, taking subjectivity seriously means considering how difference founds and frames subjects, regardless of the girls' own easy words espousing sameness.

The Limits of Racial Multiculturalism: An Example of Anxious Identity

On the other side of a disavowal of violence is the extreme discomfort that arises when racial otherness must be acknowledged and spoken, which then poses the possibility that others will discern it as *avowed*. Here Blindy (Hispanic) describes having to talk to a store employee about another employee's interaction with her.

Blindy: Like, sometimes you can't really identify somebody [by name], and then you just say, "Oh, the Asian person" or something. It's like, sometimes I feel bad saying that, I don't know, because *I kind of feel it's kind of racist.*

Mary: Shorthand.

Blindy: Kind of, because it's like I went to [a store] and, it's like, I was trying to describe the manager who talked to me, and I can't really describe her. And all I could say was black, and I really felt bad because I just *felt like I was being kind of racist.*

Nane: Yeah, I hate being in that situation.

Blindy: I just don't like being in that situation because *I kind of feel racist.* Like, *I feel like I'm being racist.*

Nane: Yeah, you don't know whether to call them African American or black or colored or something.

Mary: So if you describe someone by their race that feels racist? Just using the terms?

Blindy: I kind of—I *kind of feel like I'm being racist,* but in a way not really, but it's like, [it] *kind of is.*

Blindy's extreme distress is evident through the repeated expression of her feelings of anxiety and guilt. Nane misreads Blindy's anxiety by interpreting it as regarding proper identifiers to use: black or African American or colored; the changing norms for racial identifiers is one result of multicultural education that affirms the right of a group to self-identify and self-label. Neither the girls' anxiety about racial qualifiers nor Blindy's feelings of guilt easily fit with multiculturalism, which exists only through a celebratory articulation of racial difference as self-identification, rather than racialization, which marks the power of others to racialize. (On the dilemmas of race talk, see Pollock 2004.) The void between celebratory self-identity and the deep commitment to racial difference that identity presents here fills Blindy with guilt about her role in perpetuating difference and produces an anxiety about the possibility that she, too, might be seen as racist in a multicultural world. This insecurity marks Blindy's youthfulness, but it also reveals themes beyond age. She wants to be liked, and her anxiety mirrors Amy's ideal that people who are "not about life" are the ones who are committed to racializing difference (i.e., racism). After all, Blindy designates this woman by race and otherness and would not have been able to see *any* other subject without doing so. But the analysis of this example must go further than just the visual imperative of identifying race.

Focusing solely on Blindy's words, rather than the unconscious and conscious process that motivates them curtails an understanding about their importance. It would mean reducing a lens of analysis to only an immediate reaction or a situation that motivates the repeated phrase. It would be incorrect to use Blindy's words to construct an argument solely about the difficulty of racial definition and self-identity through her anxiety about terms and the naming of racial categorization. The other does not have to be reconstructed because the problem is how people *use* the other and create myths to understand the other. Applying a psychoanalytic reading of this interview excerpt means not fixating on the object, in this case the black woman, or the term causing the anxiety about her definition (Laplanche 1999; Caruth 2001).

The repeated phrase in Blindy's narrative is an indication of her failed attempt to communicate her own self to others, a self that is not fully, radically socialized by racial difference. The anxiety evident in the repetition indicates the *impossibility* of that desire to be seen as a nonracist and the *impossibility* of experiencing a full self. The repeated phrase is a symptom of Blindy's failed repression of the fear and anxiety that arise from her acknowledgment of a racial other, a different other who presents her with the reality that her self-identity is not translatable in a language that truncates the subject and her spaces (Spivak 1999). Unconsciously, Blindy knows that if she must racialize an other, then she also must be racialized. This racialization submits her to a symbolic system of differentiation and fracture that threatens her own egoistic stability. Her self-image is a precarious state that requires that she repress the fact of her circulation as a subject in a social system that extends far beyond her own control. She does not have the power to self-define, and this lack of power results in an anxiety about racially defining and reducing this other subject. Her fantasy of being a full self, untruncated by the social demands and practices of categorization, is in constant jeopardy. Her repeated phrase is a symptom of her anxious identity and her anxiety of being labeled by others as a possibly disavowable, outcast racist in an ideal multicultural space. Blindy fears that others—including me, her white adult audience in this case—will misapprehend her words. The repetition is a sort of pleading for me to recognize her anxiety about race and her desire to be seen by me as nonracist. She cannot know how I receive her words, which is why she continues to utter them. Blindy cannot but fail to communicate her anxiety, since, of course, even she does not know the full extent of it. In turn I cannot know the idiosyncratic story of her anxiety and what it might indicate about other issues for her because approaching a psychoanalytic diagnosis of Blindy's anxiety would be far beyond my role or interest. (Pile 2010 is instructive here.)

Youth such as Blindy have few tools for talking about racism. The injustices and anxious feelings that they experience are both conscious and unconscious when they are faced with a possibility that they may be wrongly accused. The feeling of being racist also points to the gap that is opened when multiculturalism frames racial-ethnic identity at the expense of a critical engagement with the logics of social differentiation. Such an approach to difference would demand an education for youth that includes economic, racial, sexual, and colonial histories and geographies, which would amount to nothing short of a revolution in public urban U.S. education and political systems. Furthermore, education is only one space of many in the lives of youth, so effecting such fundamental shifts in racial identifications and practices would entail more than implementing the ideas contained in simple and normative statements about what education should be. (I also do not want to foreclose the possibility of local and individual teaching practices, which may struggle to provide such a critical context to students.) I argue, particularly in the next section, that the lack of public and school spaces for interrogating difference has led to a further cementing of race-ethnicity as a personal or personalized identity, rather than as a process and effect of subjectivity that is contextualized within U.S. histories and spaces of immigration, racial segregation, and racial-ethnic exclusion.

This example also serves as another lesson: the challenge for girlhood scholars to allow our encounters with research subjects to also decenter *us*, instead of, as Allyson Stack (2005: 73) has argued, using encounters to consolidate "our identities [personal and professional] through interpretive gestures that effect centrifugal re-centering." Jean Laplanche writes that "when one follows the path of synthesis, one silences the unconscious. . . . It is not that there is no question, with complexes and myths, of discoveries which are partly psychoanalytic. But these discoveries are inadequately situated: obscuring the unconscious in psychoanalytic theory, just as they obscure it in the human being. They are transformed into something which can be used by the human being to master enigmas" (1996: 10). Perhaps girlhood analyses recenter our own feminist commitments (Driscoll 2002) and our own fantasies. In other words, commitments to a sort of multiculturalism—strength in diversity—also shape how feminists analyze race or gender identification in girls.

If we remain mesmerized by the meanings of the *representations* of these fantastical objects—the effects of race or gender, for example—and their supposed potentials as the bases for social change (e.g., girl power), then the focus remains too simply on the interiorization of the representations and the reproduction of these by human subjects. We remain fixated, in other words, on the potentials of identity politics instead of thinking through the very difficult processes of how identification proceeds and why. Analyzing gender or racial identification according to a social epistemology means that, in effect, we circumscribe the unconscious and recenter the egoistic function without attending to its buttresses and fantasies. I advocate a further consideration of the trenchant psychic attachments to difference, formed in a sort of psychic trade-off whereby a subject takes up social identity as a way to exist in the world.

Racial-Ethnic Resentment and the
Limits of Multiculturalism

Multiculturalism, I have argued, provides a normalized language for these youth to self-consciously disavow racism, but at the same time, the girls do not seem deeply invested in working to achieve multiculturalism. Their everyday lives also do not illustrate any practices that work seriously to this end; to a very large extent, they have friends only within their own racial-ethnic groups. Rather, the girls' narratives illustrate the insecurities they experience when talking about race and ethnicity (Blindy) and the daily racism they experience at school (Filipinas Zelda and friends explained that they are called "Chinky" almost daily; see Chapter 4). Furthermore, and of importance, the girls contradict their supposed humanism as they reveal their deep and perhaps unacknowledged resentment of other racial-ethnic groups. The following excerpts illustrate this resentment and show the girls' distrust of and segregation from racial-ethnic others. Because the interviews were open-ended with little direct questioning after the first few moments, these excerpts represent general conversations about social activity and school life. The speakers have close friends (with whom they socialize outside of school) of only their same racial-ethnic group (see Stearns 2004).

Grisselle, who is Armenian, is the speaker in the following excerpt, which is extracted from a group interview.

[With] Hispanics, if you fight with one, you fight with them all. . . . You can't just have one fight with just one person in it; you have to have another one. . . . It's because Armenians, they like to represent, so they do things [to show their pride]. They always have things that, like, represent Armenia, and Hispanics don't like that, and so they start giving each other bad looks, and then so [it] ends up starting a fight.

The following dialogue comes from a group interview with six Latinas; this excerpt includes two of the girls. (Unfortunately, the tape quality was too poor to consistently assign names to the voices.)[2]

Speaker 1: Armenians stick together no matter what. You have, like, let's just say one Armenian, [and] one Hispanic does something to one Armenian. About five Armenians are going to come after the one Hispanic. . . .

2. I was prepared to interview three girls, but six girls showed up for the interview in a crowded coffee shop. The resulting background noise and overlapping conversation made the identity of each speaker difficult to discern.

Speaker 2: Like last time, a black guy was getting chased. I swear about forty Armenians were chasing him across the school. This guy is running with all his might. And there's, like, forty Armenians going after him.

Amy, the speaker in the following excerpt, is Armenian.

And it was mostly, like, I don't know why or how this happened; it just, mostly, they kicked out all the Armenian boys [after the riot], and they just suspended, like, a few, like two or three, Latino boys. [*Later in the interview*] [Even in the cafeteria], some people just want to cut in line, and they do. And mostly you can notice because [with] the lunch ladies [monitoring the cafeteria] that are Latino, the Latino kids could cut, but if they're, like, an Armenian kid that tries to cut, she'll go, like, "Go back in the line," you know?

Keisha and Daija are African American students at the school. (Approximately 5 percent of the students at the school are African American.)

Keisha: But, like, out of all the people, like with the Armenians and everything, none of them, like, really, really got arrested that day [the day of the riot], but . . . this one [African American] boy that I knew, he was my friend, he got arrested. . . .

Daija: He got in a fight because one of the Armenians pushed him, so he started fighting them, and I guess they [the police] pulled him to the side and checked him out. . . . He had a knife [in his bag], so they took him to jail.

Blindy and Nane, the speakers in the next excerpt, are Hispanic.

Blindy: It's like, the impressions [Armenians have] of Mexicans is just like gangster kind of. . . . And, like, the impressions [I have of] Armenians, from what I've heard [from] a lot of people is that they are very conceited. That, like, they get a lot of help from the government. And there's more racism towards Mexicans because I've noticed a lot of the Armenian people get a lot of help from the government. . . . But for the Mexicans, it's like, I've noticed, it's like, not many make it unless they have, like, family contacts or connections around here. . . .

Nane: And so, we have our cars, you know, we need our cars because there's a lot of us, so we buy the [nicer] ones that will not mess up a lot, and it's not for conceitedness. . . . [But for the Armenians,] they're only, like, maybe, twenty [in their family] compared to us, and they have very, very, very, very, very expensive cars. They have a Hummer, and those are very expensive, and they don't use it. It's always just there in the driveway.

The girls consciously articulate a strong commitment to multiculturalism and racial harmony, as seen in previous sections, while detailing their resentments organized around racial difference. Such contradictions occur through the girls' focus on injustices. The girls themselves do not recognize the contradictions that these radically paradoxical positions create. In the first case, Grisselle (who previously in this chapter remarked, "There shouldn't be fights against race because we're all people") suggests that pride in one's heritage is resented by other groups and provokes competition between Armenians and Hispanics at school. She markedly places the blame on Hispanics—that is, the other group. In the second excerpt, the Latinas suggest that Armenians gang up on others. Blame was a common theme in the interviews, particularly concerning the race riot. The girls displaced blame from their own group and pointed to the vile fighting practices of their enemies. Here the injustice of the other group's fighting tactics (they don't fight fairly) results. However, the Latinas magnify the blame through exaggeration, drawing on images of lynch mobs (e.g., "forty Armenians going after him") to provoke profound disgust at Armenian behavior and finger Armenians for extreme racist violence.

The next three excerpts highlight the central role the girls give to the state in adjudicating disparate racial-ethnic difference. For Amy, the school's "lunch ladies" (i.e., adult employees, often teachers, who monitor the lunchroom) give special privileges to same-ethnicity students. Daija and Keisha claim that the police unfairly singled out black students after the school riot by arresting disproportionate numbers. (Eleven students were expelled from school that year, an unusually large number compared to other years; only one of these students was black, and over half were Hispanic.) Remarkably, targeted punishment was a common claim; many said that disproportionate numbers of members of their own race-ethnicity were arrested. Finally, even the U.S. government gives Nane and Blindy a case to argue for their own economic and ethnic disadvantage. They resent government aid to Armenians that they claim is not available to Mexicans. In one of our conversations, Blindy qualified the nature of this help by saying, "It's, like, welfare, or, like, tickets, money coupon things." Blindy and Nane draw further attention to the economics at the heart of this resentment: the perceived privilege that non-Mexicans receive when arriving to the United States and the simple envy that is triggered by displays of wealth and money presumably bestowed by an unfair system. Their resentment thus stems from not only unfair state favoritism but also the wealth and the "conceitedness" that grow from it. While, in

Nane's estimation, noble Mexican families have nice cars out of necessity, the Armenians have "very, very, very, very, very expensive cars" simply because of gross consumption practices, signified by the Hummer. The girls' reactionary comments are also fueled by what they assume are the Armenians' racist stereotypes of Mexicans as gangsters, not family-oriented hard workers, itself a competing stereotype of Mexicans.

According to these girls, state entities—namely, the public school, the city police, and the government (which is somewhat nebulous in their accounts)—give special status to *other* racial-ethnic groups, to the disadvantage of the girls' own groups. The girls articulate their resentment of another group's ability to take better advantage of state preference, whether it is in the lunchroom or through welfare benefits. However, the girls do not claim that these preferences should not be granted—only that they should not be granted unevenly by the state entities that they name (i.e., they should also receive state aid, or they should also be able to cut in line).

This feeling of "wounded otherness"—being the ones who are hurt by their exclusion—ties the girls intimately to their commitments to universal humanism, liberalism, and a justice and rights discourse. Of course, such a commitment is paradoxical in that it corresponds to *individualized* identity and personhood in the form of individual rights and access to the state (Brown 1996). This commitment to humanity, personhood, multiculturalism, and naturalized identity in a sense *depoliticizes* racial-ethnic disparity in the public realm by naming minority competition for the state's attention and benefits as a proper venue for justice (Brown 1996, 2001; Žižek 1997). The "good" of multiculturalism and liberalism seems unquestionable; the "good intentions" of subjects end up solidifying institutional claims and procedures of multiculturalism and racial recognition (which is why Povinelli calls recognition "cunning" [2002: 16]).

While I have been emphasizing U.S. multiculturalism, it might be worth a pause here to note that these arguments are not relevant solely for American education. The emphasis on cultural education is not just an American phenomenon. Scholars studying schools and education in disparate national contexts—from Ghana (Coe 2005) to Tanzania (Stambach 2000, 2010), Venezuela (Hurtig 2008), and India (Jeffrey, Jeffery, and Jeffery 2008)—show that schooling is a process of molding youth and their bodies according to the priorities of individualized economic liberalism and political authority (not always successfully, of course). These scholars demonstrate that education is normatively imagined and proffered as a space of the good, progress, modernity, advancement, and hope (see also Fong 2004; Lopez 2003). But as Janise Hurtig bluntly states, any notion of an individual embodying this idealized space is rife with contradiction. In her research on schooling and patriarchy in Venezuela, Hurtig insists that the image a student has of herself as an (eventually) educated adult fully implicates her investment in the terms of state promises of neoliberal education and subjectivity. Yet "at every step along that path toward educated adulthood, Santa Lucian [Venezuelan] women were faced with conflicting choices and constraints that were not anticipated by the progressive promises of modern meritocracy or the coherent certainties of classic patriarchy," such as male breadwinning and support (2008: 17).

Back in Los Angeles, these kinds of contradictions also involve the girls' resentment of other youth, wrapped up in a call for inclusion in state-adjudicated justice. While these further cement the girls' investments in a liberal and neoliberal state (more on this topic in Chapter 6), they also juxtapose the impossible reconciliation of banal multiculturalism and American racialization, identity, and racism. Even ethnic pride—a bedrock of multiculturalism that holds center stage in school programming—is considered a right in the United States granted to immigrants, per Grisselle's insistence that pride is proper. The irreconcilability between multicultural identity and rights-based claims to justice, however, follows: Grisselle claims that Armenian pride evokes Latino resentment, as if displays of pride take others' identities away. This resentment indicates the limits of rights-based discourse, since plurality does not necessarily adjudicate conflict or stratification (Brown 2006) in this case. The violence that ensued at this school from ethnic and racial pride as identity thus marks the profound insecurity of placing hope in the state's adjudication of rights and justice.

The girls *disavow* the challenge that identity and difference present universal humanity and multiculturalism. In other words, rather than seek racial-ethnic complexity, they validate the logic of liberal individuality and the underlying belief that people are the "same," not "different." They consume banal multiculturalism and its norms of peaceful and colorful coexistence and repeat its philosophies as their own. Fundamentally, however, racial incompatibility, mistrust, and injustice frame the girls' practices, perhaps to a greater extent than multicultural coming together, given their highly segregated social lives. This discrepancy marks the gap between articulations of multicultural, peace-loving selves and the fact that, as subjects, the girls do not acknowledge the investments in racial differences that so intimately guide their everyday geographies.

Curative Multiculturalism?

In the interviews, I asked all the girls the following question: What do you think the school should do to prevent future violence?

Nane: They should just tell us every day, like, encouraging words or something. Have more events where we could all, like, get into.

And, I don't know, because today, Cinco de Mayo, we had an assembly. . . . And I was actually enjoying it until some people that were mainly the Armenians next to me, they were sitting next to me, they were saying, they were saying things like "I don't want to be here; this is bullshit" and lots of other things. And I'm like, why? Just, if you don't want to, then don't look at it. Because they were just dances. And it's like, you don't have to be disrespectful. When you had their Armenian genocide anniversary or something, no one was yelling around, "Oh, screw you Armenians," or something. We actually had a moment of silence over the PA [public address system], and no one did anything to ruin their day, their day to remember the people they loved, or something, or their country. But here they are saying things about our only, one of our only holidays that is just for us.

Zelda: We should probably just learn about each other's cultures, just for one minute learn about some other culture, what motivates them to do these things. You know? Instead of just stereotyping.

Amy: Well, we definitely would have to talk about it. It can't be [an] overnight thing, you know. We definitely have to sit down and communicate with one another to know what really is the problem, what's bothering us, and why there's this border in between us that separates us from one another. And once we talk, I'm sure there's still going to be other people that won't change their mind. I've heard there are people like that.

It seems like we are back where we started. The girls' assumption in these excerpts is that conflict resolution in the aftermath of violence at multiracial schools is possible under the rubric of humanist multiculturalism. A central ideal underlines this assumption: successful multiculturalism and peaceful coexistence in a livable world is acquirable through descriptive education about cultural differences mediated by the state. (See Coe 2005 on Ghana and the cultural education of nostalgia and difference.) There is even a pop psychology aspect to this concept, seen in Zelda's "what motivates them to do these things." Interestingly, her use of "them" connects to Amy's "other people" and "people like that." Nane's desire for encouraging words from "them" refers to her school, yet she quickly recognizes that "some people" (the other racial-ethnic group—in this case, the Armenians) refuse to truly accept multiculturalism. The girls see nonmulticulturalists, presumably racists, as fringe elements beyond saving. The corresponding logic is that "normal" people speaking encouraging words and more multiculturalism are the cure for violence, segregation, and competition.

Despite Nane's pain, her Armenian nemesis in this case might be using the right words (but with the wrong sentiment): "This is bullshit." Celebratory multicultural programming is just one indication of the failures of the U.S. public education system to provide critical education needed to contextualize racism, ethnic violence, and poverty. These events and narratives must also be weighed against the *neoliberal* public education system that places primary emphasis on "teaching to the test" and school choice (although school policy is not my focus here). Such emphases result in a geographic disparity of education; simply put, resources ensure that better educations go to those students who come from privileged households and districts. Public urban schools similar to this school in Los Angeles lack sufficient funding and are shaped by (among many other things) disenfranchisement, poverty, city decay, and California's own banal commitments to multiculturalism. All of these conditions restrict the possibilities for critical multicultural education about race, poverty, ethnic difference, geography, and migration. These are relegated as the problems of the city or the nation or perhaps the economy that creates inequality but not necessarily all at once (Amin and Thrift 2007). Attempts do exist to shift education norms, but these attempts seem dire; critical multicultural education remains framed by a U.S. normative neoliberalism that details the empirics of individualized injustice and individual failures to live up to the American ideal. I thus hesitate to even suggest that critical multiculturalism could affect the racial politics of these youth, particularly as an insulated project conducted only in school spaces.

Indeed, as Nane's sentiment shows, banal multiculturalism can actually *exacerbate* racial conflict. Deborah Lustig finds that this worsening happens when multicultural events encapsulate ethnicities at school by decontextualizing complex histories, space, and subjects (1997: 587). Nane is offended when the Armenian student fails to listen to her, see her, and experience her event in a way that she desires. The issue is thus far more complicated than education politics and debates over critical versus banal multiculturalism. It is also an issue of subjectivity.

Girls may affectively articulate their hopes for humanist multiculturalism, yet they remain tied to racial difference and racism via their own identifications. Identification in this sense is not simply self-identity; subjectivity is achieved only by entering into a conditioning spatiality of social norms and categories that to a large extent preexist the individual subject. Their education as racialized subjects (Stoler 1995) involves profound investments in the idea that racial difference is a primary *personal* identity; race, in this model, is the *self* as well as a right. Multiculturalism serves as a placeholder in the process of their racialization and identification. In other words, the use of multiculturalism in the girls' narratives is a disavowal of the ways that racial-ethnic identities can operate along a spectrum of difference. Thus, analyzing the multicultural idealizations in the narratives that proclaim identity *without* difference can highlight the gap between the girls' ideal identities and selves as postracial and nonracist and their practices of racism, segregation, and ethnic violence that performatively produce their subjectivity.

For this generation of American youth, and even for other generations, multiculturalism and humanism *are* the dominant racial idealization ("despite racial differences, we are all the same"), and this operates with an assumption that people are fundamentally "wholly communitarian" (quite to the contrary of history; see Freud 1961a). As Meyda Yeğenoğlu (1998: 8) insists, critiquing the idealized humanist, liberal individual involves unveiling "the subject's abstract universal pretensions[, which is] a demonstration of the fact that its illusory self-production is a denial of relationality, complexity and dependence on the other." This argument also relies on a concept of subjectivity that recognizes that the narrated self is not the equivalent of the psychoanalytic subject; Yeğenoğlu marks the self's denial of complexity and relationality as a foundational aspect of the subject. The girls deny and disavow their own racism and racialization by proclaiming multicultural ideals and highlighting the good and essential sameness of humanity. By articulating so clearly their commitments to multiculturalism, the girls likewise perform the liberal move of eschewing differences, and even violence, and focusing on individual rights and justice.

The girls also rely on the fantasy that their own racial-ethnic identities do not encumber them in a social system of racism, segregation, and violence. Rather, they eliminate themselves from culpability by displacing blame to other groups, and they do so by depicting the others' racialized behaviors as indicative of a failure to incorporate proper multicultural respect. They strive to communicate their own full selves, unmarred by racial labeling (e.g., Blindy) or deathly hatred (e.g., Amy), yet they are as fully constituted by an investment in the symbolic as are their others.

Multiculturalism may always have been about humanism and universalism (contra Katharyne Mitchell 2004), despite its emphasis on differentiation and uniqueness. Mitchell writes, "Although multiculturalism has always been strongly linked with capitalism, it was once also accompanied by the spirit of the ethical self—the necessity to work with and through difference and to find harmonious solutions to problems in democratic process" (2003: 399). The spirit of the ethical self may be just as problematic as the link of multiculturalism with capitalism, however (compare Torres 1998). The ethical self indicates that some individuals can claim a responsibility to overcome their racism, for example. A feminist reference to girl power elicits a similar claim (see Mahmood 2005, e.g., page 13): girls are summoned in girl power discourses to have a self-conscious agency to combat gender-sexual oppression. Supposedly girls can work with good intentions (as an appeal to democracy certainly indicates) toward a better world and overcome the divisiveness of social distinctions. But as Saba Mahmood's work reminds us, agency and everyday practices "are the products of authoritative discursive traditions whose logic and power far exceeds the consciousness of the subjects they enable" (2005: 32). American multiculturalism definitively involves the coupling of color-blind racial ideology and rights-based claims of recognition; a binding requirement of this coupling is the disregard of inescapably *conflicted* identities and social-spatial relations.

In this chapter, I have articulated the unlikelihood that multiculturalism in schools could ever be fully taken up by subjects who are fundamentally, via subjectivity, vested by difference. There is no mere working through differences, given that difference *is* the subject. Remaining focused on the self addresses the superficial repetitions of what these girls, most of whom are first- and second-generation Americans, know they are supposed to advocate in normative America (even if these beliefs are heartfelt): freedom for every individual, harmonious social relationships, and multicultural "getting along." A confined focus on the autonomous, agential self, I argue, occurs at the expense of asking difficult questions of what processes racialized identifications and racist practice entail for the subject, such as how racist practice and resentment might be as heartfelt as peace to subjects. The implications of this argument call into profound question the ability of any subject to narrate its way into an ethical position through the choice of multicultural language.

A Final Note on "Stupid"

In Chapter 3, I delve into the girls' qualification of the "stupid" fighters as specifically *boys* (there are many more examples of the girls using "stupid" in that case). Here I want to make a brief interjection about the use of the term when the girls discuss the potential of a nonracist, nonviolent campus. In the two excerpts at the beginning of this chapter, the girls speak the word to make evident their disapproval of racialized fighting. However, they specifically do so in tandem with an evaluation of the fighters as "not understanding" the fact of humanism. They are stupid, as Grisselle puts it, because we are all the same, and fighting "against race" neglects sameness. Chibi-Kim uses strikingly similar terminology: "We're all the same," and it is stupid to fight as if we are not.

The affective use of "stupid" in these cases points to more than the girls' spoken commitments to peaceful multiculturalism at school. The passion and energy they exhibit as they speak also indicates the psychic energy displaced with their avowal of sameness. The affective tone, in other words, represents a sort of boundary between a commitment to a nondivisive racial-ethnic identity and their unconscious reliance on racial difference as viable subjects.

Because their racial identities are loudly articulated and expressed in conscious ways in other times and spaces, they cannot merely shun the violent practices of racial difference and identification when they arise. The girls say that they hate the violence and that others who do the fighting are stupid, but these girls also participate in the daily segregation and racial exclusion that form the racialized spaces on campus and in the city.

As Judith Butler argues, "There is no purifying language of its traumatic residue" (1997a: 38). Butler means that the identities we employ to describe ourselves and others, and through which we are "hailed," are not of our own making. They are imposed on us, and through subjectivation, this imposition is not neutral but traumatic because there is no saying no to the terms of sociality. The girls may speak about stupid racism, but they are as active in its perpetuation through identity difference and identification as are the violent fighter-boys. Their energy at the use of "stupid" gives an indication of the passionate attachment they also have to race. They desire the qualities that race affords them as a social subject within a racial logic of society. They need to be identifiable in social terms to be viable subjects. Thus, the girls espouse racial-ethnic identification as a proud act, a valuation of diversity within this context of multiculturalism. They are proud of their "heritage." Yet this pride and their hopes placed in multiculturalism rely on the masking of the traumatic aspects of racial identity, which is surely just as important a process in their subjectivity.

My point is that this pride can exist only through an investment in their own anxious placement in a social system of racial differentiation. They take on race as not only a marker of pride but also a validating superiority in which their race is not the race of others. The other is "different" and strange, in other words, and the other is stupid for its strangeness. The speaking girl can wish away the discipline of race by calling others stupid, but her words mask the circulation of her own passion for its marker of her as a viable member of her family, friendship group, and social space. While she faults the other for giving in to racial commitments and thus perpetuating violence, her own commitments are not so easily shaken either. Her condemnation assumes that there is an ontological difference between her other and herself (Butler 2001: 46).

The "stupid" other is an imaginary figure, a fantasy that the self can shake the bonds of its constitutive investments. It is a gesture that renounces one's own participation in violence, despite not having raised a fist in this case. The affect of expressing "stupid" time and again highlights the desirous need for the fight even as the critiques fall heavy from the girls; the violence is also reassuring to their sense of how the world and its subjects are spatialized and segregated, an argument that becomes more apparent in subsequent chapters. The anxiety that all subjects experience psychically that they fit nowhere is here allayed by a racial struggle in which the girls can witness "their side." They paradoxically invest themselves with a multiculturalism that means this struggle cannot be narrated. But the emotion and passion they express through the narration of its opposite points as much to the paradox of needing conflict as to the espousal of peace.

3

The Sexual Attraction of Racism

The Latent Desires of "Boys Are Stupid"

"Boys are stupid." This prototypical phrase was uttered time and again as the girls explained to me how the race riot began at their school. "Just boys being stupid and fighting." But how do the girls so easily skim the importance of race in this explanation? Certainly boys were the main instigators and battlers that messy day, but the fight was fundamentally a racialized conflict as well as a masculine one. To further confound this story, some girls also told a gendered story about the fight's ignition: a boy of one race hit a girl of another race, prompting "other" boys to come to the aid of the offended girl. The "stupid boys," therefore, are simultaneously model, racialized heterosexuals in the girls' estimations, since the boys protected feminine subjects from dangerous "other" boys. Despite the stories of racial conflict, the girls reduced the cause of the fight to the boys' stupidity.

In this chapter, I draw out the girls' narratives, which are laden with the intimacies between race, sexuality, and gender, to think through the heterosexual desire of racism. In what follows, I discuss how the girls explained the fight's beginning—what they thought caused it—and I suggest that sexuality and desire are key aspects of the racialization that happens through this school's social and segregative spaces (Epstein and Johnson 1998). But because race is subsumed by the girls' analyses of boys' gendered behavior, I detail how the convergent meanings of sex, gender, and race are condensed, interchanged, and heavily invested. My goal in exploring the convergent—yet unconscious—intertwining of sex, gender, and race is to build further on this book's arguments against banal multicultural-ism and racial identity making as fixes to conflict at school. A commitment to girls' agency toward racial understanding must be interrogated for its simplistic assumption about how racism functions and is reproduced in U.S. urban education spaces. Heterosexism and investments in gendered binaries of passive femininity and strong masculinity must be racialized; their effects are racially evident. Likewise, this chapter indicates that commentary on teen girls' sexuality should also fundamentally deal with racial difference and the racist motives that inform sexual desire. Multicultural programming in U.S. schools and urban contexts often elides the challenges that such a complex interarticulation of sexuality, gender, and racism presents.

Condensing Race, Gender, and Sexuality

How do girls accomplish the interdefinition of race with gender and sexuality? How does racism become a trenchant aspect of girls' practices through their desire of protection and love from boys? Toward the goal of addressing these framing questions, I borrow the term *condensation* from Sigmund Freud. I employ his dream work as a source to explore the unconscious motivations of definite language and muddled affect. Simple phrases or explanations such as "boys are stupid" mask complex emotions, unconscious attachment, and contradictory experiences and practices. Condensation is a useful tool to help explain how girls' narratives are laden with meaning that they themselves are unable to acknowledge and factor into their explanations for how racial segre-gation happens at their school.

In his dream work, Freud distinguishes between the latent and the mani-fest content of dreams. Manifest content is what is evident (i.e., the details explained by the dreamer). The latent content is "revealed by interpretation" only (1966: 210). The latent content is what popular translations of Freudian psychoanalysis have taught us to think of as the "hidden" messages of dreams, which can supposedly be uncovered with analysis. As Jean Laplanche and J.-B. Pontalis (1973) put it, condensation is a "sole idea" that is condensed from "several associative chains." This singular idea contains a sum of the energies concentrated on it, although it might not actually contain a unity. A condensation may result in a blurring of traits that "do not coincide so as to maintain and reinforce only those which are common" (82–83). Condensation intertwines multiple ideas and affects, and this intermingling and confusion of issues and ideas are indistinguishable to the subject itself. Condensation thus produces effects that are masked but productive of action, emotion, identifica-tion, and more. Freud writes that it is "enormous" (1966: 211).

It is vital to emphasize that condensation is not a conscious process. Even making condensation conscious through analysis does not result in a disentanglement of multiple threads; psychoanalysis does not make it possible to measure or discern each category or idea. In other words, the point of this chapter is not to take race, gender, and sexuality apart with the goal of putting them back together again in a new framework (such as intersectionality). This would indicate that race, sexuality, and gender are discernible rather than intimately made through one another. Condensation is therefore conceptually useful because it insists that social and spatial relations (including segregation) and identifications are so entwined that a mappable junction between them is a false model that assumes the separateness of each. "Boys are stupid," I argue, is the condensation of a range of conflicts, affects, desires, hopes, and contradictions. The range of affects and explanations that the girls draw on to explain the riot and boys' behavior pulls from areas of emotion and experience that are radically unconnected within a conscious understanding of racial conflict. Such an explanation makes it extremely difficult to neglect the combined implications of spatialized racial conflict, misogyny, and desire. This includes the sexual desire of racism and segregation, and girls' investments in a misogyny that happily self-relegates them to feminine passivity in the face of boys' racialized violence.

Ignition: Boy Hits Girl

In each conversation with the girls, I asked about the riot in roughly the following way, usually as a way to start and focus our conversation without placing any evaluation on the fight: "Your school has been in the news lately, as you know. I would like to know your thoughts about what happened that day." Usually the girl or the girls would laugh, given the obvious reference to the fight. Their laughter insinuated, "Yes, we do know!" In every case, the girls quickly launched into their stories of where they were when the fight broke out, how they saw it play out, and what they thought were the longer-term ramifications of the fight.

Overwhelmingly, the girls' narratives converge around surprisingly similar ideas about racial-ethnic conflict, masculine violence, and feminine desire. Of course, these convergences were not evident to the individual girls themselves because they did not hear each other's interviews, and they take dramatically different forms in each conversation. In general, however, the girls blame masculinity—and the boys who profess tough man practices—for the fighting and the violence. Several girls also detail the gendered conflict that instigated the fight. In this section, I provide numerous examples from the girls' narratives about how the fight began, and I draw out the convergences in their narratives to illustrate the ways that gender and sexual difference overrides racial conflict.

The point to keep in mind in this section is not that gender therefore overrides girls' racial identities or consciousness; rather, gender becomes a focal point in their storytelling *at the expense of* racial consciousness. Racial identification, however, remains a fundamental crutch for gender-sexual identification; the storytelling itself condenses gender, sexuality, and race. The spatiality of school, interestingly, belies the simple condensation in girls' narratives since racial segregation and conflict cannot be so easily explained as a problem of boys. (See Chapter 4 for more on girls' segregating practices.)

Denise and Violet, sisters who identify as Hispanic, explain what they considered to be the gendered manner of fighting that day. Through their ideas about the fight on campus, they tie racial conflict to a description of boys' aggressive and protective behaviors.

> Denise: Well, I think girls are more catty; they're more talkative. I don't think it gets to the point where they would be violent and things like that. But men, I think men, in general, are more macho, testosterone-driven types, so they need to fight to show that they're better. I don't know.
>
> Violet: It was mainly guys that were fighting anyway at that riot. Girls didn't really. . . .
>
> Denise: I heard rumors of, like, supposedly some Hispanic guy slapped an Armenian girl or an Armenian guy slapped a His—I don't know, someone hit someone, so someone felt they had to protect the women, or something like that.[1]
>
> Violet: And it just escalated from there.

Denise's explanation of protection is an easy one for the girls to conjure, since sexual difference is normatively defined by feminine passivity and masculine strength. The violence of boys is juxtaposed to the speech of girls, and girls' conflict is marked as catty and confined to language in contrast to boys' macho, hormonal bodily fighting. Boys' fighting norms also enable the escalation; by naturalizing their testosterone ("hormones") as causes of the fight, the girls emphasize sexual difference at the expense of racial conflict. Importantly, the girls mark racial conflict as boys' domain, and they distance themselves from the masculinized racism that caused the fight. While gender roles are

---

1. To clarify, the unnoted "someones" in Denise's account are gendered and racialized as follows: "Some [boy of one race] hit some [girl of another race], so some [boy who was the same race as the girl] felt [he] had to protect [his] women."

solidified in their speech as a heterosexual gender binary, this is accomplished by naturalizing racial violence via the male's essentialist need to fight and show superiority. Thus, Denise naturalizes boys' fighting as buttressing racial boundaries and superiority. In their story, naturalized masculine fighting overlays and obscures racial conflict. However, the message's latent content insinuates the racial conflict that also fuels the heterosexual-gender division of protection and protected. The racial content is outright but does not factor into the girls' depiction of boys' need to fight.

Denise also suggests that masculine, racial "pride" turns to arrogance and further fuels racist flames:

> It's to the point where they're so proud of their own race that they're racist against anyone who's not among them. I think that's what it is. They're so proud of their own race that they don't think anyone is as good as them. Which is not true, and they feel like they have to bring other people down along with it. I don't know. I just—I don't know; it seems kind of dumb and stupid.

The "they" are boys, the boys who fought that day. Denise notes the racial pride that segregates the students and suggests a racial-ethnic competition between groups. (There are examples of racial pride in Chapter 2.) Denise discounts that pride by saying that no one is better than another, although it is important to suggest here that she does not discount racial pride per se. Rather, too much of it, or coupling pride with "bringing down others," is where she places her disregard. Denise also relies on her theory of boys' hormones as the energies driving conflict, which needs to be placed alongside excessively prideful racism. "They"—the boy fighters—are driven to fight by both their testosterone and their pride. Denise suggests that boys almost cannot stop themselves from fighting, and their racist arrogance ("They don't think anyone is as good as them.") fuels the "dumb and stupid" outcome. "They" also distances Denise from improper racism. Through her use of "they," she names others as responsible for racism. To call "them" stupid, she must disavow her own attachments to racial identity or the ways she defines herself via race, even by marking herself as separate from its circulations and power over others. *They* fall victim to racial competition, but *she* defines her own ability to not be "stupid" through the currency and comparison of racial difference. The logic of racial difference, therefore, remains at the heart of her own identification, even though its negativity—rather than social solidarity—drives her self-understanding in this moment. Is "they" really "we"?

Nane and Blindy, both fifteen-year-old Hispanic girls, use language similar to Denise's and Violet's; they call the fighting "stupid." They also depict the fight's instigation as a masculine defense of racial violence against girls.

Nane: From what I heard, it was that these Armenian girls and Hispanics, they were getting into an argument, and, you know, the Armenian men, they started to defend them. And so, the Hispanics, they all got in, including the girls. The Armenian girls, they were actually out of it. It was just the guys, and it just went from there. I actually almost got hit by a trash can on my way to fifth period. It was kind of scary. . . .

Blindy: It was actually the girls in conflict, and then they got aggressive with each other, and that's when the guys came in and started trying to defend themselves. And from what I've heard, the Hispanic girls and the Armenian girls were fighting, and the guys came in and hit one of the Hispanic girls. During nutrition.[2] And then the Hispanic guys were, um, [they] heard about it, and at lunch they started fighting against each other.

Mary: I see. What do you think about that? What do you think about the whole thing?

Nane: I think it's stupid. It's stupid because—

Blindy: I think they try to find any kind of conflict just to get to fight. Because, right here, it's always, I think it's racism. Because Hispanics, I've noticed Hispanics and Armenians always talk bad about each other, and they can't stand each other.

Nane: In general.

Blindy: In general, yeah. And they're always apart, and they're always trying to cover, like, more turf, like, their property [at] the school. Like, all the Armenians hang around on the left side [of central campus], and the Hispanic is usually on the right.

Nane: [When our group hangs out at] lunch, [we're] in the middle [of campus] where it's all mixed up. That's where we are actually. We are with a bunch of different ethnic groups and stuff.

Blindy: We've noticed that our group is the most diverse one.

First, notice that Nane and Blindy suggest that girls began the racial confrontation by "getting aggressive," then "men" and "guys" escalated the fight by defending those girls. The violence resulted in an Armenian guy hitting a Hispanic girl—which resulted in the Hispanic boys going after the Armenians. Note also this phrase of Blindy's: "That's when the guys came in and started trying to defend themselves." "Themselves" indicates the racial grouping being defended across gender difference; girl conflict is quickly condensed in this depiction as primarily a racialized conflict. However, this story of the fight's

2. *Nutrition* is a brief mid-morning snack break.

ignition shares an essentialist assumption, also seen with Denise and Violet, of boys' tendency toward fighting. It's "stupid," but it is normalized because boys just want to fight. As Blindy says, "They try to find any kind of conflict just to get to fight." Again, masculine tendency is absorbed by targeted *racial* violence.

Second, in this exchange, Nane tries to temper Blindy's overdetermination of Armenians and Hispanics as "always" in conflict and as always poorly behaved. Blindy both acknowledges and dismisses her. She acknowledges her by saying, "In general, yeah" because perhaps she knows that such an overstatement does not reflect the complicated practices of social and racial interactions at the school. Yet she quickly undercuts her assent to Nane by noting the racial-ethnic segregation of school space. The spatialized form of racial difference illustrates to Blindy one of the reasons for racial conflict at the school: masculine protection of racialized turf (which I argue in Chapter 4 is also the work of feminine turf policing). The contest between "always" and "in general" also suggests that Nane and Blindy are aware of how their depiction of racial difference could be regarded by me as racist. Making an overly broad characterization of racial groups as acting in a determined way, in other words, represents a racist viewpoint. By correcting this characterization as a generality, Nane is hinting that she recognizes that such a comment could potentially be seen by a listener (in this case, me) as racist.

Gender difference seems easier to talk about. It presents a less worrisome topic for the girls since I am unlikely to misinterpret what they say about "stupid" boys. After all, to them I am also a girl. They are more anxious that I may think they are racist because of their words about Armenians (Nane's "in general" insert). Racial difference is much more difficult for them to discuss because it requires that their language fall outside normatively nonracial discourse. In other words, teen girls talking about dumb boys is a common, accepted cultural exchange, but talking about race is a dangerous enterprise. Fighting for racial reasons is "stupid" and "racist," but it is still compounded in their story through their naturalization of boys' hormones or need for aggression. The insistence that fighting is "stupid" illustrates the ways that these girls have internalized a multicultural rejection of racial conflict, particularly violent conflict. Racial difference has been wrapped into sexual difference in the girls' narratives, and they, in true multicultural form, skirt a deeper discussion or analysis of racism. Even as they begin to do so, the language becomes tempered and wrapped complicatedly into gender.

Also wrapped into this dialogue are two things: the everyday aspect of racial segregation on campus and the indication that this spatial arrangement fuels discord at school. Blindy replies to Nane that, yes, she should say, "in general," rather than "always" when referring to verbal racial sparring between Hispanics and Armenians. But she immediately, without a breath or moment to consider the new challenge, remarks on the spatial normalcy of groups that are "always" trying to cover more turf. She paradoxically insists on segregated spaces (both in general and always), even as she previously nodded to the need to complicate the "alwaysness" of racism itself. Gender difference is okay, but racial difference is not. Racial segregation is okay, but racism is not. Thus, the spatiality of racism is not obvious as an active contributor to the girls' own racial ideals of campus life. The girls neutralize the racialization of school space by creating a vision of the school's racial landscape as naturalized (and as inevitable—"always"). Directly following this exchange is how the girls locate themselves in the racial economy of segregation. They told me that "their group" was the most diverse on the school campus. They alone, on campus at least, are the integrated social group. The girls inhabit this space but insist that they themselves do not produce it.

Nane also told me that, at home, she is likely to have conflict with her Armenian neighbors. Notice again the repeated use of "in general" and "always":

> They [Armenians] just, because in general, it's usually with them I also have problems with, no matter. My neighborhood, I think we're the only Hispanics, and maybe some other Asians a few streets away, and everyone else is Armenians. And I try to get along with them, but they always end up calling me stuff.

When Nane is using the active voice, with the "I," she posits her perspective on "they" as "in general." When she shifts to describe their Armenian behavior, she uses "always." They "always" act poorly, but she has problems with them only "in general." Thus, Nane's insistence on racial integration on campus is her badge of honor, but racial conflicts with Armenians at home, in the neighborhood, also shapes her racializing practices (compare her stories in Chapter 2). Nane and Blindy's dialogue illustrates their conscious attachment to a nonracist idealism, but they are firmly entrenched in the spatiality of racism at school and at home. These contexts impact the racial identifications of the girls. Gender difference at school is one vehicle for the girls' maneuverings around self-evident racism on campus, since they can blame boys. But without that excuse at home, Nane points her finger to her Armenian neighbors to explain racial conflict. It's either the boys' fault or the Armenians' fault—never her own.

Mayra, like Nane and Blindy, who contextualize segregation in terms of their friendship group, frames her story of the riot in terms of her own specific social sphere at school. Many of the girls did; they describe the day's events in terms that are familiar to their social-spatial contexts and in ways that fit their own self-images. As such, their narratives are processes of self-making. Mayra also provided her credentials for her knowledge of gang activity on campus. While not involved in a gang herself, she told me, "I hang out—I—I could say myself and my friends, yeah, well, most of my friends, are a lot of gangsters. I'm not one because I would never, you know, make up a group name, and I wouldn't be willing to die for it. Because that's just not me." She continues:

> Mayra: It is, definitely, I mean, that riot was mainly started because of guys. I mean a guy foxed a girl, you know, punched her, but it ended up being this whole gang thing. It turned into a gang thing, but then, eventually, it's like, oh, they started a riot, and they call all the other Hispanic gangs, and they get together. And it turns into this racial thing, so people—who don't even know what happened to begin with—get into it.
>
> Mary: What did happen? . . .
>
> Mayra: In class, and, I mean the [Armenian guy] punched a girl, but that girl happened to be very well known for being in a gang. . . . And so she ended up calling all the other Hispanic gangs, and then they started all grouping up. And then eventually everybody starts noticing while they're all grouping up without knowing the reason, and they just say, "Oh there's going to be a rumble; let's all go." So then they get close to each other, which is the line. It's very popular at school; there's the line.

With Mayra, we have a similar depiction of the start of the fight, but she explicitly says, "That riot was mainly started because of guys." She also places some agency with the girl, who gathered support for a larger-scale confrontation. In Mayra's story, however, the girl involved with the fight is a Latina gang member. Thus, the girl who fights is marked as a "gangster" in contrast with Denise and Violet's catty girlfighters, who rarely can compete with the violence of boys' fighting. Mayra's girl who fights is thus markedly different. This girl's gang status gives her more credibility as an instigator of a riot, and her agency at starting a large fight relies on her connections with other gang members, particularly boys (see Miller 2001; Mendoza-Denton 2008; compare Miranda 2003). However, girls can never, according to Mayra, really compete with boys' power at school.

> Yeah, I mean girls, if you're considered to be one of the—the gang member girls, obviously you're going to jump into the fight. But if you're known as just one of the home girls, just one of the girls that's just there, then you hold the stuff for the guys when they go fight. And it's mainly guys [who fight] because they have to feel that they're, they have power and that their gang is going to be respected, no matter

what. [*A minute or so later*] I mean, because, the main guys, they're guys, so, it's mainly guys [who were fighting in the riot]. I mean the girls, there's some girls who want to meet up to the guys. I mean, I wish I was respected as much as some of the guys at school. Because it's not fair that they just get respected more because they're guys. . . . Honestly, at my school, no girl there is powerful.

The male mob mentality takes over from an organized gang action. According to Mayra, most of the boys that day did not even know the reason for the fight; they just stepped up to the line when they saw the racialized tension building through the massing of bodies at the understood, and thus quite literally physical, line marking segregation. For those at the line, racial difference is intractable; as Mayra tells it, the "call to colors" is an ultimate racial requirement for strong boys. The simple explanation, "they're guys," is enough for Mayra to justify the claim that they seek power and the respect that is seen to follow. Even though Latino gangs also fight with each other (e.g., Salvadorians versus Mexicans), race trumped ethnicity or nationality on the day of the Armenian-Latino riot. Mayra says, "It doesn't really matter what gang you're from at that point; it's just Armenians and Latinos."

Despite the differences in their stories, the girls' narratives share a similar logic. Each presents the fight's beginning with a boy hitting a girl, and each outlines the fight's immense growth from that gendered act into racial conflict related to segregation at school. The girls also refer to that segregation in similar ways. They point to the line—the turfs' meeting point—the center of campus between the left and right divisions. The boy-girl racial conflict comes to represent the school's segregative racial-ethnic tensions, competition over turfs, and spatiality.

Even when the girls do not rely on the myth of the fight's beginning, they draw out the gendered lessons of fighting and the riot that day. Jackie and Amy, Armenian sisters, say the fight came "out of nowhere," but boys are still to blame for such violence. (They later explain to me that there were resultant conflicts between boys and girls around the riot, which I explain in the next section.)

Mary: Well, who's doing the fighting . . .
Amy: It was just a rumble, you know? It's just out of nowhere. They hit each other—
Jackie: It's mostly the boys though.
Amy: Yeah.
Jackie: Because, I mean, girls would say stuff to each other and then, like, yeah, they might hit each other, but that's nothing. You see that everywhere. But, and then the boys, they just make everything

a big deal. They have to kill someone, get rid of someone, just for them to say, okay, it's over. . . . I can't say it was only the boys that were actually fighting that day, but I can say that they're the ones that started it because they were actually the [main part of what was] happening. And, you know, once something gets thrown at you, you know, you have to throw it back, I guess. I'm not sure. So that's how it continued. And then the next thing I know, the whole school is going back and forth like this.

Mary: Who started it, do you know?

Amy: I was there. It was just like in a war, you would expect a war, a typical war, in your head. Just, like, hitting each other—different people, like, hitting each other. It was just, like, a whole crowd of people just hitting each other. [So I] was unclear who started it. But it was in a group, like, I guess, like, three people, from the other side. But it was a big group, so I couldn't see clear through it. Yeah. And then those other big groups they just hit each other, and then the principal and the other workers, staff members, couldn't do anything about it. . . .

Jackie: There was a line. You know how you play tug of war, you see that going back and forth? That was like that, but with, like, thousands of kids, imagine. It was crazy, and everybody was screaming.

Fighting from "nowhere" indicates aspatiality and reiterates the mob mentality aspect of the fight similar to Mayra's depiction. But the girls contradict this remark by placing the fight in the segregated campus, as Mayra does also. Of course, it did not come from nowhere, and the policed "line" between the Hispanics and the Armenians on campus is heavily surveilled by segregative social-spatial practices at school. Thus, there is also an inevitability to the fight despite its coming from "nowhere," since, as Jackie puts it, once it gets thrown at you, you "have to throw it back." It's typical racial segregation to her, masculinized and normalized: an everyday space of segregation made violent through boys having "to kill someone." Boys go too far with their mob action; they must have a definitive ending to the fight.

This comment points to Amy and Jackie's explanation for the scale of the violence that day. It has to be big for resolution, for a winner. Amy uses war as an image of comparison and paints a picture of "big groups" and chaos. She thinks it might have started as a small fight, "like, three people," but the need of boys to "make everything a big deal" ensured its escalation. The racial escalation of big groups coming together is obscured by her theory that boys "have to kill someone." But certainly in this story, that someone is a *racial* someone, not just a boy's random target. The subjects of the stories are furthermore spatialized implicitly. Although Amy first suggests that the fight "came out of nowhere," the logic of the fight in Jackie's estimation resulted from crossing the "line" between the warring factions. Once the mismarked racial boy crossed into enemy turf, the boys have the reason they "need" to fight. Masculine violence is defined in and through spatiality and the segregative racism that places subjects with their proper racial contexts. The ways that the girls rely on spatial norms for racial belonging are articulated through gender difference. Put another way, the condensation of race, gender, and sexuality is spatially contingent, and the logic of segregation is the hinge on which condensation operates.

Jackie also easily dismisses girl fighting as insubstantial and everyday. Therefore, in the heart of Jackie and Amy's discussion about the fight's beginning, a story exists about boys being the primary perpetuators of fighting. Girls, according to Jackie, and also Jane, just "say stuff to each other." Jane, an Armenian, shared this logic and remarked very similarly:

> Yeah, it's definitely being driven by the guys because girls, they're not really involved in it; they're just there, looking at it, you know. I think, I mean, there could be small fights with girls, but then that just, like, basically, mainly is personal problems. "Oh, you stole my boyfriend," or something like that.

Girls fight for personal, even petty, reasons (see also Burman 2004), which Jane similarly limits to catty behavior. Feminine fighting is defined by jealousy and attacks on other girls, who are presumably usually same-raced girls, since there is very little interracial dating at the school. The opposing, unspoken aspect of Jane's analysis of gendered fighting is that boys fight for bigger issues than girls. *Boys fight to maintain group racial identity.*

These girls' stories consistently indicate that the boys at the school are the driving forces behind the fight, except for Mayra, who suggests that it was a girl who garnered the support needed for the large-scale fight to occur. Although her foundational role was stripped by the masculine mob mentality in Mayra's story, Mayra tried to reinsert the action of the girl who "really" started it. Regardless of the murky details of how the fight began across the girls' stories, the gendered aspects of the fight's ignition are clear. The girls fundamentally illustrate the gendered terms of the fight's beginning and the centrality of sexual differences to the subsequent myth making about that "big day" for the youth. However, this argument is insufficient. It takes for granted girls' own theories of masculine violence, theories that occlude the racism at the heart of the girls' stories about "stupid" boys. The next section examines in closer detail the heterosexual desire that enables this gender-racial occlusion to occur in the girls' narratives.

Desire and Racial Violence

While the girls insist that "boys are stupid" for fighting, I argue in this section that they also insinuate that girls *enjoy* masculine shows of strength. As Jane said in a previous quotation, girls are "looking" at the boys while they are fighting, which hints at the pleasure of watching racial fighting among boys. By *pleasure* and *enjoy*, I mean that girls get a sense of satisfaction from boys' protection, which is not necessarily or consciously known or addressed by the girls. Their narratives highlight the meaning that many of the girls create around boys' fighting, even while the girls may not pointedly relate it to racial conflicts at school (although sometimes they do). A paradox thus emerges, since girls both desire boys' fighting (or articulate desire for boys and their attention by discussing it) and critique it (by calling such fighting stupid). The complexities of this school's social differentiation also hinges on the idea that fighting among boys is imperative to the girls' senses of themselves as needing the racial-ethnic protection of boys. That is, while they insist that boys are dumb for racial fighting, they reward boys for their violence.

Thus, from this group of girls, we have two contradictory messages. First, the girls place racial responsibility at the feet of boys and situate boys as the perpetuators of racism. Second, the girls suggest that they, themselves, instead emphasize the similarities of people in racially neutral terms and thus situate themselves as nonracists or even antiracists. The contradiction results from the fact that the girls do not "reward" peace necessarily, but they find pleasure in the boys' fighting and racial-ethnic discord. The girls enjoy (both in a psychic sense and a social sense) the racially motivated violence. They displace the responsibility of racism onto boys while they also play an active role in perpetuating and desiring racial fighting. While the girls do not consider their active role in creating spaces of racial difference and segregation, their everyday practices of gender-sexuality and racial identification certainly are core components in doing so.

In this section, I work to draw together the girls' discussions of the racial fight with the ways they make sense of it through ideas of masculinity and, in particular, their ideas about masculine fighting and protection. They wrap feminine norms of passivity into their explanations of masculine practice. The first excerpt is from a conversation with Amy and Jackie, who are Armenian sisters.

> Amy: All the Armenian girls felt harassed, I guess, by the Hispanic boys because [when] some Latino girl tried to go in the fight to protect her boyfriend, she got hit.
> Mary: By an Armenian guy?

Amy: Yeah, and the next day [after the fight], the Latino boys were, like, "Okay, watch, we're going to get your girls." And then they [the Armenian girls] felt harassed. They were, like, scared, most of them. They didn't come to school. They had, like, 700 kids were absent the next day. It was terrible.

This excerpt is an obvious example of how Amy fears Latino boys and their possible retribution against Armenian girls. While a Latina is named as a possible "fighter," Armenian girls are fearful and victims of harassment. This exchange is further complicated, however, by what follows, about ten minutes later in the interview. Amy and Jackie shift to a description of Armenian families and the expectations for sexual and dating practices among girls. The two girls shift their discussion of protection toward pondering about girls and racial purity—protecting the race from dilution.

Jackie: I don't know why, maybe not all of them, but most of the Armenians [parents, the community] are so overprotective, you can't even imagine.
Amy: Yeah.
Mary: Just to the girls you mean?
Jackie: Yeah. I'm sure some guys, too, but not mostly. Like, it's mostly the girls that get all the attention.
Mary: You disagree with her?
Amy: I disagree with her because Armenians, we're just a group, right? We're very little, and we want our race to stay pure, and we don't like it when other races marry Armenians. We totally don't. Very few Armenians marry other ethnic groups, such as, like, Latino or African American, and there are, like, Armenians that have been here a long time—like, thirty years, forty years. We're here, um, I've been [here] my whole life, and she's been, like, fifteen years here? Yeah. And then, um, the thing is, like, yeah, if we, when we're going to get older, when we're going to get engaged and married, our parents expect us to marry an Armenian. They don't say, "Oh, go ahead, go date anybody you want." You know? They're not like that. No Armenian's like that; it's not only our parents. Armenians like to keep their group. . . .
Jackie: Please, we're not allowed to date until we get married.
Mary: How paradoxical is that!
Amy: Yeah, it's very protected. Armenian girls are very protected. But we, I'm, like, the weird person in the family because I'm, like, not racist at all. I go, "Sure, why not?" I wouldn't mind if I had a daughter, and [she] went out with, like, a Latino guy or married

Figure 3.1 The "dangerous" boys. *(Photo by Amy; used with permission and parental consent.)*

a Latino guy. I wouldn't mind, but my parents do if I do, right?
Because they were born and raised in Armenia—

Jackie: No, I bet you are not going to say that when you grow up and
you have a daughter.

It's not entirely clear how Amy is disagreeing with Jackie. Perhaps she
assumes that Jackie approves of this practice, and indeed, both girls insist that
Armenian families protect girls. Also, Amy seems more intent on highlighting her "weirdness" compared to her sister. Amy claims to be the nonracist in
the family, the girl willing to date a Latino; she explicitly insists on her ability
to consider Latinos as possible dates. Of course, this sits uncomfortably next
to her previous words about fearing Latinos. She also documents her fear in
a photo project for me, by taking a picture of "*cholos*" just outside the school.
She calls them "dangerous," and she carefully hid her camera behind her
friend's backpack so the Latinos would not see her taking the photograph of
them (Figure 3.1).

My point here is that there is consistency between these two moments,
as the girls articulate the masculinist protection by Armenian men and family. Embedded within them is Amy's contradictory message: Latinos are
dangerous, and I'm scared of them, but I'm not racist and would even date a
Latino. The consistency lies between the related themes of the Armenian boys'

protection of Armenian girls and the protection of the Armenian family or bloodline with the regulation of whom Armenian girls can date. Racial differences at the school directly confront this family's ability to remain Armenian.

Amy's narrative here is also contradictory. She situates herself as the oddball family member who isn't racist, but she *doesn't* say, "I will marry a Latino guy." She says it would be okay if she had a daughter who did. She takes the voice of her parents when considering her own ability to date a Latino ("my parents [mind] if I do"). Jackie, in her reaction, seems to take for granted that this future daughter of Amy's will have two Armenian parents. Amy did not then refute that the daughter might be the product of a Latino father. The conversation even points to how any potential boyfriend or love interest is fundamentally racialized in the girls' imaginations. The boyfriend is impossibly race neutral, as the girls cannot imagine a boy who is not racialized somehow; thus, he is always fundamentally identified. The girls assume that racialization will always be the case, even in the distant future, even as they become more "American" the longer they live in the United States. (Amy was born in the United States shortly after her family emigrated, but Jackie was two years old when the family left Armenia.)

A group interview with four girls (three Armenians and one Anglo) similarly raised the topic of why men fight. The Anglo girl in the group did not speak during the following exchanges, since the other girls were discussing specifically Armenian practices.

> Grisselle: It's guys [doing this fighting], and then girls take advantage of it; they want to get in.
> Mary: Why do they take advantage? What do you mean?
> Grisselle: Like, the girls try to find fights. They think, "Oh, there's a fight, so let's just go in it," you know? So then they [Latinas] start coming to us [Armenian girls] wanting to start fights with us, but we're, like, no.
> [*Unclear who the speaker is*]: We don't pay attention [to them].
> Mary: Who's we?
> Grisselle: Like us, the girls.

The girls who "try to find fights" are expressly Latinas. Grisselle describes the aggressivity of the Latinas and their own (Armenian) heroic refusal to engage in such petty fighting. She sees herself as an agent who resists the racial opportunistic fighting of the Latinas. Embedded here is Grisselle's theory of the primary fighting of boys and the secondary, nonfeminine or even masculinized behavior of Latinas who then "want to get in" and take advantage of Armenians' feminine propriety and their own proper passivity. The girls continue by considering why boys fight:

Alexis: I think it started off from animals—when, like, monkeys try to dominate, and the best monkey gets the best female. I think that's what they're doing.

Grisselle: Talk about monkeys.

Alexis: Hey, remember we were doing research for science class last year. That's how I think it's turning out to be.

Grisselle: Yeah, they say that we evolved from monkeys.

Alexis: If you just look at the whole concept, that's exactly what they're doing.

Mary: So the women are the prizes. Do you feel like you're a prize?

Alexis: Well, you know [shrugging, nodding].

Mary: Do you like it when guys compete for you?

Alexis: No.

Grisselle: Yeah.

Anne: Yeah, like, you feel special. But I mean if they start hurting themselves, no; but if they're just, like, doing things, like showing off and like that, that's okay. But if they start hurting themselves, it's like, never mind.

Mary: Then that's not attractive.

Anne: Yeah, because then they'll have a bleeding lip and no eye.

Grisselle: And then you're going to feel guilty.

Anne: I won't feel guilty. I'd just feel like, "You guys are retarded."

Mary: Yeah, all of a sudden they're not as attractive, huh?

Anne: Yeah, they have cuts on their faces.

My use of "attractive" was not meant to indicate physical attractiveness, but Anne was literal in her critique of boys "hurting themselves" and quite clearly continued her assessment of boys hurting their bodies and the ways that make them *less* attractive to girls. (Perhaps the alternative meaning of "attractive" in my phrasing was lost on these teenage girls who were all born in Armenia, even if they are all fluent in English.)

This exchange is stunning in how clearly it makes the connection between racial fighting and girls' heterosexual desire. First, the girls analyze boys' fighting by naturalizing the competition for women. In the girls' estimation, boys fight because they have an inherent need to win the best girls. This story points back to the previous examples of a naturalized masculine strength and fighting, but it *results* from the girls trying to explain racial conflict at school. Alexis digs into her academic training to seek an understanding of why boys fight, and—in particular to the race fight on campus—where girls should draw the line at appreciating such masculine shows of strength.

Second, the exchange follows from these girls' ideas about aggression by Latinas, which the Armenian girls insist that they ignore. The girls suggest that the "females" from the other racial-ethnic group—Latinas—are more aggressive than they, the Armenians, are. Such aggression is defeminization of Latinas, of a sort, since feminine passivity—the proper way to be feminine to these girls—is taken away from Latinas in the way they depict Latinas as aggressive. Latinas, in other words, are depicted as aggressive, potentially violent, and dangerous, which is a further articulation of racial difference being defined through and mixed into gender difference. The Armenian girls form their own gendered and racial identification only within the context of evaluating Latinas. They define their passive heterosexuality in contradistinction to Latinas' different, aggressive heterosexuality. This heterosexuality is a process of racism: determining the other girls to be different and, furthermore, dangerous through a primarily ranked racial identifier.

Third, the Armenian girls ignore any aggressive culpability in the monkey story. How *is* the best female decided—by self-evident beauty? They certainly do not seem to compete with each other to win the title. They are just waiting to be won—passively. Perhaps the self-evidently best girl chooses the winner of the fight. Regardless, the story insinuates a heterosexual pairing and a reproduction of feminine domesticity and maternity via the use of "protection." Regardless, the test is the sexually charged, desirous fight. Girls don't obviously compete here—only boys do. What if four girls wanted one boy, perhaps the one boy is the winner of an observed fight (i.e., the best monkey who gets the best female)? Then the girls *are* pushed to enter into sexual competition and fight each other. This competition is exactly the scenario from a previous example that the girls gave for the aberration of the girl fight. In other words, girls fight for catty reasons, such as over boys. Pursuing the story in either direction—as boys fighting for girls or girls fighting over a boy— still insinuates violent heterosexuality as centrally defining the practices and struggles of racial-gendered subjects.

Finally, and most obviously, the girls value boys' beauty and lament its scarring. They feel pleasure in looking at boys' bodies and talking about their appearance, and all of these practices are sexually desirous. They want the boys to fight for them and enjoy the boys' physical strength and attractiveness. If a boy is physically marred by violence, however, perhaps that indicates his weaker state and his lack of strength compared to his competitor. The girls desire sexual-racial violence but do not want to confront its materiality and how it marks the masculine body.

In all of these ways, the girls articulate a clear pleasure with the boys' fighting, even as they proclaim their lack of interest. They feel "special" when boys fight over them. With these examples, the girls also value the racial protection of "their" boys. I could conclude through these examples that the girls enjoy all fighting, not only racially motivated fighting. However, I suggest that, in these excerpts, the girls explain their desire, which is bound with gender-heterosexuality, *in terms of the racial-ethnic violence at their school.* Gender and heterosexuality, therefore, are formative of racial differences; racism articulates itself as gender and sexual pleasure (Ferguson 2005). In their complaints about boys' violence, the girls' heterosexual valorizations of boys' strength indicate their desirous attachments to racial differences and racialized fighting. Binary heterogender and desire for boys' protection is foreground, precluding homosexuality or queer desire and even misperformed gender roles. But at the core of these narratives lies the inextricable articulation of racial and gender difference; both are primary investments and result in the particular gendered, sexual, and racial practices of the girls. Bound into these investments are their criticisms of other girls' racism and misogyny—never their own. Their conscious investment, in other words, is, on the surface, an investment in the ideas that they are not violent, racist, or interested in conflicts with other-raced girls. Their narratives, however, illuminate just how facile their criticisms of boys' violent and fighting behavior are. The girls do not want to be held responsible as violent subjects, so they reject boys' bloody faces and bodies. Their dismissal of boys going too far in violence suggests that the girls want to have their cake and eat it, too. They desire fighting but want no responsibility for its marring effects and results. They say boys are "retarded" *only after* they cheer the fight on and feel "special."

The girls differ in their explanations for how masculine protection and fighting developed, of course. While Alexis and friends employ human evolution as their mythology, Sammie and Lola theorize a shorter temporality of gender behavior and indicate a regional place-based geography of masculinity for exploring gender. Sammie is Armenian, and Lola is Latina. Their friendship was one of the few that crossed the racial divide outside of school. (The girls shared a "rocker" identity that overcame the racial segregating forces on campus.)

> Mary: The conflict is driven by the boys?
> Sammie: Yeah, that's what I think.
> Lola: They're all being macho.
> Sammie: Oh, god, I hate that; it's stupid.
> Mary: . . . So why are guys like that?
> Sammie: Um, I don't know. It's been like that for so long. I think now it's less; there's some guys that are not as sexist or—
> Lola: I think it's just—go ahead—
> Sammie: I think it's just how everything's been from, like, the 1800s and all that. Women have always been kind of the house-maker, the one that takes care of the baby, and the guy has to be a tough person, like taking care of the family.
> Lola: Yeah because, like, my mom's boyfriend now, he is from Uruguay, and I guess over there, they're, like, it's not like when

they're young or whatever; they're not sexist. It's just when they reach a certain age, they have to act more manly or whatever. I guess the whole thought of being manly, you have to be strong and manly to protect the woman and then [she] will, like, go under your shield, you know? And that will be like a whole little ritual or something. . . . It's like, "Here, I'll go slay a lion. Will you go out with me?" . . . I think it just comes from little things. And, I don't know, let's say they're fighting with each other to impress a girl or whatever, and they just get used to it and that becomes kind of their personality, so they just move on to bigger things—bigger fights and riots.

Adolescence is an age when boys have to become manly, according to Lola—and protecting their women is a way to masculinize. This rite of passage, naturalized over time and space (seen as less than modern, a more machismo trend), results in masculine violence and feminine domesticity: "It's just how everything's been from, like, the 1800s." The girls seem invested in the inevitability of it despite their critique, "Oh, god, I hate that." It has been around for so long that it is difficult for them to imagine a way out of it.

In the article "'Over There' and 'Back Then': An Odyssey in National Subjectivity," Melissa Hyams (2002) notes a similar narrative device of conflating generational change and geographic difference. In her study, Mexican American girls living in Los Angeles used such stories about life "over" in Mexico as depicting the past—that is, antiprogressive gender and generational practices. The girls thus insinuate that they are more modern than Mexican girls, and they argue that their Mexican immigrant parents must realize this distinction and allow them more freedom (e.g., more mobility and less parental surveillance). In doing so, Hyams argues that the girls posit themselves as "forward-looking agents of change" as opposed to Mexican girls whom the girls consider "passive and unchanging" (470). This, Hyams suggests, is a way that Mexican American teen girls reproduce normative American identities and reinforce the border between Mexico and the United States (473).

In Lola and Sammie's conversation, history and geography similarly become the tropes of social, racial, and sexual difference. This storytelling invokes an inevitability and thus a naturalization of sexism and machismo, despite the girls' critique. In other words, the girls ascribe masculinist protection as a centuries-long process—a process that disseminates from other, less progressive spaces to the present space of the racial fight. In a sense, they rely on a myth of cultural diffusion: a spatial spread of certain power. The sexism and masculinist power eventually becomes so big that the racist riot also becomes an inevitability. Of course, the girls elide male and racial fights, similar to the narratives earlier in this chapter. Their summary of the fight condenses race and gender while it hides the girls' need to explicitly address racial differences. It operates just out of reach of the girls' story, masked by the geographic and national reference, the animal tendencies of boys fighting their nature (slaying lions), and the spatial representations of gender-sexual difference (homemaking, home protecting, and family making). Boys must become men and prove that manhood by protecting women, but the *racial protection* of women is masked by the girls' story.

A group interview with Latinas articulated similar understandings of masculine protection, but their evaluation is more approving than Lola and Sammie's, except for the lone voice among them that gets lost in the crowd. (This interview had six participants. The quality of the taped discussion is poor, so the speakers are identified with numbers.)

> Speaker 1: It's their nature, and that's what makes a girl want him: that toughness, even though it might be annoying, and you're like, "Why do you got to be so tough?" But then when he's up there [fighting], you're like, "Yay!" It's just a guy thing [to fight]; you can't change anything about it. It's like, why are girls so emotional? Because they're girls.
>
> Mary: So do you think that women like men to be violent?
>
> [*talking over each other*]
>
> Speaker 2: Not violent, but they like to be tough.
>
> [*talking over each other*]
>
> Mary: So you're attracted to really masculine guys?
>
> Speaker 3: Uh huh.
>
> Speaker 4: Not really.
>
> Speaker 5: Someone who can take care of me, you know?
>
> [*talking over each other*]
>
> Speaker 6: I wouldn't want a feminine guy who, like—
>
> Speaker 7: [Is always] running away—
>
> Speaker 8: You want someone who's going to . . . protect you when something happens. You're like, "Hey, something happened," and he's there, you know?
>
> Mary: To take care of you?
>
> Speaker 8: Yeah, pretty much.
>
> Mary: Is that what you meant?
>
> Speaker 8: Yeah.

The essentialism in the dialogue that starts this excerpt is clear: girls are emotional, and boys by nature are tough and want to fight. This essentialism defines the sexual relations of gender difference: "That's what makes a girl want him." Running away is cowardice.

Time and again the girls made these remarks and drew precarious lines in them to demarcate improper violence from masculine toughness and so-called appropriate fighting. The differences between the two are not very important and, I believe, exist because the girls have internalized the message that violent fighting—taken too far—is degraded in multicultural settings (even as it is glorified in media such as films and gaming). Their words might point to the ways girls yearn for an end to "stupid fighting," but, to the contrary, I have argued that the complexity of their affects and subjectivities point rather to sexual desire of racism and racist fighting. Agential claims stemming from a gendered identity ultimately ring hollow when contextualized by the desires that drive the valorization of racism, segregation, and violence.

In condensation, there is always censorship by the unconscious. This fact makes the term useful for thinking about how racism and racial difference have come to play roles in the practice of heterosexual desire and sexual difference in the girls' narratives. The girls claim a postracial identity (as seen in Chapter 2) and condemn boys' racialized fighting. Yet we can see in this section that racialization permeates the girls' evaluations of boys, boys' masculine strength, and the girls' myths about why sexual difference exists (monkeys, eighteenth-century homemaking, and lion slaying). The condensation at play in their ideas about boys' "stupid fighting" not only reflects their investments in sexual difference but also instigates an abiding heteronormativity based on racial difference. In other words, sexuality and gender-sexual identities are practiced through intimate racial beliefs and normativity. Thus, desire is not simply to be read off sex-gender identities or the sex of object choice. Rather, gender and sexuality are intimately entwined with race. As Siobhan Somerville puts it, sexuality is conceptualized "through a reliance on, and deployment of, racial ideologies, that is, the cultural assumptions and systems of representation about race through which individuals underst[an]d their relationships within the world" (2000: 17). Again, it is important to remember, however, that racial ideology can be circulating in the girls' narratives without girls' own conscious or obvious understandings of those circulations. In turn, reading gender and sexual ideologies of the girls' narratives without race merely strengthens a binary and occludes the complexity of the subject.

Criticizing Other Girls: Misogyny and Racism

In this section, I draw attention to several narratives in which girls evaluate other girls. Chapter 4 considers girls' interracial relationships and friendships in greater detail, but the narratives in this section in particular insinuate heterosexual racial differences, and they do so by focusing directly on racialized femininity and girls' attitudes toward other-raced girls. The excerpts point to the ways that the speaker highlights her own superiority in comparison to other girls. The first excerpt is from a conversation with Nane.

> Mary: Do you always know, do you always have a clear sense of when someone's racist to you? . . . How do you gauge racism?
>
> Nane: For us, it's kind of weird because we don't, we're not like the other girls who put on lots of makeup and make themselves look pretty and stuff. We're [not] like . . . the usual girls walking around showing their ass, or their stomach, their breasts, with a lot of makeup that they look like fake Barbie dolls. So, most of the time I get bad looks from people on the way I am, that I'm not, like, all fancy; like, I'm just in a plain T-shirt with jeans and ripped up shoes sometimes or something. But it's just the way I am. I like being comfortable. But usually I get bad looks from people on the way I dress, or, like, I hear them saying, "devil worshipper," or something. My own family members in Mexico, they're like, "She worships the devil. Don't mess with her; just let her go wherever she wants to go."

Nane marks the "bad looks from people" as racialized and racist, and her response to the question about racism evokes anxiety about her femininity or lack thereof. I can infer only that the "Barbie doll" girls are Armenian because she distinguishes "other" girls in the context of the racism question. The looks she gets from "people" are therefore those she sees as hyperfeminine: Armenian girls. I asked Nane about racism and how she might gauge when someone is being racist toward her. She answered unexpectedly by marking her gendered practices and identity—as *not* a pretty, superficial girl. Her answer reduces girls to their apparent superficiality, rather than giving, say, a critique of sexist demands that ask girls to dress up like dolls. Nane points to the Armenian girls as pretty and as actively and superficially evaluating her own sexual-gender misperformance of femininity. She wants to be "comfortable" as a Hispanic girl, and she marks her racial difference from the hyperfeminine Armenian girls whom she criticizes. She feels the pain of "bad looks," but in turn, she is also looking badly at the Barbie dolls. This is how girls' misogyny works against a gender solidarity in service to racial-ethnic segregation. She then extends this misogyny to her own family, as if to say, "even" my own family questions my normalcy. Of course, this is achieved by distinguishing the Mexican family members who are less savvy, in Nane's eyes, of the style of American girls who just want to be "comfortable"—and fashionable to the rock 'n' roll crowd in torn shoes and T-shirts.

Nane's emphasis on consumption and products places her narrative on familiar ground: femininity is articulated through those consumer objects that provide its meanings and racializations. As the Modern Girl around the World Research Group (2008) has so excellently illustrated, there is no separating the exchange of goods, race, sex, gender, location, and time. Commodities such as the Barbie doll place Nane into contemporary girlhood and offer her a mode to distinguish herself from the overly sexualized Armenian girls, even if race is lost in her critique. Her own modern, edgy appearance distinguishes itself from the hyperconsumption of femininity (yet it is notable that she refers to those Barbie girls who make themselves look "pretty"). This distance from consumer culture (contra the Modern Girl project) provides voice to Nane's agency to be different and antifeminine, but it simultaneously prohibits racial familial inclusiveness as well as schoolgirl friendships. "Usual girls" in Nane's story "function as a racialized category" (11).

Jane, an Armenian girl, told me that Armenian boys treat Armenian girls respectfully because these girls are appropriately feminine. In contrast, she says,

> Like, not to be racist or anything, but sometimes Latino girls, I see them walking around, and guys would be treating them, like, I mean, like, they [Latinas] would be dressed, like, not appropriate for school. They would be wearing baggy pants and very open shirts. And this actually goes for everyone, you know, people that dress, like, slutty. That's how they're treated, like [the way] they dress, you know? If they present themselves that way, then obviously they're going to be treated that way. Um, and yeah, guys do things that make the girls look low. They build a reputation like that.

Therefore, for Jane, slutty girls deserve being treated poorly by boys, particularly Latina sluts whose shirts are open too far. She extends her evaluation to include "everyone" in a similar move to Nane's that broadens the critique so that racist labeling is not too apparent or obvious. Emilie Zaslow, in her account of how girl power has framed media and style for girls, shows that "the dressed body represents a site on which gender, emotion, and self are narrated and on which identity is visible, surveilled by outsiders, and enacted upon by its owner" (2009: 85). Jane here gives a counternarrative to girl power consumption that focuses on sex appeal and agency through dress, however. Style is racialized, so the Latinas' baggy pants and open shirts indicate sexual promiscuity (see Hyams 2000); Jane surveils their bodies and behavior via dress.

In Jane's response, she also points to the power of boys to affect the reputations of girls. Girls decide to self-present in sexual and "slutty" ways, but boys then use that for their own purposes. Again, Jane loses the opportunity to find sympathy for these other girls whose reputations are easily affected.

Rather, she racializes the slutty girls and precludes an opportunity to critique gender and femininity norms (like Nane's failure to question Barbie doll norms). While she stops short of endorsing boys' behavior, the responsibility for girls' reputations in her account is that of the girls (Skeggs 1997). Latinas have an excess of agency and sexuality, even if Jane is careful "not to be racist or anything."

As a final example, Denise (a Latina) explains in the following excerpt how girls and boys differ in their delivery of racist commentary.

> Denise: I think they're more like, boys need to show it [racial aggression], and girls keep it to themselves amongst themselves, amongst their group of friends. And the guys will tell you straight off. They're more direct about it. I think that's a difference. I've heard [Latina] girls [point to an] Armenian girl, and they'll point out her characteristics and be very nasty about it. I've heard that, but they'll say it to themselves and maybe in Spanish or in a different language. And I don't know if Armenians are doing the same thing, they probably are, Armenian girls. I don't know.
>
> Mary: So what are some of the ways that they are derogatory against Armenian girls at school? What are their kinds of stereotypes about Armenians?
>
> Denise: Big nose, hairy. They smell. They call them armpits. Because there's a gang, AP, Armenian Power, they call it. They call it—I heard people say it stands for armpits; they smell so bad.

Here we have a similar process of a girl depicting the girls of the other racial-ethnic group as being different. Rather than Nane's pointing to hyperfemininity, here Denise points to the Armenian girls as hairy and smelly and also similarly "catty" as Latinas are in their racism. Again, racial difference trumps gendered solidarity, while Denise also insists that girls share affinities in opposition to boys' fighting. But in the same breath, she points in a misogynistic manner to the ways that girls are mean to each other: "nasty."

Conclusion

As I argue in Chapter 2, many of the girls claim a postracial identity (by insisting, "We are not racist"). In this chapter, I argue that they condemn boys' racialized fighting ("boys are stupid"). Yet racialization permeates their evaluations of boys, masculine strength, and the myths they create to explain why sexual difference exists. The condensation at play in their ideas about boys' "stupid fighting" not only reflects their investments in sexual difference but also instigates an abiding heteronormativity based on racial difference.

In other words, sexuality and gender-sexual identities are practiced through intimate racial beliefs and normative spatial segregation.

The girls reject the norm of racial and racist fighting by placing the blame for the riot on the shoulders of boys. They also reject the possibility of their own racism by displacing it onto boys, but this rejection is unspoken (and perhaps unconscious). They displace the blame for racial segregation by belittling boys for their stupidity, in a sense sweeping away their own pleasure experienced through racial segregation by marking the riot as a silly, stupid boy act on a single day. This is a practice of displacement and deferral, I find, not a simple summation or even evaluation of that day's events. The narratives are themselves part of the girls' practices of racial and gender-sexual identification and must be further contextualized with their everyday stories of their behaviors of segregation, which is seen in other chapters. The practices and stories ensure a repetition of racial segregation day in and day out in their lives. As Freud claims in his *Introductory Lectures on Psychoanalysis* (this one on dreams), "When you reject something that is disagreeable to you, what you are doing is repeating the mechanism of constructing dreams rather than understanding it and surmounting it" (1966: 179). Psychoanalytic theory therefore helps to get past girls' own agential voices that disparage racial violence.

In Freud's words, the girls do not do the work of figuring out the mechanism that propels segregation. They lament it but concurrently desire it. In this sense, the girls value racial segregation and its sexual rewards. Girls desire boys' fighting, especially as they reframe it via protection. The complexities of this school's social differentiation and segregation hinge on the idea that boys' fighting is imperative to the girls' senses of themselves as needing the racial-ethnic protection of boys. The material might suggest that the girls enjoy all fighting, not only racially motivated fighting. However, these interviews revolved around the topic of the school's riot: the girls' narratives are indicative of their desire, which is bound with gender-heterosexuality, in terms of racial-ethnic violence. Gender and heterosexuality, therefore, are formative of racial difference; racism articulates itself as gender and sexual pleasure (Ferguson 2005). In other words, the girls' complaints about boys' violence and the girls' heterosexual valorizations of boys' strength indicate their desirous attachments to racial differences and, perhaps, even in this case, racialized fighting. Certainly the contradiction between the girls' criticism of boys' fighting, and their enjoyment of it is not itself that befuddling. Rather, it is more important to ask what the effects of this contradiction are. The girls condemn racial fighting, and in so doing, they speak the language of progressive racial projects at school. Yet since they also valorize boys' strength and protection, ultimately, I argue, they support the racial segregative practices at school, in family life, and in the city as everyday inevitability and everyday pleasure.

Racism is a part of American society. This is not a statement that necessarily raises ire or demands justification. But claiming that racism is foundational to subjectivity in the United States does. Freud writes that (referring to the fantasies for the death of one's own parents) "there is an unmistakable inclination to disavow their importance in life and to make out that the ideal demanded by society is fulfilled far more often than it really is" (1966: 255). Fantasies of racial harmony, nonracist spatiality, or nonracism in one's own self are ideals that are rarely realized in society. One goal of this chapter is to hint at how such fantasies buttress the disavowal that one is not a racist.

A more explicit goal, of course, is to consider how disavowal proceeds through the condensation of gender, sexuality, and racial differences. They are utterly merged in the girls' stories about the riot, making it possible for girls to answer questions about racial violence with words on boys' behavior. The slippage is unintentional, unconscious, and thoroughly effective of further segregation and racism. The complexity and contradictions involved in these girls' racial, feminine, and sexual identifications and practices make it impossible to take girls' agency for racial harmony or feminized peace and harmony for granted. We cannot assume that feminine identities for these girls are necessarily potential sources for progressive politics—that girl power provides the space and time for a feminist project. Girls are heavily invested in binary meanings of gender-sexuality that relegate their social roles via the masculine and racial difference to be fairly passive. Of course, in everyday life, they are not passive subjects. But it is vital to think about what these narratives insinuate for a theory of subjectivity—how the girls' narratives naturalize and valorize masculine protection in the face of racial conflict. I suggest that the qualities of racial and gender difference are at the heart of each subject and, by definition, instantiate racial and gender-sexual identification along the spectrum of these qualities. That means any words spoken in support of racial understanding must also be made with the contours of racism, sexism, and heterosexism in mind. There is no racial identity without racist differentiation, and there is no strong femininity without misogyny. These social meanings are, by definition, made also through punitive evaluative processes (see Aitken and Marchant 2003). The girls' narratives point to the difficulty in imagining a subject who has an agency unmarred by its own defining process of that differentiation.

4

The Pain of Segregation

School Territoriality, Racial Embodiment,
and Paranoid Geographies

Mayra: At school, my [white] friend today, she walked over to the spot [where I was with my Mexican friends]. And what did they do? Everyone just looked at her like, "What are you doing here? Get away from me." And I felt so bad for her, so I told her, "You know what, let's just walk this way." . . .

Mary: Is it mostly the girls who looked at her funny?

Mayra: It was guys, too. Guys, too. Like, "There's a white girl here? And you're talking to her," like, you know, "What's *wrong* with you?" . . . [Because] then you're, like, [accused of being] whitewashed. You know, "Get away from me."

This chapter explores the "misplacement" of racialized bodies in this high school's segregated territories of racial-ethnic difference. In particular, it considers the importance of the subjective and emotional experiences of the girls, such as fifteen-year-old Mayra, who either venture into strange racial territory or find themselves receiving friends who have crossed racial-ethnic boundaries. Over the course of my interviews, Mayra's story became a familiar one. The "funny" looks, the discomfort, the hurt feelings, and the accusations of being a race traitor, I argue, are important clues for examining the role that the social body—and how others evaluate it—plays in subjectivity. While subjects like Mayra are categorized by others according to their bodies of difference and are policed to maintain behaviors following those stereotyped bodies, feelings of pain and discomfort simultaneously indicate the subject's failure to be fully captured by the categories that mark her. What are the repercussions of girls' experiences of being labeled and evaluated by others? At the center of this interest is the importance of the context of encounter, exchange, and conflict. In the excerpts through this chapter, space affects the subject's perceptions and responses (conscious and not) of the other. The space of interaction or social relations is just as important as the subjects doing the interacting.

The first space to consider is the immediacy of one's body in context. The narratives I culled from the interviews to frame this chapter illustrate how thoroughly the girls specifically negotiate the placement, reception, visibility, and mobility of their bodies on the school campus; other urban spaces also come up in their stories and are discussed here. These negotiations are comprehensively aged, gendered, racialized, and sexualized. As Mayra's story illustrates, racialized girl bodies have a proper place in the segregated spaces at school, and girls maneuver through these spatialities with an acute awareness of where one's body "belongs" and where one's body is improperly situated. However, the process is not one of the girls merely figuring out the rules of racial segregation; rather, the girls' narratives indicate that they often conform to the rigid spatial logic of racial segregation. Thus, the spatiality of the social-racial body is acutely experienced as part of the pressures to conform and solidify identifications, but the girls also reproduce racial-ethnic identification and segregation by accepting and often reproducing the same categorizations of difference that pain them.

The second spatial contingency is embedded within the complexity of the first (and in no way is separable from the body's spatiality): the urban campus itself. The campus space is both an existing configuration of social relations and a performative result of those social processes that materialize it daily (Thomas 2005b). The girls encounter the spatiality of segregation as soon as they walk onto the school grounds, and they are acutely faced with the materiality of the campus space. They see and experience the ways that the campus is already acting as a segregating force, as a competing array of groups and territories based on the social forms that Mayra described in her photographs of the school grounds (see Chapter 1). Of course, the patterned everyday practices of the students simultaneously form the segregated space as soon as they walk one way and not another or sit with one group at lunch and not another. While they might have the agency to disrupt the patterns of segregation evident on the school campus, they often do not act on their desires to integrate racial and social groups. This chapter considers why this occurs.

Certainly the formation, existence, continuance, and possible disruption of the school space are intimately tied to its history of experience and its mobility and connection to other spaces. (Chapter 5 extends this discussion to the family.) Everyday practices, including those in other spaces, such as the home or the city, are the building blocks of social spaces on campus. In this case, the girls' identifications are not isolated or essential to their bodies or selves, and they are not functioning only in the space that they happen to be discussing or experiencing at any given moment. Race and gender relationships at school do not develop only within the confines of campus. The urban campus space is materialized by all these processes and the many bodies maneuvering it each day.

By articulating the complicated spatial relations of campus segregation and delineating the pain that results in its surveillance and enforcement, I hope to suggest the broadest possibilities of antiracist work for multiracial urban schools. I offer this analysis as an indication of the restrictive scope of multicultural ideals to foster idealized campus spaces. Treating the school campus as a certain, bounded, and predictable space or context dooms such programs to fail because the spatiality of the campus is formed in tandem with the many other spaces of the lives of youth. Even the seemingly finite space of the body extends beyond its immediate temporal and spatial context because it materializes through spatial processes that far exceed the materiality of the body itself (Butler 1993). Youth may speak consciously about their hopes for racial integration (and place such hopes within the frame of multicultural celebrations of diversity, as seen in Chapter 2), but their spatial practices often yield other, unconscious attachments to segregation and racial definition that prohibit these yearnings from materializing into changed space. The arguments in this chapter present a critique of school programming that assumes that a renewed spatial arrangement can affect social change or integration. Identity and spatial relations cannot be simply manipulated as a variable policy in multicultural programming.

To work through the implications of this argument, I scrutinize racial territoriality, one of the spatial, normalizing processes of racialization for youth, alongside the *excesses* of that process. Hints of those excesses, I argue, include the girls' insistence of being more than just a racialized body. The concept of embodied subjectivity includes contingent social practices; personal desires for belonging; investments in race and ethnicity; and daily geographies that include youthful insecurities about not being seen, liked, or truly honored by friends. The girls react to campus segregation and its pressures to conform to that spatiality by resisting the categorical summaries of who they are based on what race they are. In other words, their narratives insist that others should not summarize them with categories of racial difference (defined visually and linguistically in the girls' stories, as forthcoming sections show). The discomfort and unease that their stories illustrate insinuate the struggle to overcome the other's confined definition of their subjectivity. Discomfort and unease are symptoms of the psychic pain that results from this struggle.

The Wrong Body for the Territory:
The Politics of Racial Reduction

In this section, I draw attention to the prevailing feeling of discomfort that the girls highlight when they tell of entering into the "wrong" racial-ethnic territory on campus. Discomfort indicates the girls' painful experiences on campus, and it points to the gap opened up between the girls' racialized bodies and how they themselves subjectively embody difference. In other words, the girls' peers at school racialize bodies by marking improper mobilities. When a girl enters into a racial-ethnic territory that she is seen to not properly embody, she is met with stares and verbal assaults and is quickly and sometimes silently encouraged to leave. The girls who are thus marked feel hurt, I argue, because their subjectivities far exceed the categories of difference that police their behavior and social practices. They yearn for friends and peers to see them for "who they are," not what "race" they embody.

Sara Ahmed (2002) theorizes the relationship between painful feelings and the encounters between the body's surficial boundary with others. She suggests that "one is more and less aware of bodily surfaces depending on the range of intensities of bodily experiences" (21). For example, a painful experience, either physical or emotional, as she puts it, "rearranges" bodies because one's body is never the same after pain. The memory of pain creates a historical and spatial legacy that determines a new identity for one's body or one's encounter with others (26). The intimate connections to others that produce pain determine that subjects are never fully alone with their pain. She writes that "it is because no one can know what it feels like to have my pain that I want loved others to acknowledge how I feel. The solitariness of pain is intimately tied up with its implication in relationship to others" (23). Literally, bodies form through painful experiences; they are the material effects of affect (27). This encounter of bodies and the subject's desire to have her pain acknowledged by others indicate the fundamental relationality of bodies and subjective embodiment.

I employ Ahmed's relationality of painful encounter in this chapter to explore the girls' narratives about the discomfort of being reduced to a racialized body, of being reduced to an other, rather than being recognized as a subject. While the girls do not use the word *pain* explicitly (they do use the word *uncomfortable* a lot), their stories evidence their painful experiences of racial reduction. In other words, their discomfort of being "out of racial space" invokes the pain of being reduced to their racialized bodies. My focus on identity, territoriality, and bodies further indicates the ways that normative spatial constraints are taken up by youth and thus operate to insist on proper racialization and subjecthood. Yet the social and subjective terms of spatial organization are not fully accomplished and not merely a matter of agents pursuing their interests. The production of space and territoriality includes the *simultaneous doing and undoing* of the subject's sense of identity and self. As Ahmed indicates, the desire for recognition (from peers in this case) is an indication of how one's pain produces embodiment through the encounter with others. The failure to achieve recognition provokes a psychic defense that affects practice and identification.

While Mayra's narrative at the beginning of this chapter provides one example of the problems that exist for those who are visited by friends of other races, most of the girls described how they felt to be the ones who ventured into the wrong territory at school. This first excerpt, from a group interview with three Filipina girls, illustrates the often extreme racism and verbal assaults that resulted from their misplaced racial bodies.

> Sephi: I walked in the Armenian territory, and they just started saying bad stuff at me.
> Chibi-Kim: . . . They do that.
> Zelda: That's really stupid.
> Mary: So what did the Armenians say to you when you walked over there?
> Chibi-Kim: Chinky!
> Sephi: Yeah, Chinky.
> Mary: Chinky?
> Zelda: Yeah. . . .
> Mary: Why do they say Chinky?
> Zelda: You know, your eyes are kind of slit. Not all Asians have those eyes [though]. . . .
> Sephi: They imitate Chinese. [*Mimics stereotyped sounds imitating Chinese language*] It doesn't really make sense.
> Zelda: They think, they automatically assume we know martial arts, and they go, "I heard you Asians can fly."
> Chibi-Kim: From *Hero* the movie.

This exchange shows how the girls share a clear understanding of which territory belongs to which racial-ethnic group. Venturing into Armenian territory elicits a verbal onslaught of racial epithets, which these girls said they tried to ignore. The girls explained that Latinos similarly called them "Chinas" in Spanish when they went into Latino territories, and they received these kinds of remarks on a weekly basis, at least. These three girls, however, do not claim that such epithets hurt their feelings because the racism does not come from friends. Of course, being on the receiving end of such remarks must be painful (Sephi calls it "bad"), but the girls shrug off that possibility by reducing the Armenian attacks to stupidity. Chibi-Kim told me, "We're the minority at school; there are, like, less of us than them. . . . We don't have the power over them; they have the power over us." Ignoring them is the girls' only stated agential act that they claim to reduce both the epithet's impact and the power of Armenians and Latinos to name these girls as "Asian" through racist bodily stereotyping. Of course, narrating to me the story of these encounters illustrates the girls' inability to just ignore the *effects* of these painful memories.

Zelda's remark about "your eyes are kind of slit" brings the racial exchange back to her body and those of so-called Asians. Certainly this racial category is stretched hard by the girls to incorporate both Filipinos and Chinese. Sephi reproduces the imitative mimicry used by the Armenian students to make fun of "Chinese" language. This exchange by the girls indicates how their bodies' placement in Armenian territory enables an encounter of racial difference that defines them and their bodies as primarily (or even solely) "Asian." However, Zelda says, "Not all Asians have those eyes," as a way to insist she is more than her eyes and the racialized markings on her body. At the same time, her remark also points to her racialized Asian self-identity because indicating an Asian category beyond stereotypical eye shape is a way to open the category for her own inclusion. Here the girls' use of "Asian" also points to the power of racial categories over those specifically relying on ethnicity and language. Ultimately, it is important to note that the girls partake in the economy of racialized difference that they also resist and protest.

The use of "they" and "us" (e.g., "*they* have the power over *us*") also demonstrates the girls' participation in an Asian-other division at school. These girls' close friends are also Asian, in particular other Filipinos. (In fact, there are very few Chinese students at this school.) These words invoke Zelda's racial-ethnic identifications and point to the ways that bodily norms "cultivate" investments in the self. I borrow this terminology from Judith Butler (2002). She argues that norms preexist the subject (like racial and gender-sexual difference) and therefore mold how bodies are visible and identified, yet norms are in no way the summary of the subject's embodiment or subjectivity:

> We will become attached to ourselves through mediating norms, norms which give us back a sense of who we are, norms which will cultivate our investment in ourselves. But depending on what these norms are, we will be limited to that degree in how we might persist in who we are. What falls outside the norms will not, strictly speaking, be recognizable. And this does not mean that it is inconsequential; on the contrary, it is precisely that domain of ourselves which we live without recognizing, which we persist in through a sense of disavowal, that for which we have no vocabulary, but which we endure without quite knowing. This can be, clearly, a source of suffering. But

it can be as well the sign of a certain distance from regulatory norms, and so also a site for new possibility. (17)[1]

The conditions of subjectivity include entering into social visibility; that is, bodies are legible only given their recognizability. (You cannot see something you do not know how to see.) As Butler notes, however, the subject also *exceeds* its social visibility because it is founded on a governing disavowal of what falls outside normative social life. One must reject social forms and norms in order to identify with those norms through which we "cultivate our investment in ourselves."

The fantastic claim by the Armenians that "Asians" can fly—a joke made by the Armenians and repeated by the girls to me—also places Zelda's racialized body in a media exchange after the Chinese martial arts film *Hero* (in which the heroes can "fly") and out of reach of Zelda's control of her own defining embodiment. "They have the power over us" literally means that these Filipina girls are powerless to affect the ways their racialized bodies are marked, defined, policed, and mocked. Norms (and discourses that include stereotypes) such as these provide the girls with ways to recognize themselves and recognize themselves in the eyes of others. However, while they take up certain modes of identifying (as Asians with Asian bodies), they also maintain a distance from the norms that regulate their bodies (Butler 2002), which is evidenced through the comments about not having *that* kind of Asian eyes. Here their ethnicity (and their own racial stereotyping) asserts itself by marking their Asian eyes as supposedly less "slit" than those of Chinese.

Girls suffer when their subjectivity is reduced by the visibility of their racial-ethnic bodies (i.e., what others see), but their narratives also indicate that they do not know how to contend with this pain. Instead of Butler's ever-optimistic indication of possible—and progressive—social change (Mahmood 2005), the girls I met end up reinscribing racial-ethnic difference by shrugging off their pain and then accepting these identifications and productive powers as inevitable and natural (such as with Zelda's rebuttal that "not all Asians have those eyes"). This normalizing of racial difference, despite the pain it invokes, is a step that should discourage easy suggestions of embodied agency within the confines of a highly regulated and invested racial economy of subjectivity. Possibilities exist, but the forces to conform are strong (compare Morris-Roberts 2004b). As I show in the forthcoming sections, the girls note their disappointment in not achieving these possibilities. However, this disappointment relies on a victim standpoint. The girls never seem to be enforcers of segregation; they are only victims and sufferers of segregation.

1. Here Butler is discussing Michel Foucault's work on power in terms of what it teaches about subjectivity.

Violet and Denise are Hispanic sisters whose peer groups are largely composed of Anglo students. (Denise goes to a different high school, however.) Violet, a cheerleader, insists that race is not an important determinant of belonging in her group of mostly sports-identified youth; rather, individuality and "coolness" count.

> Violet: [In my social group at school] each person has their own individuality and, like, we really don't, like, we don't, like, *really* look at your race. And, like, [we don't say,] "Oh, you can't do this because you're this race." If you, if you're really cool, then we're with you; it doesn't matter. Like, our group of friends has a mixture of race, of race and stuff. . . . It just so happens that we just, we just, like, click together.
>
> Mary: Do you have a certain territory at school?
>
> Violet: We all, our group, we always hang out by the senior sign. And that's where the football players and the cheerleaders and the white people are right there, and the black people too. And then the Hispanics are in the cafeteria; that's where they . . . have lunch. . . . And the Armenians are in the front of the school. . . . Each person has their own set. But, like, I—I go to different groups, like, I'll go to, like, the metal people and, like, the rockers. I change a lot.
>
> Mary: Would you ever walk up to the Armenian group? . . .
>
> Violet: I have, I have been there, like, with my friends. Like, some of my friends are Armenian. I'll go there, I'll say hi or whatever. I really—I feel really uncomfortable sometimes, but I do go. Yeah. But I really don't want to.

It is hard to know whether Violet does indeed have the racial mobility she claims, given her discomfort and seeming lack of words to break the discomfort when visiting Armenian friends in their territory. But her insistence that race does not really matter to her friends and her example of being in cliques that form based on music and alternative identities and activities (such as rockers and cheerleading) indicate Violet's investment in her identity as different from the other highly racialized, regulated students at school (see Morris-Roberts 2004a).

What does it mean, though, that Violet emphasizes "really" when she says, "We don't, like, *really* look at your race"? In part, at least, it points to the impossibility of *not* looking at race. Violet knows that she cannot avoid looking at race because race is marked on the body, but she disavows the power of that visibility to determine friendships. She resists the power of embodied ethnicity-racialization, but her comment also acknowledges the inability to escape the confines of normative racial-ethnic difference. While she resists the normative differentiation, she also marks the constraints of that resistance. "Coolness" is instead the litmus test she espouses for belonging to this peer group, but Violet does not have any African American or Asian friends, and most of her white friends are Anglo, not Armenian or Hispanic. Violet claims that the mobility of friendship groups is related to music and sports-based groups, not racial-ethnic groups.

Violet's story of friendship is not remarkable for its contradictions. In fact, as Jane Dyson (2010) tells us, there are important connections between "friendship and the reproduction of dominant ideologies and practices" (482). Friendship can be both a source of solidarity and empowerment even though it might form around "instrumental concerns" (491) or exclusionary social or kinship structures. Dyson's work insinuates that friends must have an underlying agreement about morals and social expectations and, as her research shows, a shared commitment to gendered work regimes for girls. But, she insists, "the particular form that friendship takes, and the manner in which people discuss friendship, varies geographically and historically. Among a set of young people living in [her case study site] contemporary north India, friendship was primarily imagined as a relationship of trust and affection that simultaneously facilitated effective labor and was formed through that labor" (495). In the case of this American urban high school, the way coolness works for friendship is mired in normative white bodies and mobility. Friendship can offer discomfort when the spaces mismatch the ideology of "cool," such as when a friend is visited in Armenian territories. This discomfort marks the limit of that friendship to resist racial segregation across particular campus spatial regimes, and the moral commitment to being open and accepting (i.e., cool) is dropped outside racially safe zones.

Violet and Denise noted their inability to "fit in" with many Hispanics because of their own poor Spanish language skills. They often felt uncomfortable in what they call "Hispanic locations" where Spanish is dominant.

Denise: Only when I go into, like, Hispanic locations, like, to certain stores, when I go in there, they look at me because I'm different from them. . . . They just stare at me. Like, I feel uncomfortable, and then I feel like leaving. But my dad, he's buying something, and, like, he speaks the language better than I do.
Mary: Right.
Denise: And I just feel uncomfortable. That's why I don't really like going with him to, like, Spanish places and stuff like that. . . .
Violet: I never ever, since middle school, hung out with Hispanic people. I just never got really along with them because I'm not like them. But I do associate with them sometimes, but only during class for, like, projects and stuff. Other than that, I hang out with

the white kids, white people and football players and, like, people
who don't really look at my ethnicity, just who I am.

These girls find more social comfort around other English speakers, nota-
bly "white people." White people, according to Violet, "don't *really* look,"
which is remarkably similar wording to her statement that she and her friends
don't *really* look at your race when interacting with peers at school. In this
second case, however, it is Violet's own racialization that is not *really* noticed.
(It is noticed because there is no such thing as not noticing.) But Violet insists
that she is not reducible to her "ethnicity." It is not "who I am" to her. The
discomfort she and Denise describe by being reduced to the Hispanic girl in
Armenian territory (Violet), or the poorly performing Hispanic girl who cannot speak good Spanish (both girls), points to the anxieties of being partially
or incompletely seen as merely an ethnic and racialized body. Violet desires
recognition, but certainly she desires a wider recognition than one based on
her ethnicity. Whiteness to Violet marks the ability to look beyond race, while
the Hispanic Spanish speakers reduce her to her ethnicity and note her failure
to live up to it properly (compare Dwyer and Jones 2000). Denise, as the following excerpt illustrates, insists that her brown skin should mark an inclusion
into a racial group that she does not fit into linguistically.

> Denise: Or like older women because older women will ask us for help.
> Because, you know, they always ask young people for help because
> they know we speak English and they think, okay, you're bilingual.
> And I'm, like, oh, I can't help you. And then all of a sudden they're,
> like, so upset because they're like, wait a minute, you're supposed
> to know, you know, you're supposed to know how to do it so you
> can help us older people who can't speak, who can't speak English
> that well. And I guess because I can't help them, they get so upset.
> I've had that happen a couple of times.
> Mary: So do you think they get upset because they think that you're
> selling out to American life, that you're not Mexican enough?
> Denise: Oh, yeah. They think we're big sellouts. They call us *gringas*
> or things like that all the time. I'm like, no, I mean, I'm brown-
> skinned! This may be a nice cover-up—but no.

In this example, Denise feels the stares of Spanish speakers in Hispanic
spaces as marking her difference: "They look at me because I'm different from
them." Here she insists that her brown skin should prove her fundamental
racial solidarity with other Hispanics, despite her inability to speak fluent
Spanish. Skin—the body—in her mind should trump language. The body's
phenotype is a fundamental connection to other Hispanics in her mind. This

is another kind of racial reduction, of course, than the one Denise criticizes from school. Here she values the possibilities that racial reduction to skin color affords because her body marks her claim for inclusion to a group that seeks to exclude her. Her brownness validates, in her mind, spatialized racial categorization: the brown skin is her entrance ticket to Hispanic spaces. White social spaces, on the other hand, in Violet's estimation are inclusionary based on class markers such as style, social and sporting activities, *and* the supposed disavowal of skin's colored materiality. Whiteness serves as a fantasy to Violet that she can be seen as "who she is" and not what color she is.

While actively recognizing race, a comparison of the two narratives brings to the fore the conflicting forces of seeking racial recognition and resisting racial reduction. On the one hand, Violet insists that "I'm not like them"—the Hispanic people that she references particularly at school. On the other hand, Denise pleads to Hispanic people to see that "I'm brown-skinned!" Both are right, in a sense. In a context of complex processes of subjectivity, there is an ambivalence of racial identification: one is both *more* than one's race and always socially and spatially *accountable* for the materiality of one's body. But Denise's plea hints at a hope that she will be identifiable as an authentic, Hispanic body despite her linguistic inability to communicate that identity properly in words. She hopes that her skin will do the work to provide the recognition she seeks, but she fears that her skin and her embodiment of race is not adequate to avoid the racially charged and class-coded "sell-out" label of *gringa*.

To be clear, I do not want this argument to indicate a position that validates the politics of recognition. I am swayed by Lois McNay's *Against Recognition* (2008) that cautions theorists not to rely on prescriptions for agency and resistance in terms of identity. Rather, McNay urges scholars to remember the power relations that shape the terms of calls for recognition. Following her lead, my use of recognition here is meant to mark the *failures* of identity politics. Denise wants her identity of Hispanic to be self-evident through the marking of color on her skin and calls for inclusion based on that simple identity. This is, of course, resisted by those who define—in exclusionary ways, to be sure—the broader contours of race and ethnicity as language. Denise's hope to be recognized as a brown-skinned Hispanic girl neglects the powerful racial and class relations that shape ideal norms for behavior in particular spaces. Violet's hope for recognition as a more-than-Hispanic girl at school similarly neglects the social-spatial power relations that already influence her *need* to be seen as such. She also relies on an idealized fantasy of inclusion to white segregated spaces at school. I do not mean that she is allowed to access these spaces; rather the fantasy is that she thinks she can overcome her racialized embodiment by simply being with white people. She problematically situates whiteness and its spaces as racial-free zones of openness. Whiteness becomes vacated of power relations through this narrative and occupies a central focal point for Violet's ideal of peace at school. Whiteness solidifies its hold as the normative spatial ideal through Violet's commitment to its supposed neutrality.

Resisting Segregation? Shrugging/Acquiescing and Reproducing Separate Spheres

Language, style, dress, music, body features, and media are all examples from the girls' narratives that mark their racial-ethnic difference and serve as modes through which they self-identify as feminine, racialized subjects. The range of these examples illustrates the ubiquity of how ethnic and racial difference saturate the girls' narratives and identifications. These practices also show how the girls' subjectivities develop via the norms that circulate in their particular social and spatial contexts. The girls have a deep sense of themselves through these social and class markers, including visual bodily markers, yet they also often gloss the attachments to ethnic and racial difference that their practices of language, style, or dress simultaneously invoke. Even explicitly resisting race's defining powers over the self marks the subject's intimate connection to normative difference. Thus, resistance to norms is highly constrained, contrary to Butler's hope for "new possibilities."

"Rockers" were one clique at the school that did partially transcend racial-ethnic divides between Latinos and Armenians. (I did not hear any examples of African Americans in this group, and apparently there were very few recent immigrants because of language barriers. From what I could tell, the group spoke English only.)[2] Lola, a Latina, and her friend, Sammie, an Armenian, shared an identity at school involving music and style. I interviewed the girls together. Lola shared a story similar to Violet's about entering Armenian territory.

> Lola: At our school, it's like, there's a little zone of Armenians, and then there's, like, Hispanics. Well, one day there's this [Armenian] girl that my boyfriend was talking to, and she, like, kind of wanted to leave her group because she was a really, like, hard. Like, she was a [hard] rocker or whatever, and they were kind of criticizing her for it, so she came over to our group. And then one time, she didn't come, and there was a guy in our group that kind of liked her, so we went over [to visit her in the Armenian zone]. And, like, all of

2. Because Latinos and Armenians are the overwhelming majority at the school, it may be that I just did not meet girls who fit this possibility or did not specifically talk to girls who mentioned black rockers.

the Armenians, when we pulled her over and talked to her, they just, like, all, like, *gazed* on us. . . . Like, all of them were looking at us, and we're just like, yeah [*nodding*], ohhhhh, okay.

Mary: . . . They're staring you down.

Lola: Like, as long as you're not, like, well, we didn't do anything bad to them. They were just looking at us, so we were just, like, felt a little uncomfortable. . . . It's just like, if you're one of those people that just likes to talk about people a lot, then that's when you get in trouble, you know? But if you just, like, mind your own business and just, like, stay with your own, like, I guess, like [*trails off, shrugs*].

Chibi-Kim, Sephi, and Zelda did find that they do just "go off" for no reason, as evidenced in the racist epithets they encounter when they venture into Armenian territory. However, Lola's story shares some similarities with Violet's, particularly the "gaze" (Violet spoke of looking at race), and of course, the feelings of being "uncomfortable." (On the discomfort of proximity, see also Thien 2005.) Both Lola and Violet are Latinas who found themselves in the Armenian zone or territory. Lola here also notes that staying with "your own" prevents such discomfort, and in her case it refers to her own clique and its zone at school. "Trouble," as Lola notes it, is the conflict that is reflected by the gaze—the looks—that tell her not to be in that territory: she does not belong in Armenian space as determined by the visibility of her racial (and stylistic) difference. "Minding your own business" means minding your racial-ethnic territory, an explicitly *spatial* behavioral expectation. There is also some confusion in this quotation because she insists that they "didn't do anything bad to them" and were not people who would "talk about people a lot." Therefore she distances herself from being in "trouble" with the Armenians because there was no overt challenge or verbal assault. Instead, the gaze indicated potential trouble and is reason enough to Lola to "stay with your own."

The gaze—the viewing of the visible racialized body as well as being viewed—is inevitable in Lola's account. I think the important aspect of her narrative is the discomfort that she notes, rather than the marking of the othered body. The regulation of this discomfort means that Lola will stay with her own group because she says that if you "stay with your own," you can prevent tense interactions arising from interracial and interclique confrontations. The discomfort may be an example of what Butler both calls "a source of suffering" and marks as a potential point for resisting "regulatory norms," but Lola's shrug also suggests that she prefers not to make waves. Thus, status quo segregation remains the normative and normalizing spatiality of the school. This segregation and racial territoriality may be painful, but at the same time they are comforting to the girls. The fact that they have "their own" people to be with is both inclusionary *and* exclusionary.

Armenian girls likewise experienced similar situations. Jackie told me about running into her Hispanic friends at the mall and being "cold-shoul-dered" by them. Her sister, Amy, then chimed in with her own story.

Jackie: Like, me and my [Armenian] friends went to the mall, and I saw . . . a couple of my Hispanic friends there. So we gathered all together, and they were with another group of [Hispanic] friends. And then they just started ignoring us. And then, like, my friends were like, "Okay, well, we'll just see you later" [*shrugging*]. So then they just passed by. And then, like, I felt that, like, . . . they were just leaving us because we were there, you know? . . .

Mary: So they were avoiding you because they didn't want to—

Jackie: Be seen [with us] or be around, I'm not sure. They're like, after that, still me and my friends are still friends, but [*trails off, shrugs*].

Mary: Right.

Jackie: I didn't say anything, but you still felt it, you know? . . .

Amy: Incidents like that—when I was walking, I saw a friend of mine. She was Latino, and she was with a group of her other Latino friends. It's like, I wanted to say hi to her, but I didn't feel comfortable because her other friends were there, and they were looking at me in a weird way. So I was like, okay, stay away from trouble. I just, like, ignore it, and I just smile, you know?

Jackie: Yeah, when they're individuals, and you're friends with them, you can say hi, but if they're with groups and you're alone, you can't just pretty much go say hi to your friends.

Amy: Yeah, you feel, like, outcast. You know?

Jackie's shrug showed me that she did not trust her Hispanic friends after this experience, and she did not confront these friends for what she thought was their poor behavior toward her at the mall. The racial territories at school are not place specific to the school campus, but the spatiality of segregation is enforced even in what could possibly be more fluid spaces for teens, such as the mall. The peer pressure of staying with "your own" is a strong segregating force. Jackie's discomfort and hurt feelings of being ignored by the Hispanic girls whom she thought of as friends further encourages her to stay with her Armenian friends and in Armenian territory at school. The mall interaction suggests to Jackie that her "real" friends may be only other Armenians, thus her hurt feelings indicate the rejection she feels from her Latina friends. It is also notable that she initially refers to Armenian friends simply as "friends," but Hispanic friends are racially qualified. The pain of being an "outcast" to the Hispanic girls is one effect of Amy's racial-ethnic identification and embodiment, and it marks the ways that identification proceeds through the rejection and disavowal of the encounter, just as much as similarity and solidarity do.

It is also important to note that in all of the girls' narratives, they posit themselves as the heroes of their stories. That is, they are the ones who attempt to transcend racial segregation and enforcement, only to be rebuffed. No one told me, for example, of incidents in which they coldly rejected friends who came to visit them. Furthermore, very few of the girls I interviewed had close friendships with girls of other races and ethnicities (Sammie and Lola were exceptions), and few girls had been to the homes of their friends who identified as other races or ethnicities. Many of the Armenian girls even said that their parents (all of whom were born in Armenia) forbade them from being in non-Armenian homes.

Whitewashing Race

Mayra, whose story begins this chapter, told me the following about the same white friend, whom she described as "one of my best friends":

> Mayra: I know her, and I know that, you know, she loves every race, you know, she loves every person. And with her I feel the same way. She's not—she's not white to me, you know; she's just my friend. . . .
>
> Mary: What about when you go home with her? . . .
>
> Mayra: We've never hung out [outside of school].
>
> Mary: So why is that? I mean, why don't you hang out at each other's house?
>
> Mayra: That's—I think it's because, I mean, I would be scared to meet her mom because she'd probably be like, "This is the kind of person my daughter hangs out with?" You know?

I do not know if Mayra's friend had, in fact, ever invited her home. Mayra, who faces the scorn of her Latina friends for being "whitewashed" by having this white friend (and for other reasons seen in Chapter 5), herself devalues her ethnic body and worries that her white friend's mother would think she was a dangerous gangster-Mexican who, as she qualified to me, had failed four classes (her white friend had also failed four classes, as Mayra made sure to add).

Arlene Dávila, in her book on the public whitewashing of Latinos in the United States, analyzes how model minority discourses of hard work and family values "frame the trajectory by which minority groups can claim to belong to the nation, turning some groups into living proof of the ideals of individualism and meritocracy at the core of the US national ideology"

(2008: 7). Here Mayra turns that trajectory to herself, and her shame at failing this meritocracy frames her friendship with her white friend.

As Dávila also suggests, "Racial politics highlight the importance of 'culture' in terms of the intangible but very real markers of language, dress, demeanor, and cultural capital that, in addition to phenotype, make race so pervasive in everyday life" (17). Mayra said to me, "I was, you know, growing up I was taught, oh, [to] look like a gangbanger is what's 'in.'" Mayra's white friend may "love every race," but Mayra relents to the negative racist views of Latinas in Los Angeles who come from low-income families (i.e., look "gangster"). Her shame in the way she represents her ethnic body, through dress and academic performance, is notable. The white home is not spatially appropriate for her self-identified "ghetto" Mexican presence. She is acutely aware of the ways "race is so pervasive in everyday life," although she is less able to frame her own self-racialization (i.e., racial identity) through the terms of whiteness and its unrelenting meritocracies of privilege.

It is also remarkable that Mayra insists that her friend is "not white to me." This phrase points to Mayra's desire not to be reduced to her racialized body and its failure to achieve normative white visibility. However, the desire to surpass her racial appearance and body has not been able to achieve a friendship off campus. Mayra does not have a language to discuss this friendship's ability to transcend the pressures of racial-ethnic segregation without resorting to an ideal of racial harmony; fundamentally, this ideal is based on the love of racial difference ("She loves every race."). In other words, if this friend were not white, or Mayra were not a Latina (both impossibilities), perhaps they would be able to hang out outside of school. Despite "not being white to me," their bodies mark the limited potentials of the friendship.

As with the previous discussion of Violet's reliance on whiteness, here again is an example of how the category works psychically as a symbol of belonging and recognition. While not a universal (Wiegman 1999), whiteness functions in highly particular ways as an anchor to lodge girls' faith in multiculturalism. It provides them an idealized context that they think will enable their "full" subjectivity despite fundamental racial differences. Their practices, furthermore, belie the fantasy. Mayra loves her friend, and her white friend "loves every race," but neither girl has extended her love beyond the sociality that school provides. In Mayra's narrative, she indicates that she cannot get past her own racial embodiment and the stereotypes of Mexican *chola* that her friend's *mother* will see. Mayra is self-imposing this shameful restriction on herself (or saving herself from having to admit to me that her friend has not invited Mayra to her home). Yet whiteness does not fail. Mayra fails herself instead of critiquing racist ideologies. Thus, while she resists the segregating behaviors of her Mexican friends at school, she ends up inscribing this segregation in her own life. McNay writes that recognition "cannot be dissociated from misrecognition or the process whereby individuals are accommodated to their own oppression" (2008: 33). While Mayra says that her white friend loves every race and loves her despite her Mexican race and ethnicity, Mayra couples this narrative of recognition with the misrecognition that she thinks the white girl's mother is sure to have. In effect, it is Mayra's accommodation to her own racial embodiment and oppression that fuels the fear of the mother's misrecognition.

Like Mayra and Jackie, many of the girls claim to have friends of other races and discount the power of racial difference to prevent friendship. Yet all of them also tell of the effects of racial difference on their friendships at school, in public, and in homes. Very few of them actually have friendships that extend beyond school spaces, and even the friendships they claim have difficulty finding space to be at school. The girls indicate the multiple ways that they are marked by their racial-ethnic bodies, and these marking epithets (Sephi and friends), looks (Violet), gazes (Sammie), and rebuffs (Jackie and Mayra) cause them discomfort, hurt feelings, or shame. These subjective feelings hint at the anxiety the girls have for not being adequately or fully acknowledged, seen, and befriended. The everyday racial policing of body placement steers the girls' social-spatial practices of segregation on campus. As I show in the next section, the girls' *perception* of such spatial policing of racial territories—whether that perception is accurate or not—is just as important a process as the so-called actual social pressures to segregate.

Paranoia: Suspicion, Fear, and Self-Segregation

The girls indicate that the practices of segregation and the feelings of discomfort and pain at racial territorial transgression are often based on a perception of some type of threat. The ways that the girls talk about the "gaze" of others, the foreign tongues that must be discussing them but that they cannot understand, the assumed reactions of others to the girls' actions, and what someone is *about* to say about or to them (but doesn't) show that these suspicions are all quite capable of altering girls' behaviors. Ultimately, these perceptions and uncertainties play a vibrant role in the ongoing processes of girls' identification and their social-spatial practices. In a sense, "perception" gives too much of a cognizant meaning to the process, so in this section I draw out the theoretical importance of both the conscious and unconscious aspects of these stories. This section analyzes more directly how the girls evaluate, judge, and fear the actions and thoughts of racial others. There are two distinct geographies of these actions and thoughts that the girls described to me: school and shopping. After I provide a conceptual framework to introduce this section, I divide the examples into these two subsections, providing more particular context to each space.

The girls seem, in simple words, to be paranoid of others around them. They tell of their territorial transgressions with a constant accompanying theme of the other's potential reactions to their actions. Rarely does this reaction extend beyond a look—cold or threatening—in the girls' stories. But the regularity of this repeated situation begs the question of its importance and its function in the segregation practices of girls. Their perceptions of the always watching, judging other are both conscious and articulated and, I argue, unconsciously operating to powerfully shape the spatial behaviors of the girls in any number of different contexts, from school to other urban geographies.

Of course, I do not want to indicate that the girls are clinically disturbed. Sigmund Freud's own primary source on paranoia (Freud 1958) was a case study of Schreber, the probable schizophrenic. Freud characterizes Schreber's paranoid symptoms as a defense against homosexual impulses (Oldham and Bone 1994). Rather than turning to Freud's analysis of Schreber, I instead develop several general behaviors of racial paranoia based on Stanley Bone and John Oldham's clinical overview of paranoia.[3] Again, I caution that exploring paranoia in this case in no sense indicates that I believe that the girls are pathological or clinically ill. Rather, paranoia indicates several "normal" psychoanalytic foundations of subjectivity, including narcissism, which is a necessary psychic function in the development and ongoing health of the ego.

Drawing conceptually on paranoia helps to further think through how girls aggrandize their own racial identities as based on respect and love, as intense distrust and suspicion surrounds their dealings with girls in other racial groups. This section focuses on girls' social and racialized practices of suspicion, surveillance (perceived toward them and targeted at others), and antagonism. Suspicion is perhaps the most important of these three because it leads the girls to blame *others* for racism and segregation. They tend to aggrandize their own racial practices as laudable and love filled at the same time.

Bone and Oldham (1994: 4) list the American Psychiatric Association's (APA; Crapanzano 1998) clinical criteria of paranoid personality as follows (these were not significantly altered in the APA's fourth edition of mental disorders, published in 2000):[4]

A pervasive and unwarranted tendency [unassociated with schizophrenia or delusion] . . . , to interpret the actions of people as

---

3. Explorations of paranoia in fiction and film studies are also numerous, particularly in explorations of American genres (Carr 2004; Coale 2004; Tuhkanen 2001; Farrell 1996).

4. Interested readers should read John Farrell's book, *Freud's Paranoid Quest: Psychoanalysis and Modern Suspicion* (1996), for a trenchant critique of Freud's theory of paranoia. He argues that Freud's thesis of the psyche was a direct consequence of Freud's own paranoid tendencies.

deliberately demeaning or threatening, as indicated by at least four of the following:

1. expects, without sufficient basis, to be exploited or harmed by others.
2. questions, without justification, the loyalty or trustworthiness of friends or associates.
3. reads hidden demeaning or threatening meanings into benign remarks or events. . . .
4. bears grudges or is unforgiving of insults or slights.
5. is reluctant to confide in others because of unwarranted fear that the information will be used against him or her.
6. is easily slighted and quick to react with anger or counterattack.
7. questions, without justification, fidelity of spouse or sexual partner.

This list is not meant to prescribe any one girl's behavior, but taken together, the girls' multiple narratives illustrate the paranoid tendencies of segregation and racial suspicion. There are many more examples than the ones I raise in the following subsections, and examples in other chapters might bring this argument to your mind as you read. But before I jump to the empirical subsections, let me tailor this clinical list to the case of territories of racial segregation that this chapter examines.

I initially was drawn to the concept of paranoia for its compelling attention to the ways that the subject's self-centering occurs through its often warped assumptions about how others were scrutinizing its own appearance and actions. Additionally, this self-centering proceeds through unconscious motivations and forces, not just through any sort of conscious ability to judge with objectivity the fact of others' motives. Thus the subject's depiction of others' practices and opinions provide a certain function in the making of a self (which Freud develops through his theories of narcissism). Many of Bone and Oldham's symptoms seem relevant to the girls' narratives that describe their interactions and relations with peers at school and, as I show, their experiences as nonwhite shoppers and consumers in urban Los Angeles. The girls repeatedly discussed how those they identified as racial-ethnic others were watching their activities and bodies reproachfully, sometimes with a fear that the other would follow these looks with some sort of action against them. Thus, they articulated a clear suspicion of the racial-ethnic other based on their interpretation of the others' watching them. According to Bone and Oldham, the girls "expected that look," and they read "threatening meanings into these often benign events." Even a look or a glance, or an overhead conversation in a language they did not understand, made them react with suspicion and sometimes fear. They told stories of other groups laughing as they walked by; they were sure it was directed at them, even though the language of the other groups was incomprehensible. And finally, as in previous sections, their encounters with so-called friends in segregated spaces or in chance meetings (such as at the mall in Jackie and Amy's story) led them to question their friends' loyalties in the face of racial difference.

Thus, the overall effect of the pervasive relations of suspicious paranoia results, I argue, in an assumption of these youth that the racial other is always watching and surveilling. Thus, the girls fill in this other subject beyond themselves. Their paranoid practices and narratives are the fuels that drive the girls' ways of seeing the other. They assume to know the other subject based on their own paranoid observations and interpretations. They depict another's activities and intents, and these depictions motivate them to alter their own behaviors. At the same time, this depiction and analysis of the other is a process of unconscious self-making for the girls. That is, their reactions to that other subject and its spaces are productive of the girls' own racial segregating practices and identities. The slippage between these delusions and the girls' interpretations of their delusions means that the "truth" does not matter; only their perceptions of it matter (compare Carr 2004: 284). This does not mean that girls are always wrong about the intents of others, but they repeat time and again certain social spaces as saturated by the behaviors of others in terms that explain these behaviors as direct reflections of their own centrality. In other words, many girls think that the other is constantly focused on them, whether or not this is true. This thought process, not the other's force, results in patterned self-regulation, such as segregation and self-surveillance. Thus, paranoia directed against the watching, threatening other points to the subject's self-aggrandizement (as occupying a central focus to the other). Paranoia encourages a reiteration of racial identification via relations with the *perceived* other. This relationality proceeds in a context of intense and particular power relations that are spatially contingent. It also points to the limits of a self-aware agency based on one's identity as a nonracist. The girls may claim that the other is to blame for always misevaluating their intentions and actions, but paranoia fundamentally refocuses such motivations *to the subject herself.*

Paranoia at School

I group the excerpts in this subsection to mark the repeated nature of the symptomatic narratives that the girls share (an arrangement similar to that in Chapter 2). You may recognize some of these excerpts from other chapters, as I reinterpret them here with the particular argument of paranoia in mind. Unlike most other sections of this book, I highlight with italics the recurring themes in the interviews that point to what I am identifying as symptoms of paranoia.

Denise and Violet, of the following excerpt, are Hispanic sisters. In response to my question of what they think started the fight, the conversation proceeded as follows:

> Denise: I heard rumors of, like, supposedly some Hispanic guy slapped an Armenian girl or an Armenian guy slapped a His—I don't know, someone hit someone, so someone felt they had to protect the women, or something like that.
>
> Violet: And it just escalated from there.
>
> Denise: From there. And it's always been tension. . . . You can notice the tension between them.
>
> Mary: How do you notice it, like, what do you, how do you?
>
> Violet: The *stares* at each other.
>
> Denise: The stares and, like, they talk in their own languages: like, the Hispanics will talk in Spanish, and the Armenians will talk in Armenian. *And you have the feeling that they're talking about each other, but you can't really prove it because you don't know the other language.* So it's just like, I think it was just emo[tional]. Like the reason why, they've just always wanted to fight each other, but this gave them a reason to do it. And I think they always wanted to from the beginning.

Amy and Jackie, the speakers in the following excerpt, are Armenian sisters.

> Amy: All of the Armenian girls felt harassed, I guess, by the Hispanic boys because some Latino girl tried to go in the fight to protect her boyfriend, and she got hit.
>
> Mary: By an Armenian guy?
>
> Amy: Yeah, and the next day [after the fight], the Latino boys were like, "Okay, watch, we're going to get your girls." And then they [the Armenian girls] felt harassed. They were, like, scared—most of them, so they didn't come to school. They had, like, seven hundred kids were absent the next day of school. It was terrible.
>
> Mary: So is there a lot of harassment across groups between boys and girls? I mean, are the boys harassing usually?
>
> Jackie: You can't really say harassment. But, *you feel pressured*, that's all.
>
> Amy: And *you're just, like, scared to look at them. You think they're going to start a fight with you. I'd just rather go, like, this way, you know, instead of that way.*

Mary: So there's just this kind of threat all the time.

Both girls: Yeah.

Jackie: It's not really harassment, like, it's just like, *you feel pressured.*

Mary: Is there a particular group, or is it just in general you just try and stay away?

Jackie: Mostly, to be honest with you, it's the Latinos against the Armenians.

Mary: Yeah. Armenian boys don't bother you; you don't feel threatened by them.

Jackie: No, no.

Mary: But you do by the Latino boys?

Jackie: Yeah. [*Later in the conversation*] Not a lot of people got suspended. The Armenian guys got all the [expulsions], . . . and the Latino guys got suspended for, like, a week. And then they came back. That's why *everybody [Armenian] was scared* because they [Latinos] came back and, like, they still needed to take something off their backs, you know. And then they started *threatening the girls* because one of their girls got hit. And I don't see why we have to, like, be scared to go to school because of that. Because we had nothing to do with it. Like, I was minding my business in the College Center for my SATs, you know?

Mary: What do you think—like when you feel scared like that, what are you scared of? What do you think could happen? . . .

Jackie: *They stare like they're going to do something to you, and you get really cautious about yourself, like, why is he looking at me that way?*

The following repeats and then continues the excerpt at the beginning of this chapter.

Mayra: At school, my [white] friend today, she walked over to the spot [where I was with my Mexican friends]. And what did they do? Everyone *just looked at her* like, "What are you doing here? Get away from me." And I felt so bad for her, so I told her, "You know what, let's just walk this way." . . .

Mary: Is it mostly the girls who looked at her funny?

Mayra: It was guys, too. Guys, too. Like, "There's a white girl here? And you're talking to her," like, you know, "What's *wrong* with you?" . . . [Because] then you're, like, [labeled,] whitewashed. You know, "Get away from me."

Mary: So are they going to say something to you tomorrow?

Mayra: No, I mean, they just, *they just looked at her funny and with that, that was enough to let me know,* "Hey, get her away from here."

Mary: What'd she say about it?

Mayra: I just told her, I was like, "Yeah, let's walk this way," and she's like, "Why?" I was like, "Because *they're looking at you funny.*" And she's like, "Why?" And I was like, "Because they're either about to hit you up, or they're about to come over here and tell you something. So let's just leave."

Keisha and Daija are African American, and in this excerpt, they talk about Armenian girls. They think of them as "Middle Eastern kind of."

Keisha: Some of them are, like, real cool, like, friends, I have friends that are—

Daija: Some of them are racist.

Keisha: Some of them are real, yeah. Some of them are real mean, too.

Daija: Yeah.

Mary: How are they mean—like, what do they do? Like, how do you know they're racist?

Keisha: Just like the way they act.

Daija: *They'll look at you,* like.

Keisha: *. . . You could, like, feel that negative energy.*

Daija: Yeah. . . .

Keisha: They even say something sometimes. Like, like, mean stuff.

[*both girls talking*]

Daija: *But you can't understand them.*

Keisha: Yeah, *they just say it in their language.*

In the following excerpt, the same girls describe how African Americans are stereotyped as being in gangs.

Keisha: Yeah. No, it's just, basically they look—like, *people look at you* [and think,] . . . he dresses, like, "Oh, yeah, you're in a gang."

Daija: Yeah.

Keisha: This is what I don't like about school, like, some, like, Latinos and all them, like, the guys, *they look at me* and they, like, and they just say, like, "Tanequa," like, [with a] real ghetto [voice]. . . . I'm like, "That's not my name!"

Mary: They'll make up black names for you?

Keisha: Yeah, like Shaniqua or something like that.

Daija: Shakina.

Keisha: Yeah, I'll be like, that's not my name.
Daija: Because you're a black girl!

In the following excerpt, three Filipina girls discuss the judgments of the popular crowd. Please note that none of their depictions actually occurred as conversations between them and the so-called popular people. These are the girls' made-up stories based on what they *think* the popular people are saying about them.

Sephi: All the popular people, like, hang out by the trees.
Chibi-Kim: No one's popular, god.
Mary: They're not?
Chibi-Kim: They just act snobby. . . .
Mary: What do they—what's a snob like?
[*talking over each other*]
Zelda: They put you down if you're—
Chibi-Kim: They really put you down.
Zelda: *If you're inferior to them.*
Mary: How do they put you down? . . .
Zelda: Um, *looks.*
Mary: Do they look at you?
Zelda: Well, *they look at you funny.* "This person's poor because . . . he wears this all the time."
Chibi-Kim: Oh, "I have the newest shoes."
Zelda: I've never experienced this before, but, I mean, I've seen some people.
Mary: So it's based on money and style?
Zelda: Appearance.
Chibi-Kim: Money and style and appearance . . . and the new brands.
Zelda: Yeah, if you don't wear—
Chibi-Kim: If you don't have them—
Zelda: If you don't have them, you're—
Chibi-Kim: Excluded. . . .
Zelda: And then some of them are, like, into, like, Gucci, or . . . they're probably fake Gucci.
Sephi: They probably stole it, so don't worry.

One remarkable aspect of these interviews comes when I directly ask many of the girls for examples to explain the fears they somewhat blithely mention. Their stories first articulate their fears and the threats made against them. These trepidations usually involve other-raced boys, although in the last excerpt the threat of humiliation is resoundingly class based in addition to race based. However, when I push the girls to give me more details about these threats, they often resort to the explanation that they were on the receiving end of looks—or that they merely "felt" hostility or harassment.

When I ask Denise and Violet how tension is noticed on campus, they say, "The *stares* and the feeling that they're talking about each other, but you can't really prove it." While Amy gives an example of Latino boys explicitly saying, "Watch, we're going to get your girls," Jackie negates that by replying that the boys don't actually harass. She says, rather, "You feel pressured." When I also ask Jackie to further explain the basis of her fear—"What are you scared of? What do you think could happen?"—she replies, "They stare like they're going to do something to you, and you get really cautious about yourself." Amy says, "You think they're going to start a fight with you," which she explains then motivates her to change her spatial maneuvers on campus: "I'd just rather go, like, this way, you know, instead of that way."

Keisha and Daija are the exceptions because they give me an example of "Latino guys" calling them stereotypical black names like Tanequa and Shaniqua. But they also extend their remarks to include the "looks" they get that indicate, "Oh, yeah, you're in a gang." The called-out fake names are also prompted first with a "look." In addition, they describe the differences that gender and ethnicity make: the Armenian girls do not speak directly to them but "look at you" so that, as Keisha says, "You could, like, feel that negative energy." Both girls also bring up the example of language and intent: "They even say [mean stuff] sometimes." "But you can't understand them." This begs the question, of course, of how Daija and Keisha know that mean things are being said, since they do not understand Armenian.

Finally, and perhaps most interestingly, the last excerpt shows a fabricated exchange by Sephi, Chibi-Kim, and Zelda. They identify a "popular" group of students who "look at you funny." After Zelda makes this remark, she gives words to the person whose funny look was cast her way. The look becomes an interpretation of class difference. Zelda herself has not experienced this look, so she never actually heard these words spoken. In the end, she and Sephi degrade the possible class superiority of these "popular people" by insinuating that they stole the designer goods they flaunt in such a snobby manner. This is the girls' way of responding to the other's ability to "put you down." Instead of acquiescing to their "inferiority," they try to prove the others' supposed criminality and poverty. Again, this exchange began when I asked the girls, "How do they put you down?" Zelda replies, "Um, looks."

The reactions of the girls to all these looks and foreign tongues range from fear to humiliation. Fear, when it results, has a decidedly gendered context. Amy and Jackie are both scared of Latinos, even though they cannot point to actual examples of harassment. Their racial fear (also seen in Chapter 3) is compounded by their ideas of Latino sexual power and potential violence. Feeling "pressured" indicates their feminine self-perceptions of being less powerful and vulnerable to the anger and vengeance of Latinos after the school riot. They told me that they "never" feel threatened by Armenian boys, even ones they do not know personally. Remember, too, that Amy vociferously insists time and again that she is not a racist, despite the numerous examples that illustrate her sexualized, racist fears of the Latino. In Mayra's case, she fears *for* her white friend, rather than for herself. But the threat exists as potentially violent, even if it is more like verbal. Humiliation often rises when the girls assume that the talk of others is directed at them in menacing or belittling ways. They feel poorer, less well dressed, tentative, and racialized in demeaned ways (such as ghetto or gang devaluations of black), and these are all feminized in the examples. In a sense, their feminine identifications present them as weaker, more vulnerable, and sexually primed to *expect* insults.

The narratives also indicate the centrality of the girls. They place themselves in the center of the other's attentions and ascribe the other's intentions with no or little actual case for doing so. This is not to undermine the effects of the very real and violent racial conflict that erupted at the school. However, none of these girls was directly involved and had never been party to any actual violence or fighting on campus that I know of. The repeated phrasing of each subject "feeling" harassed, targeted, or put down points to the emotive results of the severe racial segregation that impresses on them every day. As the girls tell their stories of suspicious interactions with others in segregated spaces or the liminal zones between them, they do not realize or articulate the layered and long training that such responses indicate. They also do not necessarily realize the ways they perpetuate these spaces of racial segregation through their unconscious responses, even given the conscious decisions to "go this way instead of that way." Many of the girls place the blame for their spatial, bodily actions at the feet of their racial others, who are often boys. Thus, they assign blame in incomplete and often unfair ways. This banal everyday maneuvering is not an issue for justice, however, but a regular process of specific identification with social-spatial differences.

The self-centering, the expectations of exploitation, the threats read into "looks" and foreign conversations, and the feelings of being slighted by friends of other races when not properly welcomed by them in their racial-ethnic cliques and zones are all indicative of the paranoid processes motivating girls' spatial practices at school. More than that, these behaviors also give clues for the unconscious progression of racial entrenchment at school. When girls feel embattled and attacked, regardless of whether they are correct in their feelings (and sometimes, of course, they are), segregation takes a naturalized form, solidifies, and becomes all the harder to address.

Paranoia in Shopping and Consumption Spaces

Mary: Have you ever felt like you've been a victim of racism or ethnocentrism in any way? . . .

Denise: When I went to stores once—I went to Afterthoughts at a mall, and it's, like, this little, like, jewelry store. It had mirrors on top of the wall and I didn't [realize] it was a part of the design. I had no idea; I was completely oblivious that those mirrors are meant to look at people who might be stealing. And, um, this girl [shopkeeper] *kept on staring at me*, and I didn't notice it; my mom pointed it out. And she—she had me walk out of the store. And I guess, *she was probably staring at me because I was Hispanic.* But I've never really, other than that, I've never experienced it, but that, that was, like, that was a bit of a shock. Yeah, never thought that would happen. . . . When I go into, like, Hispanic locations, like, to, like, certain stores, when I go in there, *they look at me because I'm different from them, . . . and they just stare at me.* Like, I feel uncomfortable, and then I feel like leaving. . . .

Jackie: Me and my friends were at the movies once, and there was a security guard that just kept on *following us, like, as if we were going to do something bad.* . . . [W]e watched our movie, we got out, and then they were just following us, thinking we were going to sneak in somewhere else or something. And then, I saw other kids in front of me, like, they were at the movies with us, and then they sneaked into the other movie. But we just left, and then *they just kept on following us.* Like, their attention was so much on us that they didn't even get to see the other kids sneak in.
Mary: Right.
Jackie: But I didn't really know if it was their job to do it, like, just in case, like, because there's a lot of kids that sneak in and stuff. *Or maybe it was just us because we were the Armenians.* I'm not sure. Like, I'm just saying that was an incident that happened.
Mary: Right. What about you?
Amy: For, like, incidents like that, when I was walking, I saw a friend of mine, she was Latino. And she was with a group of her other Latino friends. It's like, I wanted to say hi to her, but I didn't feel comfortable because her other friends were there, and *they were looking at me in a weird way. So I was like, okay, stay away from trouble. I just, like, ignore it and I just smile, you know.*
Jackie: Yeah, when they're individuals and you're friends with them, you can say hi, but if they're with groups and you're alone, you can't just pretty much go say hi to your friends.
Mary: Right.
Amy: Yeah, *you feel, like, outcast*, you know. . . . I'm not that type of person, I'm so not racist, you know? We're all people, why can't we be friends? That's what I think, you know?

Mary: Is that the first thing you think when someone looks at you, that they think you're racist?

Mayra: Yeah, I think the first thing they look at is that they're being racist and *that they're looking at me [thinking], like, "Oh, she's Mexican, watch out."*

Mary: What do you mean "watch out"?

Mayra: Like, because, like if you walk into, let's say, a store in Beverly Hills, they'll be like, *"Watch out, she might steal something."* That's not even the case because my mom, she—she loves going to, like, expensive stores and stuff, and she wants me to dress, like, you know, wearing Abercrombie and Fitch and stuff. You know. . . . And my mom, she doesn't pay attention to that [looking]. Like she, you know, I mean once in a while she'll be like, "Oh," you know, "they were being racist." But it's not, like, an everyday thing for her, *and for me it is.* I won't—I mean, if I go to the store, she's more like, she's like, "Hi, how are you?" you know, "Do you have these jeans is this size?" And if they look at us the wrong way, I'll be like, "Mom, look at them, *she just, you know, looked you up and down, you know, just because we're Mexican."* And part of that is because at school you get that. "Oh, wow, you're Mexican? The Armenian girl was looking at you the wrong way because you're Mexican." And at times I know it's not even that, but it's really ignorance.

Ultimately, the spatial experiences these stories reflect are not separate from campus; they illustrate how the subject comes to see its "place" in the world through racial identifiers. In fact, in Amy and Jackie's exchange, the story begins with the movies and ends with a focus on school friends at the shopping mall. These same friends will be the ones at school with whom Amy and Jackie continue to negotiate segregated spaces.

The shopping examples also pull out the class dimensions of racial difference in Los Angeles. Mayra, the Mexican American girl, specifies a Beverly Hills store to draw attention to a place that has extreme race differences with her home context in the San Fernando Valley. Beverly Hills symbolizes the ultra rich and chic and the shopping that caters to them. Mayra juxtaposes her own Mexican body to these high-end retail spaces and expensive brands and senses the watching eyes that wait for her to "steal something." Unlike her mother, it's "an everyday thing" for her. She may relegate the looks to "ignorance," but the effect of the looking is a process of self-racialization. Mayra's Mexicanness is enhanced by the spatial contexts that she depicts: the class difference, being out of place, and being a central focus as a Mexican in the places Mexicans are not supposed to be. Denise shares this type of story, but while

Mayra expects it, Denise finds it a "bit of a shock." She also feels ostracized in even Hispanic locations "because I'm different than them, . . . and they stare at me. Like, I feel uncomfortable, and then I feel like leaving." She does not easily conform to the racial definitions of the LA spaces she describes because she does not simply fit into a Hispanic or an Anglo category.

The girls' depictions of urban spaces such as shopping are indications of how they understand their own bodies and selves (see Cahill 2007b: 204). When told through paranoid language, the narratives illustrate how fundamental race and class are to the ways that the girls expect others to react to them and, likewise, how these frame girls' expectations of others. The consumption city is at the heart of girls' identifications and, of course, their interactions with peers. The shopping mall is not an idealized format for girls' friendships across race, as opposed to the perhaps more heavily surveilled spaces on campus, according to Amy. And Denise's account of her racial failings in the city's "Hispanic locations" show that she can never be at home in her racialized body, with the fear that she might be summoned to perform a service she cannot fulfill. Yet she is fully racialized despite this failure in other shopping places, like the mall where she is watched for possible shoplifting. These events and spaces are racial-class identifications for Denise.

I do not want to give the impression that the girls are wrongly paranoid of racial profiling in consumption space (Chin 2001). It happens with incredible regularity, and probably more often than not, the girls are savvy to its existence and the surveillance. Rather, the argument relates instead to the issue of what the effects of this profiling are and how profiling intersects with the subjective excesses that drive paranoia. I do think that the girls *feel* surveilled as racialized bodies more than they probably are, and these feelings of observation and racial marking have a deep impression on the terms of their racial identifications and how these affect their spatial behaviors. They are more likely to self-segregate to avoid what they expect to happen, whether it will eventually happen or not. And their experiences in the mall or in white hegemonic spaces such as Beverly Hills educate them to act differently at school, to avoid interaction or spatial transgression of segregated territories because it could lead to trouble.

Conclusion: Embodiment, Territoriality, and Subjectivity

While feminist geographers have worked hard to insist that the practices of young subjects are always embodied (Cahill 2007a; Evans 2006; see also Aapola, Gonick, and Harris 2005), the girls' narratives may also indicate the importance of considering the failure of embodiment to fully represent the subject. The uncomfortable awkwardness of being in the wrong racial territory, as laid out time and again by the girls at this multiracial high school, marks how complexly the social body is taken up. These discomforts are also productive of the pain of not being recognized as a subject, as being reduced merely to one's visible racial difference. These moments surely draw out the embodiment of subjectivity, such as how social norms and categories are "stuck" to and taken up by a subject, but they also insist that the body's boundaries are fluid, intersubjective, and multispatial. In other words, the body is recognizable only because of social meanings and norms; therefore, every body is an effect of its relations to others and the process of painful encounter (Ahmed 2002). The girls' depictions of their bodies in other territories point to the intersubjective, spatial negotiations at the heart of coming to terms with social relations, norms, and differences. Embodiment is both integral *and* exterior to the subject herself. They find the investments of difference only through their encounters with others, the subsequent surveillance of racialized space, and their own emotive processes of dealing with the encounters of theirs and others' bodies (see Ahmed 1999; Chin 2001).

That the girls indicate their pain of being not fully seen illustrates that the categorical empirics of bodies—for example, how bodies are seen according to race, ethnicity, or gender—do not fully capture the subjective effects of those empirics (i.e., how those bodies are experienced). However, the girls' claims to be seen for "who they are," or "as more than their race" (as opposed to being seen foremost as their race and ethnicity) rely on the fantasy that they themselves are not also fully and fundamentally invested in those social categories of difference. The girls may insist they are more than their race, but their narratives also show how they rely on a logic of racial difference in their own practices of identification. They shrug and leave the territories of their friends, they live segregated social lives, and they claim racial-ethnic identities smoothly and without irony in their self-descriptions and through their casual marking of others' racial-ethnic identifiers.

There are thus limits to their self-knowledge because the self is fundamentally socially informed and founded. In other words, subjectivity does not denote a self-reflexive process. Instead, the social and psychic processes through which norms become personally invested as aspects of the self are not wholly conscious ones, and past and present processes are not necessarily recallable. As Butler puts it, the identifications used to recognize—and to be recognizable—are not "ours" (2005: 19). In a sense then, one's body is also not one's "own"—and the discomfort, pain, and hurt feelings of the girls point to that. Their desire for recognition will never be fulfilled because they are always experientially more than the sum of their social, racialized parts and bodies. Paradoxically, subjectivity, that highly *personal* experience of being a self, is achieved only by entering into fundamentally *social* spaces of difference, although the origin of those founding moments are lost to the subject herself (Butler 2005: 38; Ahmed 2002: 27).

As Ahmed insinuates, the face-to-face encounter of bodies "does not simply happen in the privatized realm of the subject's relation to itself. Rather, in daily meetings with others, subjects are perpetually reconstituted: the work of identity formation is never over, but can be understood as the sliding across of subjects in their meetings with others" (2000: 7). The girls' pain and discomfort indicate the personal struggles each girl experiences as her own, yet these painful encounters and processes develop through the ongoing formation of each girl's subjectivity and sense of self and are intimately *social*. The complicated geographies through which race came to be—and continues to be—personally invested, are fundamentally socially defined. The girls' pain marks the limits to which they conceptualize and extend their racialized bodies beyond their own individuality, despite their bodies and selves being produced through a long history and multiple spatialities. But it is important not to reduce subjectivity and identity to that suffering because it erases the *rejection* of social norms that is not acknowledged through the disavowal Butler describes. Banal multiculturalism, for example, focuses on the experiences of identity and suffering without considering how identity is also a rejection of other bodies and other norms. When multicultural programs fail to consider these unconscious processes of rejection, they stagnate without much chance of getting past pain to new forms of social exchange (McNay 2008).

5
Geographies of Migrant Girlhood

Families and Racialization

Between 1980 and 2000, the Armenian-speaking, foreign-born population of the United States increased from about 70,000 to 156,555.[1] In 2004, the city of Los Angeles had 70,000 Armenian speakers in its households. In fact, according to 2004 data, Armenian speakers over the age of five are the third largest non-English-speaking category in the city (3.3 percent), after Spanish (74 percent of non-English speakers) and Korean (4.2 percent). Tagalog is close to Armenian (3.2 percent). Most of these Armenian speakers live in the San Fernando Valley. Glendale, a Valley city not included in LA data, has 54,000 Armenians according to "heritage" data from the 2000 U.S. Census Bureau (its total population in 2004 was 195,000). Burbank, next door to Glendale, has about an 8 percent Armenian "heritage" population. Thus, Armenians have a far larger presence in the San Fernando Valley than the Los Angeles data illustrate; the LA metro area has the largest Armenian urban presence in the United States.

This density of Armenians in the Valley is both a blessing and a curse to the Armenian girls whom I met. For these first- and second-generation teenagers (and many would be considered 1.5 generation since they

1. These data are derived from the U.S. Census Bureau's "Language Spoken at Home for the Foreign-Born Population 5 Years and Over: 1980 to 2000." The number who self-identified their "heritage" as Armenian was, of course, much higher, at 385,488.

migrated as very young children), life in the United States presented them with a wonderful advantage over those in their families who remained in Armenia. But compared to "American" (i.e., Anglo) kids, they thought their lives were very different. Immigrant parents, they explained, were stricter and insisted that their children retain Armenian language and customs. For most of the girls, this meant Armenian school on Saturdays and Armenian church on Sundays. They may have complained about the extra homework that weekend language and culture school presented, but they also overwhelmingly valued their families' "Armenianness." They voiced a strong desire to retain their cultural cohesion and insularity, even as they vociferously protested their parents' rigid rules and expectations.

The stories that the girls tell about their family migration experiences indicate the ways that they develop their own national and racial-ethnic identities in the United States. These identities result from understandings of filialness and the girls' attempts to distinguish themselves as different kinds of Armenians from their non-American parents. The centrality of their racial-ethnic-national identification as Armenians obviously affects their lives at school and in the city. The close friends of almost all the Armenian girls I interviewed were also Armenian. Among those girls who did have integrated friendships at school, the friendship often remained only on campus. For example, one group of girls I interviewed together, three Armenians and one Anglo (Grisselle, Anne, Britney, and Alexis), explained that the Armenian girls had to miss their Anglo friend's sweet sixteen party because their parents would not allow them to socialize in a non-Armenian household. That means that three of three sets of Armenian parents enforced this rule in just this one case. Jackie and Amy, sisters, also told me that their parents rarely let them go to sweet sixteen parties and then only when they knew the other Armenian parents personally. They also had never been to an Anglo house for a party.

This chapter is not just about the Armenian girls, however, although the fact that I interviewed more Armenian girls who were first- and second-generation Americans than other groups certainly weighs the chapter's examples about migration and identity. Like the Armenian girls, the Filipina girls I spoke to all shared similar understandings about the conditions of life in their natal countries and their parents' attitudes toward the Americanization of their daughters. A few Mexican American girls also articulated complaints about what they saw as their parents' (especially their mothers') backwardness in and hesitation to raising American children.[2]

All of these narratives, I argue, indicate that the girls differentiate themselves from their parents as a way to project their ideals for the ways they wish

---

2. Laura Pulido offers a chapter on differential racialization in Southern California in her 2006 book, *Black, Brown, Yellow, and Left: Radical Activism in Los Angeles.*

to be seen and recognized by others. Yet the narratives that express these ideals also contain hints pointing to girls' commitments to maintain their "special" racial-ethnic status. Their pride in American life and their excitement about Los Angeles as a great melting pot has its limits when contextualized with the foundational investments they have in their ethnic, national, and racial otherness. These investments are contingent in that they situate their identifications with existing meanings about social difference.

By foundational investment, I refer to the ways that social relations and objects become aspects of the self to the girls. Such core, socially framed identifications are the foundations that gird girls' self-understandings and also frame their subjectivities, including unconscious investments in social systems of differentiation. Thus, their stories about family history and their parents' sacrifices when moving to the United States are indications of how the girls' personal identifications around family, race, ethnicity, and nationality are fundamentally *impersonal* (see Dean 2000: 54). That is, these social meanings are taken up, as Sigmund Freud puts it, by the ego through psychic processes that seek stability and belonging (1961, e.g., page 19). In sum, individual mental lives and psyches are social phenomena (Freud 1959). The question is, what is the effect of such psychic-social contingencies on the ability of girls to quell contradictory racial and gender desires, such as whether to be protected or independent, to evaluate racial difference or seek nonracism?

Freud writes in *Group Psychology and the Analysis of the Ego*, "Identification is known to psycho-analysis as the earliest expression of an emotional tie with another person" (1959: 46). His most famous example of this, of course, was the Oedipus complex. The competition with the father for the mother's love illustrates the ambivalence of identification "from the very first: it can turn into an expression of tenderness as easily as into a wish for someone's removal" (1959: 47).[3] Freud believed that this type of identification was a process whereby objects of cathexis (love-objects) were taken into the ego as aspects of the self; cathexis was replaced by identifications (see Laplanche and Pontalis 1973: 207; Freud 1957). The ego is itself a "history of those object-choices" (Freud 1961: 24).[4] Identification (in part achieved by the taking on of objects as aspects of the self) is a way for the ego to mediate the external world's

---

3. In the Oedipus complex, Freud distinguishes "between an identification with the father and the choice of the father as an object. In the first case one's father is what one would like to *be*, and in the second he is what one would like to *have*." Freud found that it was "difficult to give a clear metapsychological representation of the distinction. We can only see that identification endeavours to mould a person's own ego after the fashion of the one that has been taken as a model" (1959: 47–48).
4. "We are reminded of how many of these phenomena of dependence are part of the normal constitution of human society, of how little originality and personal courage are to be found in it, of how much every individual is ruled by those attitudes of the group mind which exhibit themselves in such forms as racial characteristics, class prejudices, public opinion, etc." (1959: 63).

demands to conform and obey. In taking up objects as the self, there is a bit of destruction involved, for as Freud puts it, when one assimilates an object, one also destroys it (e.g., by eating something we love, we also destroy that which we love [1959: 47]), hence identification's ongoing ambivalence.

The motivations and processes of identification are unconscious ones; the ego is also unconscious in that it is not capable of describing its functioning and dynamics in self-evident terms. Therefore, the words about who one is or what one believes—or even the stories of one's life—are never so simply ostensive. In them lurk clues for their necessity in the first place and the energetic priority that each subject has for a semblance of personal unity. Of course, this unity is self-delusional, in that unconscious contradictions and ambivalence are wholly definitive of psychic processes of identification and subjectivity. This self-delusion, for me, is the heart of the matter. Psychoanalysis lends help in theorizing the *vitality* of the subject's inconsistencies. They frame the subject and, as such, must be accounted for in analyses of girlhood, identity, or school conflict.

The stories in this chapter should therefore be placed in juxtaposition to those in earlier chapters on girls' words about the "stupid" fighting of boys, the need for multicultural understanding, and, of course, segregation from and resentment for other racial-ethnic groups. Families provide the girls with a core grounding in life about "who they are" (all the girls I interviewed lived with at least one parent, and all the Armenian girls lived with both parents). Family stories are important ways that the girls learn scripts about what identifying as "an Armenian," "a Filipina," or "a Latina," requires of them—in terms of psychic processes and social or socializing expectations. Their racial-ethnic and national identifications are their homes, in a sense, are embodied by them, and are gendered and sexualized, as I show in this chapter. These home spaces and psychic necessities "travel" with them to the school. The girls can hope for peaceful relations with racial others and seek recognition from other-raced friends even within the confines of an enforced segregation, but their racial identifications prevent them from aligning so simply with these others in that quest. They can express such hopes and even do hard work toward achieving their goals, but psychoanalysis teaches us that there are always limits to a personal coming together.

The evidence of girls' racial, ethnic, and national identifications is illustrated in this chapter by focusing on their migration stories and attempts to resist so-called conservative parental expectations or rules. This chapter has three sections exploring these themes. First, migration stories illustrate the girls' commitments to a better life in the United States than their parents had in their natal countries. I argue that the girls' home lives and ideas about what their families have sacrificed and gained through migration must be a central consideration when facing the issue of segregation and racism in schools. Family histories and home spaces, in other words, are important considerations for understanding youth behaviors in integrated spaces. Second, I briefly consider an example of two girls complaining about their parents' stories of their difficult lives "back then" in Mexico. Finally, I turn to the girls' discussions about their parents' rules for dating and socializing. Many girls say that their parents are committed to maintaining racial-ethnic purity, and their responses about their parents hold lessons about the girls' contradictory commitments to resist these ideas. The theme of migrant parents' conservativeness is evident throughout the chapter.

American Dreams: Migration Stories

Jackie: Back then, people didn't even have money for food and shelter, like, they were bare. Like, they had it, but they were barely, they were struggling. . . . And over here, when they came [to the United States], it was weird for them because they were in a different country, they didn't know the language, and they didn't have—the way we were living there, like, we had our house and everything. When we came, we started off on a little apartment, and then we built into the house. But, like, it was hard for them, too, because they came, and a lot of different people were here. Over there, it was all Armenians, imagine. And, like, they didn't see anything in their life. They just came, and they just started seeing it [racial diversity], and they're like, oh my god, what did we do, you know?

Mary: Why did they come? For economic opportunity?

Jackie: Yes. Like, it was really hard because around the '90s to '96, it was very hard over there; it was like, people didn't have lights. . . . They didn't have lights; they didn't have shelter; they didn't have food; they didn't have anything. They were struggling. When we went back to visit Armenia in '95? They had no lights. I was so scared when we went.

To Jackie, who was born in Armenia and came to the United States in 1990 with her parents as a small child, the context of Armenia represents a bare struggle for survival. She continued by adding, "The thing about Armenia is that [people are] either really good or really bad. There's no middle class like us." The move, in her mind, was a quest for a rich or, as she says, "good," life, since hunger and want depict "bare" life in post-Soviet Armenia. She fears electricity shortages, the prospects of poverty or even homelessness, and the threats of a nonnormative middle-class American ideal. She later explained to me that her family has not visited Armenia since 1995 because they cannot afford the gifts they would have to buy for friends and family if they returned, let alone the cost of five international airplane tickets. The material benefits of migration, while gradual with her family's move from an apartment to a house, outweigh her concerns about her parents' struggles with their transition to a new country and new careers (more on that later). The relative prosperity that came for this family since migration gives Jackie a wholehearted investment in being in the United States. When I asked her and her younger sister, Amy, what they thought about being in the United States, they said:

Amy: I—I love the U.S.
Jackie: I love it. I can't see myself living another place.

Jackie cannot imagine living in a place with the levels of poverty she saw in Armenia, the lack of consumption, and the fundamental threats against a "good" life. She differentiates herself from being an Armenian who struggled and instead marks herself as an Armenian who is also an American. Even in her story about her family's move, she speaks of "them" in Armenia and switches to "we" only after the move to Los Angeles was accomplished. Of course, she was a part of "them" since she herself was in the family (albeit as a toddler). But these pronouns distance herself from "them"—the Armenians who faced bare life.

One difficulty she prioritizes in her initial explanation about her parents' move is the shock of moving to a racially diverse American city. Accustomed to being with Armenians only, her parents faced a fundamentally whole new reality of racial difference. Jackie represents this as a panic-stricken moment for "them" and takes their voice to say, "Oh my god, what did we do?" She even notes that there was nothing to "see in their life" in Armenia. The diversity of Los Angeles and the relative wealth of life in the United States are Jackie's focal points for what is worthy and livable but also problematic. She fantasizes that she has the ability to not only cope with racial difference but also thrive in its spaces. She marks the difficulty of diversity as one her Armenian parents face, not one she faces as an Armenian who has the capacity to have an American language for diversity.

Jackie and Amy continue by marking the career plunges that their parents endured with migration to the United States. Her parents' educational achievements in Armenia did not translate to their new country where language skills, the nonrecognition of foreign degrees, and the lack of capital prevented an easy transition to similar status jobs.

Mary: What's your dad do here?
Jackie: He owns, like, taxis, and they drive it. He drives a taxi.
Mary: And so what does your mom do? Does your mom work or does she stay [home]?

Jackie: My mom is in a salon; she does, like, eyebrows and makeup and stuff. . . .

Amy: My dad was really smart. He had—he was an engineer.

Jackie: My dad was an engineer there; he was a professor there for five years. Right before we came here, he was a professor there.

Amy: He has two majors.

Mary: Does he get frustrated?

Both: Yes.

Jackie: Okay, when we came here, he tried—let me just say this—because when we came here, he wanted to go to college and learn the language. . . . Obviously, he graduated college here, and he has a diploma from there. He has his engineering diploma there.

Amy: It's just different, you know.

Jackie: It's different because, I don't know, like, he came here and then, like, a couple of years later he was working with jewelry. At the downtown. And then when he got his language and everything, he started driving a taxi, and he just kept on doing that. Like, I still tell him, I go, quit, like, go do something you, like, you know. Because I know he's so good in, like, math and engineering and—

Amy: Electronics.

Jackie: Electronics.

Mary: Is it because he makes enough to support the family that anything harder—

Amy: No, he's just scared to not support us, you know.

Jackie: He's scared to try something new. . . . He's just scared; that's all I can say.

Amy: He would love to go back to school, he would love to. . . .

Jackie: My mom was a big coordinator there. Like, even when they were married everybody was like, oh my god, look at them, they're such a young couple, but they have their future already. . . . Imagine, from an office, to a salon. Like, or, like, from being the biggest professor over there [*voice fades*].

These girls are proud of their parents' abilities and the accomplishments they had in their Armenian careers. They lament that their parents had to give up their successes, although relatively unremunerated successes, in Armenia to make more money doing less prestigious jobs in the United States. This money, in the form of parental sacrifice and devalued labor, ensures their new "good" life. Their sympathy seems limited, however, at least in their father's case. Both girls mark his fear as the barrier for him to change jobs and work on his education and skills in the United States. Amy even uses the past tense in her remark that her "dad *was* really smart." Their vision of U.S. possibility propels their hope that their father can be whatever he wants since he has skill and motivation. Amy recognizes his fear is partly based on losing the ability to support the family, but Jackie's comment that "he's just scared, that's all I can say," seems to mark a bigger limit to her dad's motivation.

While the sisters value U.S. hopes for economic progress, they also pity their father who must face the challenges that the U.S. context also presents. The family's migration meant that their parents had to confront "shocking" racial difference and competition for viable jobs for non- or poor English speakers. As non-English speakers, these parents *are* the "diversity" in the United States, even as Jackie and Amy situate their Armenianness as their norm and frame of reference. That is, the parents' view is that they are non-racialized after entering the United States, but Jackie and Amy point to the challenges of being non-Anglo migrants with poor English language skills.

White hegemony is extremely effective on many of the girls' ideals of American families, as I increasingly illustrate through the rest of this section. The Anglo "norms" that the girls draw on in their narratives show their assumptions about two parents who are open-minded, particularly about teenage sexuality, dating, and middle class, with few migration struggles. The ways in which the girls compare their lives to Anglo girls (often by relying on the media, such as television programs or stereotypes) are not just productive of their own identifications as Armenians, but they also use such stories to show how much more they have to deal with than others of their peers. In other words, their lives are more difficult or tedious given their migrant parents' inability to assimilate.

Jane, who came to the United States from Armenia with her family as a small child, told a story quite similar to Amy's and Jackie's, as the following exchange reveals.

Mary: Does your mom work?

Jane: She does; she works at Macy's. But she's trying to get licensed for insurance, I think. Life insurance. And she's going to go into real estate and stuff.

Mary: And what does your dad do?

Jane: He drives a taxicab.

Mary: I've interviewed a couple other Armenian girls whose fathers do that. Is that like a social network, that they get their friends jobs?

Jane: Actually, no, it's basically, like, Armenians come here, and they don't know how to speak English, and they, basically, that's the only job. I think it pays well. You know, it pays okay, not like a lawyer or anything, obviously, but it's . . . good. It's a stable job, so I think that's the only good thing they can do, you know? So that's why many people do that.

Mary: So has your dad done that since you guys came here?

Jane: Um, no, he actually used to work with shoes and stuff. Like, he modeled, he designed them. . . . In Armenia, that was, like, basically, his job. But he graduated in Armenia as an engineer, but then when he came here, he couldn't work as that because he didn't know the language.

Mary: Why do you think your parents came here?

Jane: I think they came here because there weren't good jobs in Armenia, you know. And, basically, economic reasons, you know, money, financial problems.

As with Amy and Jackie, Jane points toward what is "good" about living and working in the United States. While she unfavorably compares her father's work to that of a lawyer, she marks the lesser job of taxi driver as "good" and stable, as the "only good thing they can do."

The spatiality of otherness for the family and the girls radically alters their own identities of what is center and what is marginal. The parents are the racial others to the American-native ideal, something that the girls think they approximate more with their English skills and racial mobility than their migrant-marked parents. Racial diversity is for their parents to cope with, but the girls are also products of this intimate connection to Armenia. This intimacy presents a challenge to their Armenian identities, which is a "new" identity in comparison to their parents. The spatially specific process of their identifying as Armenian—but not the same Armenian as their parents—belies the intimate modes through which the girls have become a different kind of Armenian. Their parents' foreignness mars their own attempts to be American kids.

This foreignness was painfully evident to the girls as they listed their hopes for their own American futures (and especially when they resisted what they considered to be their parents' outdated expectations for dating).

Mary: You want to stay here to go to school?

Amy: I don't plan to stay here [in Los Angeles for college]. I want to go to University—

Jackie: You're not going anywhere.

Amy: University of Phoenix in Arizona. But I'm not going to be [i.e., I don't want to be] in California, [but] I talked to my parents about it, and my dad said no.

Mary: Because he doesn't want you to go away?

Amy: Yeah. [So, the thing] about Armenian families is, like, the girl has to stay in the house until—even the boys—until they get married.

Jackie: Like, you know how—

Amy: And girls they're more strict with.

Jackie: Usually, I can say, not just racist or anything, like, the whites and the Hispanics, they move out right when they're eighteen or right when they're about, like, ready to support themselves. But [not] Armenians!

In this exchange, the girls interpret the gendered results of Armenian rules—the results of being subject to more rigid expectations and limitations than boys. Amy yearns to be independent and to be allowed to have the American (white) ideal of going away to college, but Jackie scolds her for even dreaming of such a possibility. Jackie also hints that she values this rule. She warns that although she is talking about other races (whites and Hispanics), she is not being "racist or anything." But these words insinuate that what she is saying is a comment devaluing these other racial practices. Thus, to her these whites and Hispanics have bad practices to let their kids go so young (although, as I show later in the chapter, Jackie wants badly to be allowed to go herself). Jackie's words, I argue, point to her desire to be free *and* valued enough by parents to be protected.

The narratives of Jackie and Amy point to what I have referenced as the ambivalences of identification. Like their words in Chapter 4 about the possibility of their daughters marrying a non-Armenian, the girls espouse Armenian family values while they simultaneously push against them. They want to be both Armenian and Anglo-American, and they delineate each in a fairly stereotypical fashion (e.g., Anglo-Americans are more lenient, but Armenians are more strict; life in Armenia is bad, but life in America is good.) There is not necessarily any critique to be made of the girls' narratives, since these counternarratives are fundamental to normal identification for any subject. But they do indicate the complicated spatiality of the meanings and practices that the girls employ to shape their beliefs (conscious and not) and that therefore shape their identification and social lives. Their memories of visiting Armenia, and the active and passive listening to their parents' stories about life there before migration to the United States, saturate the girls' investments in being "Armenian." They are different, in their minds, for their families' struggles and the understandings they have about life in poor, past homes. They bring this affect and identification to the space of the school where and when they are confronted by those many unknown others. The deep invisibility of such investments and identifications make them virtually impossible to share with those who are not seen to have a valid ability to understand the importance of such experiences. Again, these investments and identifications are not necessarily conscious, since the self forms in largely unconscious processes. The girls insist that they can learn about one another through multicultural exchange, but they are also trenchantly and unconsciously resistant in the belief that such exchange is actually possible. In other words, the recognition they seek might be socially desired but not psychically possible. The unconscious prevents even the self from understanding its own foundations in otherness.

Like Jackie, Jane compares the strict rules of her Armenian parents to a supposed white American leniency (of course, Jackie refers to both "whites and Hispanics"). Note that Jane talks especially about white, American girls who are allowed to express sexuality and date boys.

> People from the same culture are more similar in the way they are with their families, you know, but outside of their families, they're more alike with other people. You know, like, let's say Armenians, for example. They would be like everyone else outside, but when they go to, like, their separate family things, like, a lot of things change. Like, some parents are very strict, you know, and they're, like—like, Armenian parents, for example, are more—a lot stricter than others. Because, I don't know, when I watch TV and stuff, sometimes the things that, like, the parents say, like, I don't know, [the television show] *Full House*, for example. There's this fourteen-year-old girl, I don't know if she's fourteen or sixteen, but yeah, she's allowed to have a boyfriend, and she's allowed to date and stuff, you know? And I wonder—their family is so, like, let go, let loose, you know? Like, they're not—I mean they have rules and stuff, but, like, I feel like that portrays, like, American—like, other American families.

Jane's words are confusing or confused. She believes that "culture" (race, ethnicity, and nationality) molds people to have similar behaviors, such as in families. Yet she also thinks that family "culture" has limited scope and that people are essentially alike or at least have the potential to be. Perhaps this example is a neat encapsulation of my argument that identification is spatially contingent: people change depending on where they are and whom they are with. But then Jane negates these thoughts by marking the special status of Armenians, by pointing to their parents as "stricter." She uses a U.S. television show to illustrate the distance between Armenian and Anglo-American parenting. American families are "let loose," informal, and open to a girl's sexuality and the possibility of her dating even at the young age of fourteen (Jane's own age). Jane also corrects herself by referring to this white family as American when she adds "other American families." With this phrase, she adds Armenian as an American family, by indicating that "other" families, like Anglos represented by the white family on *Full House*, have different rules from her own. This is an obvious example of the making of "common culture" as Willis (1990) puts it, as youth draw on media to make sense of their hybridized position as migrants in multicultural America.

It is worth a pause here to consider Anne-Marie Fortier's point that youth occupy the central consideration in "the nation's value, achievements, and future horizons" (2008: 40); her case is Britain. She continues: "The young person of today figures as the multicultural citizen of tomorrow, whose development is constitutive of particular ideas about 'mixing' that found local or national capacity-building strategies aimed at increased integration and cohesion" (40). Jane's desire for that "mixing" is remarkably nationalized in addition to racial and is framed within a "loose" youthful heterosexuality. Jane must walk a careful line between her two nationalities, and she struggles with heterosexual expression of girls as good and carefree and the oversexualization of girls blamed on ethnic carelessness. (Jane criticizes Latinas for being slutty and thus deserving poor treatment by Latino boys.) She desires the promises of mixing, of the future horizon of cohesion, but in her stories over the course of the interview, she also marks the limits to that desire and the punishments and failures that lurk for young women if they do integrate. Fortier notes the dangers of placing responsibility on youth to achieve the ideal multicultural subject, since, of course, the youth subject cannot possibly be successful at embodying the ambivalences of "mixing." She writes of "the deep ambivalence of Britain's conception of 'the other within' who is expected to display not too much, not too little, but just enough alterity *of the right kind*: moderately religious, successfully heterosexual, not-too-White but White-enough" (64, emphasis in original).

We see more of this dancing between not too much and not too little when I asked Jane to further compare life between America and Armenia. She pointed to consumption as a primary difference. Like Jackie, she also says that the fact of racial diversity in the United States is a challenge to Armenians in Los Angeles. (I also used part of this exchange in Chapter 2 in my discussion of the girls' multicultural-infused reactions to the riot.)

> Jane: I think there's a big difference. Because life there and life here
> is very different, you know? In aspects, let's say small things, like
> going shopping at least, like, once a week and stuff. People there
> wouldn't even think of going shopping once a week. It's not nor-
> mal for that to happen there.
> Mary: So, here, there's more money?
> Jane: Yeah, there's more money, and the people are like, I don't want
> to say spoiled, but you know, they kind of take advantage of it, I
> think. You know, and, I don't know, school there is kind of dif-
> ferent, too. Because, okay, back in Armenia, you would be with
> Armenians, and here there's, like, people of different ethnicities

and backgrounds. So this [the riot] is the result, which I really don't like. When people fuse, this is what happens. I guess they just try to keep—the reason there's riots and stuff is that they're trying to keep who they are. They don't want to fuse and become like one. And they're trying to keep their culture and stuff, so they have their place [together at school], and they talk with their own, you know?

After the absence of racial-ethnic difference in Armenia, the confrontation of it by immigrant students at the LA school, according to Jane, results in violence. Jane insinuates that the only other option is to fuse, to "become like one." She values ethnic uniqueness and wants each group to have the ability to "keep their culture and stuff." In fact, segregation to her is one such attempt to maintain Armenian culture. At the same time, she does not like the alternative result, that of fusing because to her it necessarily leads to violence. Presumably it leads to violence because cultures will resist the fusing that spatial proximity supposedly encourages. It is as if Jane wishes to have segregation *without* conflict, as a way to deal with difference on campus and in the United States. Segregation is her solution to the fact of difference, since in Armenia being solely with people ethnically and racially like you did not result in any sort of violent conflict in school. (She was also much younger when a student in Armenia, so any conflict in school there would have been limited in scale.) Jane is both invested in the fact of being "different" from other youth and in the ability to overcome the outcomes of difference.

Finally, Jane identifies life in the United States as spoiled and shopping centric. I am not sure what she means by her phrase that people "kind of take advantage of it." I think she means that they take advantage of the fact that shopping is always possible. Perhaps her reference to "spoiled" also gives more depth to her comment about American girls being allowed to date earlier than Armenians; that is, those American girls are spoiled for their parents' leniency. Jane also does not refer to the inability of many Americans to shop every week. Every day, she sees students at school who are very poor (and remember that three-fourths of the school's population is federally subsidized to have lunch available to them). The conflict of fusing is also a class conflict between the haves and the have-nots. In my group of interviewees, the Armenian girls' families had two bread winners and higher paid occupations (and often better housing type), so the class issue at school is most probably also compounded by the Armenians. Certainly in my interviews, many Latina girls disparaged Armenian girls' abilities to buy name-brand clothes more often than they could. Jane is here critiquing American consumption and Americans' spoiled natures, but she also points to the segregation that it contributes to in the form of class difference. More than just pointing to it, she thinks segregation and staying with one's own is a strategy for better relations—the effect being that better relations are no relations.

In a final example to close out this section, I draw out the ways that a group of girls differentiate U.S. childhoods from those in the Philippines.

> Chibi-Kim: We were all born in the Philippines. ["We" refers to the three girls in the interview.]
>
> Zelda: I've only been here for six years. I was in the Philippines for nine. I've been here longer than her.
>
> Chibi-Kim: I think I've been here longer than that.
>
> Mary: So what do you think about the U.S.?
>
> Zelda: I think it's—it's okay now.
>
> Chibi-Kim: It's very easy.
>
> Zelda: Before I was really—before I was really enthusiastic because I haven't been in another country.
>
> Sephi: Many of our relatives says it's more better to live here than in the Philippines.
>
> Zelda: . . . There's, like, widespread corruption in the Philippines. [*Moments later*] There are a lot of pollutions in the air [in Manila] and a lot of pollutions and, like, and traffic especially, traffic is, like, so huge.
>
> Chibi-Kim: And children in the Philippines, like, they have to not— they can't go to school and [must] help their families. Go out there on the streets and wash cars to get money. And, like, that's [the money that] they use to, like, feed them[selves].

Compared to child labor, pollution, and political corruption, the United States is an "easy" place to live. Poverty in the Philippines forces children to stop going to school and help support the family (not an uncommon story among LA high school teens, for that matter). The girls listed difficulties by adding to each other's comments about hardships, indicating a shared story about family progress and American life. The idea that children would go into the streets to provide pennies to make the difference between hunger and starvation was one that the girls could not fathom of their own lives. Chibi-Kim's expression at this story was accompanied by a tone of incredulity.

Yet Zelda raises a hesitation about adjusting to her family's move to the United States. She says that it's easy "now." Her insinuation that it has gotten easier is tentative, given that she then says that she *was* really enthusiastic "before." Sephi also gives the agency of preferring life in the United States to her "relatives" rather than preferring it herself. I think that the stories of such hardship in the Philippines make it difficult for the girls to claim sorrow, loss, and struggle with migration to the United States, since the alternative (living in poverty in Asia) is so much bleaker to them.

The irony of bringing up air quality and traffic density in Los Angeles was not lost on me, since the city is known for these very issues. But the girls were right to insist to me (later) that it is much, much worse in Manila. These girls differ from the Armenians by not discussing shopping and consumption and focusing on politics and the environment. This difference is in part a reflection of the wider income disparity and larger population in Manila to anything the Armenian girls would have seen (or heard about) in Armenia. The Filipina girls' ideas of what is gained and lost through family migration is therefore quite specific to the actual country they left. In the main, they also have more memories of their natal countries since they arrived in the United States later in life than did Jackie and Jane (and Amy was born in the United States).

These girls who migrated to the United States with their families, or who were born shortly after that move, all reiterate their families' stories about a better American life than the poverty and struggle of natal spaces. Migration to the multiracial United States also racializes the girls, and we have seen the evidence of how that is achieved in school contexts in previous chapters. For example, the girls from the Philippines become "Asian" and "Chinky"— identifiers and identities that become possible in the particular context of U.S. spatiality. (The girls, as I show in the next section, also take up that Asianness in specifically gendered and sexual ways.) Despite the racial conflicts at school and the segregation the girls encounter, reproduce, and sometimes criticize, they also embrace the resulting identifications of the racial-ethnic and national difference that coexists with that segregation. The family stories about a "better life" form a central component of the abilities of the girls to imagine themselves as *different* from the other youth at school.

Those resulting identifications are formed, fundamentally, through the spaces and spatial processes of their family lives and its consequences. The girls hold to their racial-ethnic otherness because of the migration that continues to define their embodiments, relationships, and practices of difference. The particularity of each home's space define familial relationships and frame the girls' own understandings of what is possible in their lives and who they are as articulated selves. And, of course, the changes over time of where they live, from natal to adopted nations, means that these are mutable categories and sometimes shift from same/center to otherness. This otherness is clearly evidenced in the ways that whiteness forms a core reference for girls' evaluations of what types of futures are possible and desired by them. Finally, family myths and stories about life back "then" or over "there" (Hyams 2002) provide the fictions and justifications for their parents' big sacrifices; these are validated by these particular girls in their repetitions of the stories, yet the validations are tempered by their frustrations at being responsible for these histories themselves. The next section illustrates this point in more detail through another example.

"My Parents Hate Me": Two Girls' Failures to Be Race Heroes

Even when the girls complain about their parents' migration stories, their own ambivalent attachments to those stories arise. In this excerpt, Nane and Blindy (both Mexican American) start by showing their annoyance at their parents, but the accompanying tone, as with the previous excerpts, was of respect for their families' struggles.

> Nane: People think that, like, adults or something, they think that we [kids] have an easy life, that we don't appreciate things. And we do, at least specifically.
>
> Blindy: . . . Really, the way we show it, they think we don't appreciate what we have—what we have and they never had. And I've had one of those talks, like, [with] my dad.
>
> Nane: Every day, it's, "You don't appreciate what you have." [*mocking tone*]
>
> Blindy: "You don't appreciate what you have." [*mocking tone*]
>
> Mary: That's a parent thing to say.
>
> Blindy: Yeah. They always say, "You don't appreciate when I was in—I had to, like, work my way out." . . .
>
> Nane: It was always "back then, back then," [in] their countries.
>
> Blindy: . . . Back then when they were, like, when they turned eleven they just went off and worked. Like, right after school or something, or they'd just drop out.

Blindy told me that before her father emigrated from Mexico to the United States, he was kicked out of the house as a teenager and had to live on his own with no family support. Her grandfather, who was an alcoholic, also kicked out her aunt when she was young.

> Blindy: When he [grandfather] kicked out my aunt, she was just, like, ten years old. He just kicked them out one day, and it's like, they couldn't go back to go get their stuff. It's like, he wouldn't even let them go out to get, like, their property. He wouldn't let them. It's like, I think that was stupid of my grandfather. And I been going around saying that he was a really, really bad person. And they think that he's the cause why my grandmother died because they

told me that when he got drunk, he used to beat her. And, like, my aunts and uncles would, like, tie him to the fence. . . . That's why my [maternal] grandma didn't really like my dad at first because they usually reflect the father on the son. And they, like, they knew how my, my grandfather was, so they thought my dad was going to be like that. That's why. Because he was a bit violent. Well, that's what they tell me. . . .

Nane: I hate it when that happens. They expect you to be exactly like your parents.

Blindy: Yeah.

Nane: They expect you to be, like, just as hard working or something. And we are; it's just that, like, me, for example. I'm stuck with homework almost every day, so I never really have time. But when I finish, I try to do things, but my mom, she just doesn't think it's enough. And, I don't know. She has something against me.

Blindy: Yeah, they just think it's not enough. It's like, our parents don't think—

Nane: Or if you don't do exactly how they want, they exaggerate—

Blindy: Back then, like, classes were a little bit easier. They didn't really have that many, like, textbooks or stuff. It's like, right now we have a lot of textbooks; like, you can get any kind of information. That's why they assign a lot of essays or a lot of homework.

In the girls' minds, parents (and the vague "they") fault youth for things that are beyond their control. Life in the United States does not require—or allow (at least in the letter of the law)—early paid labor by children as young as eleven. Nane insists that they do appreciate "specific" things, and I do think they also appreciate their parents' histories of struggles. The parents are "supercitizen immigrants" (Honig 2001: 77) to their daughters: hard working, overcoming, and "the screen onto which we project our idealized selves" (78).

Bonnie Honig's supercitizen, however, evolves around "the play of xeno-philia and xenophobia," particularly "when [one's] expectations of a particular sort of relationship are disappointed and met instead by another. Often, this disappointment is expressed by way of the charge that the other is a taker who is just using us rather than a giver who really wants to be one of us" (79). While Honig certainly was *not* imagining that relationship as one between parents and children, the dance between hero and devil is clearly evident here—that is, the parent is both hugely admirable and grossly negligent, and both result through migration, generation, and race.

The girls want to be seen by their families for having their own legitimate struggles, even struggles that might not stack up to their parents'. They partic-ularly want their parents to understand that they have to confront violence at school and pressures to be sexually active; as they say in the previous exchange, the work they have to do for school is harder than what their parents had to do. The girls want these problems to be seen as justifiably difficult, even when their parents supposedly belittle today's struggles in comparison to their own "back then" in Mexico. Nane and Blindy also indicate that their "easier" life is a burden to them, since they do recognize their own relative wealth and comfort as opposed to what their parents had at their ages. In addition to the previous comment that her mom "has something against me," Nane even told me, "My parents hate me." Blindy added, "My parents think I'm weird." The girls take on a somewhat victim identity with me and look for sympathy for their parents' (supposed or actual) lack of love. They seek a particular struggle of their age to define themselves around, and the struggle as one who is love-less is noble to them. What is worse than a child whose parent hates her—particularly a child who works hard in school?

In this narrative, there are competing messages from the girls. They seek to distinguish themselves from their parents and define themselves as their "own person." This message is easily recognizable in teen narratives, and in the previous excerpt, we see a clear indication of this quest for independence. Blindy notes that "they usually reflect the father on the son," and in her example it was almost to the detriment of her father, given others' poor and unfair evaluation of him. Nane then contributes, "They expect you to be exactly like your parents," to which Blindy adds, "Yeah." However, at the same time, the girls insist that their parents should acknowledge their struggles as valid, within the frame of understanding that struggle narratives are fundamental to their family's definition and thus to the girls' own identities. In other words, the girls want to have a struggle narrative, too, like their parents. While their struggles are, of course, particular to their own lives and times, the importance of these struggle narratives in their own migrant families' self-definition means that the girls need these similarly themed narratives to think of themselves as properly belonging in the family. I believe this process is wholly unrecognized by the girls themselves; they do not consciously realize that they seek a struggle narrative as a practice of identification within their families.

At the same time, and despite the initial mocking tone and the fear that their parents cannot love or respect them because of their failure to live up to great expectations, the two girls give me their families' histories of hard times with a complete absence of mocking words and a sense of admiration and respect. Perhaps in part they are mocking themselves for not being able to prove their own worth by working as hard as their Mexican parents did. Thus, as the girls complain about their parents, they take up these stories as practices of self-evaluation and self-justification for their own hard work, albeit in different forms (such as schoolwork or saying no to early sexual activity in a later exchange). They want to be seen as legitimate hard workers themselves and to be recognized as worthy of their parents' respect, just as their parents expect them to respect their own difficulties in life. (See Hyams 2003 for a look at "home spaces" and the social reproduction of gender through struggles with parents.) That their parents fail to see their struggles as valid is also reflected in the girls' claims that their parents hate them.

In addition, the girls' racial-ethnic investments are embedded within and practiced through these narratives. These girls are the ones in Chapter 2 who described conflict with their Armenian neighbors and who described the "very, very, very . . . expensive" Hummers of the Armenians. They then contrasted this depiction of Armenian wealth and waste with their own, Mexican families' needs for reliable cars given their big families and the need to dependably get to work. The generational differences cited here should be taken within this overall narrative about "Mexican hard work." Nane and Blindy, despite their mocking of "you don't appreciate what you have," desire the respect of their parents and mark their stories as particularly Mexican. In contrast, they depict Armenian migration as government supported. (In Chapter 2, they also described the "money coupon things" that Armenians received on entry into the United States.) All of these examples are gestures— indeed, identifications—of racial-ethnic and national solidarity through family storymaking, not to mention through competition with Armenians for who is the harder working and more deserving ethnic and migrant group.

Nane and Blindy think that they have valid claims for parental respect given their own struggles with schoolwork and conflict. They desire to live up to what they read as their parents' desire; they assume they know what their parents' desire for them is: to be a hard-working Mexican who rises above strife. Of course, their parents' desire is itself partly unconscious, fully unknowable to the girls; thus the girls' desire to be seen as hard workers and as appreciative is directed at a phantom parental desire. The girls will never gain this full approval, since this cannot possibly actually reflect their parents' desire. (Even their parents could not articulate their full desires to their children, as these desires are not completely articulable.) However, the girls' quest to gain parental approval is fully successful in one way: it buttresses the girls' need for racial-ethnic and familial identification through a shared understanding of belonging in some way with their parents through these shared understandings of generational struggle, despite the generational divides of what those struggles entail.

> Blindy: It's like, my mother, my mom, has this thing about black people because every time she sees one, on the news and stuff, she always—she has an impression that black people, well mainly the Americans, black Americans, are bad, and they come from the

hood and stuff. So she has, like, a bad impression about them. And it's like, when I was growing up, she always told me not to hang around them. . . .

Nane: My mom, she's against blacks and Armenians. She's always getting so mad at them.

Mary: Why does she—why do they [both mothers] get mad at them?

Nane: They just—because in general, it's usually with them I also have problems with, no matter—my neighborhood, I think we're the only Hispanics, and maybe some other Asians a few streets away, and everyone else is Armenians. And I try to get along with them, but they always end up calling me stuff.

Mary: What do they call you?

Nane: They call me, like, "trash" and "Mexican trash" and other stuff in Armenian. They, like, flip me off.

Mary: Why do they call you "trash"?

Nane: I don't know. . . . It's only to my family. There are other people around there that are maybe pure American; they don't say anything to them. And they're the ones who are running around screaming all day long. I would just go out to maybe sit and draw outside or something, and they start, like, pointing at me and saying things. So, in general, I have problems with them because they have problems with me. I usually never give them any reason to, but that's just how it is, but, like, I have many Armenian friends that I, like, hold very close to my heart. But, in general, it's like, they hate me.

Both girls are quite frank about their mothers' obvious racism, and Nane shifts the conversation quickly to her own "problems" with Armenians in her neighborhood. Rather than explaining their mothers' racism in terms of their mothers' lives, the girls do so in terms of their own lives. In a sense, Nane justifies her mom's racism as motherly protection, perhaps gone somewhat awry in its extreme. Partly, I think, the girls do not directly answer my question about their mothers because they then avoid having to say bluntly that their mothers are racist. Throughout my interview with the girls, they avoid this label at all costs. Nane also tempers her assessment of the Armenians but assures me that she has Armenian friends, another guarded attempt to prevent me from considering her remarks to be racist. Nane's grievance against the Armenians is specified by their name calling toward her, situated by her own innocence ("I try to get along with them, but . . .").

Nane uses "also" to shift from the question about her mother to her own story, indicating a shared understanding with her mom about the Armenians ("I *also* have problems . . ."). She goes further by saying that the neighbor

Armenians call only her family "trash." Anglos, or "pure Americans," do not get the same treatment as her Hispanic family. In the following excerpt, the gradations of familial racial-ethnic identification are given broader context by the girls' theories on why U.S. diversity through migration results in conflict. The two interview excerpts provide a deeper understanding of the familial, neighborhood, school, and national spatialities of racial identification.

> Blindy: It's like, because since Mexicans started coming and Arme-
> nians—that's—that's the truth that there's differences, and there's
> a lot of people going to come for better ways to live in the U.S.
> because it gives a lot of opportunities.
> Mary: So why do you think that people are so scared of newcomers in
> the U.S.?
> Nane: I guess we're all like that. We just like to be in power.
> Blindy: Yeah, they just want to be in power.
> Nane: We like to think that we're the best. We like to think that we are
> right. That our way of life is better, not theirs.
> Blindy: That's why, like, religions.
> Nane: It's, like, the sad truth, but some people just can't accept it, so
> that's when the fights begin.
> Blindy: Yeah.
> Nane: When the name calling and stuff.
> Mary: So they're threatened because they're afraid they're going to lose
> something?
> Blindy: Like their way.
> Nane: They—they feel like they won't be, like—
> Blindy: The same.
> Nane: Yeah, that they won't have respect, but it's not true. If you actu-
> ally accept others, then you'll have more respect than you ever
> thought you can. So, I don't know, it's just our sad truth. We,
> we're, like, very over-something—
> Blindy: Protective of our, like, culture, kind of.

The girls tie the violence at their school ("the fights") to migrant conflict to maintain "power" over self-identification. This power, combined with the haughty thinking that "we're the best," indicates that the girls understand the primary power of racial-ethnic difference as a segregative force. This power that they point to indicates a sort of everyday maintenance of racial-ethnic and national definition, as well as its spatiality. This "overprotective" maintenance, in the girls' estimations, leads to a group identity and threat of dissolution (compare Jane in the previous section). The practice of one's national identity even after migration, through new generations, is the practice of segregation and self-bounding from other races, ethnicities, and nationalities. This practice extends to other contexts and creates the social-segregative spatiality at this particular LA high school.

American Children: Sexuality, Sociality, and First-Generation Parents

Here I turn to girls' narratives about their parents' expectations about socializing, dating, and sexuality. Often these narratives were complaints about how parents were too restrictive, conservative, or biased against racial others; other narratives include girls' ideas about dating racial others. I highlight the tensions in their words between their desires to be "American" girls (normalized as white) and their identity investments in being racially and ethnically distinct given family histories and racial difference.

Attempts to resist their parents' expectations, I argue, binds the girls as tightly to their racial identification as "different" as much as simple compliance with their parents' wishes would. The process of being a racial other or articulating how one is "different in America" remains, even as the girls try to integrate into multicultural Los Angeles. I deal with this issue more extensively in this chapter's conclusion, drawing together the lessons from all the material about so-called pure Americans or normal Anglos (or even television characters, as previously noted). Here I focus on the connections between sexuality, race, and ethnicity and consider how gender and sexuality norms in the girls' families impact the possibilities of their commitments to racial integration. Importantly, I show that girls' own investments in their sexual and romantic lives and futures often reproduce trenchant racial beliefs, despite their voices of complaint.

I begin again with Jackie, who explains to me that her parents are "old style" Armenians, which prevents them from letting her socialize. More drastically, she insists that they cannot possibly *know* her given this "old style" limitation. However, she extends this concept to ask whether it is possible for anyone to know her.

> Jackie: My parents are, like, still, like, their brains are in Armenia, and they—they're also, like, old style and stuff. They feel—I feel like I'm not understood. Like, because all they've seen is that, "Oh my god, they're going to go out there; they're going to do this; they're going to do that." They don't know who you really are, even though they're, like, your parents. And that's how it is around you, too, like, your teachers don't know who you really are. Like, your friends, even though they're really your friends, they still don't understand what you really, like, what you want or

who you are. What you really want to do in life. And, like, when you tell your parents that—oh yeah, I'm like, "The big major arts school is in Philadelphia; I want to go there, or New York." They go, "No, you're not going anywhere." It's, like, okay. And then you want me to be a better person in life? And then they don't understand that. And then you feel frustrated because they don't really understand—

Amy: Know you.

Jackie: And, like, like, the party was just like, you want to go to a party; they go "no." You go, "I'm not going to do anything." "It doesn't matter, no." And, like, you feel like you're left out in life because—not only in life, it's just the fun because I don't really go out and have fun or anything. So, like, I felt bad.

Jackie accused her Armenian-brained parents of overvaluing the dangers of urban life when she later explained to me that when an Armenian teen encounters violence (that is, any story of a violent event that then circulates among Armenians), their parents reiterate their insistence that she and Amy may not go to parties. Their fear leads to what Jackie thinks is severe spatial restriction; she can't even enjoy a normal teen life by having "fun." Worse, the spatiality of restriction indicates to her that her parents do not see her for who she "really" is, do not acknowledge her ability to be safe, and do not appreciate her dreams for her life (e.g., art school, experiencing new places). Jackie's parents do not recognize that she is a good girl who is "not going to do anything" to get in trouble; she just wants to have "fun."

However, Jackie's narrative indicates that there is something more at stake than a girl with immigrant parents who just wants to have fun. She shifts from pointing to her frustration at only her parents to a fear that no one can possibly really "know" her: "They still don't understand what you really, like, what you want or who you are. What you really want to do in life." Jackie's reduction to just wanting to have "fun" by going to parties masks the deeper message of her words. She marks the failure of friendship, families, and other relationships to accomplish full recognizability. This desire for recognition is an indication of both the limits of self-expression—that is, her inability to fully communicate who she is—and the limits of language to communicate one's experience of self. I do not want to reduce Jackie's worries to some type of subjective angst, although certainly subjectivity is relevant. It is also vital to frame this exchange within her understanding of her Armenian family and the limits it imposes on her idealized subjectivity. She is literally indicating that she is being left out of fun because she is Armenian, and she is unknowable because she is Armenian. Jackie believes that her parents contextualize family space as if it were in Armenia, and she resists their embodiment of the Armenian home ("their brains are in Armenia"). Yet mostly she grieves that being an Armenian leaves her utterly alone in her subjectivity, unseeable and unrecognizable to even the closest of friends and family. She laments her Armenian identity because it is no fun, but "fun" itself indicates more than parties. It encapsulates a future possibility for being an "American" who can go across the country for art school, have close and enriching relationships with parents and friends, and hope to be a "better person in life." Remember also that it was Jackie whose words in Chapter 4 show her investment in the sexual restrictions that Armenian families place on their teenage daughters. She reprimanded her sister Amy when Amy articulated a wish that eventually Armenian families would allow girls to date non-Armenian boys.

This issue came up again when I met with Amy alone in a follow-up, individual interview. Amy tells me about an eleventh-grade boy whom she thinks is cute but whom she won't talk to. I asked if she hesitated to talk to him because he was older.

Amy: No, it's not because—that's not—it's more of the race.

Mary: What is he?

Amy: He's African American.

Mary: Oh. So why—

Amy: [My parents would] not like that.

Mary: . . . Oh, you tell your mom everything. [Amy previously told me that she shares everything with her mom.]

Amy: Yeah.

Mary: I remember that.

Amy: We have the bond.

Mary: Yeah, that's right.

Amy: [She would not like the fact] even if I [only] liked him.

Mary: Does she know you think he's cute?

Amy: Yeah.

Mary: And what does she say?

Amy: Like, "Are you serious?" I'm like, yeah. But she's not like, oh my god, no, you know. She just thinks it's nothing serious, you know, she—I just think he's cute, you know; we all go through that.

Mary: Well, what happens—what would happen if you had it—if, like, a black guy asked you out? And you went home and said, "Mom, I really like this guy. I want to go out with him."

Amy: She wouldn't let me.

Mary: Would she let you if you were older?

Amy: No, she wouldn't let me.

Mary: She wouldn't let you go out with a guy, or she wouldn't let you go out with a black guy?

Amy: Black. Because, like, Armenians—have you ever seen an Armenian with, like, a different race? Married? You don't see much, you know? We Armenians, like, like to keep it one race, you know?[5]

Mary: Well, what do you think will happen, in another generation?

Amy: It's still going to be like that. Armenians are strict. No matter where they are, they're strict. They have their own rules, you know, their own religion. . . . We're not racist; we like other races. We don't like to, like, you know, interact with other races. . . . They're not, like, "Oh," you know, "African American people are bad." Never, you know. We have, like, very close family members or, we have, like, workers or whatever, that are, like, African American and, like, oh my god, they're the best, you know? We even go to, like, out to eat together or, you know.

Mary: But you just can't date them.

Amy: It's like, we like to be, you know, just Armenian.

Her desire for this boy at her school is far outweighed by her desire to be a "we"—to identify as part of the "Armenian race." The "we" illustrates her investment in her otherness, the category of racial differences that marks her identification in the group identity. "Race" is a primary category that she takes on as a normative condition of her subjectivity: "we" Armenians, and "they" others (e.g., even though they are black, "they're the best, you know?"). She shows the vitality of this identification by indicating the practices that maintain it, for example, by being strict, labeling racial difference, discussing with her mom sexuality and race in everyday conversation, reducing its import as mere crushes that all girls go through, and finally, summarizing the Armenian quest for remaining racially pure as her own quest.

I even tried, in my questioning, to draw out Amy's resistance to her mom's hesitation and racial rule making, but Amy did not take up the room I gave her to blame her racist parents. She insisted that these practices were not racist, and she consistently used the "we" pronoun to show her solidarity with Armenian rules. I frame the question as "your mother wouldn't let you," and she explains in detail the reasoning behind her mother's rules as "we Armenians like to keep it one race."

The psychic disgust at the possibilities of miscegenation and the fact that it has occurred to a limited extent in the family already comes out at the end of this exchange. Amy unconsciously qualifies the contaminations of racial difference and mixing in her example of food and eating together. Food and

5. Keep in mind that Kim Kardashian's relationships with black men were not public fodder until her reality television show, *Keeping Up with the Kardashians*, initiated her celebrity status in 2007.

eating are symbols for disgust, and they directly represent her fears of ingesting the other into one's own body. By bringing into the example her family's subordinates, the workers they pay who are black, she unconsciously demonstrates her abjection of black. She also says that they "go out" to eat, not that her family would bring an African American into their home to eat—a disgust distinctly spatial and a practice of spatially defining racial others. Race is also a spatial difference, one that cannot impact the "pure" Armenian home space without risking what *it is to be* Armenian.

Amy's words illustrate her conscious interest in being a nonracist. While Armenians are separatists, a separate race, she insists that they are not racist because they do not label African Americans as "bad" people. She cares very strongly about working to counter racism at school, and she voices throughout the interview the pain that racial violence and segregation at school cause her. But this voice sits in sharp contrast to her fundamental investment in the Armenian category and her psychic need to belong to the "race" and her family. I think it also indicates the effect of this racial identification of otherness— her own and of other non-Anglos. The effect is one of racism, even though this racism is not spoken or consciously articulated by Amy. Her disgust of others (even the desire of disgust by admiring an African American guy at school) and her acquiescence of keeping the family and its spaces pure, I argue, are practices of racist subjectivity. I suppose it is accurate to say that Amy is both racist and nonracist, and the bigger argument to make is that both are possible. However, a voiced nonracism should not overdetermine the racism inherent in her practices of identification. Both must be theorized.

The issue of cross-racial dating also came up with Chibi-Kim, Zelda, and Sephi, all born in the Philippines. Zelda marks race here as "Asian," not with the ethnic or national identity of Filipino.

> Mary: A Latino, what if you brought an Armenian home and said, "I'd like to go out on a date—"
>
> Chibi-Kim: Well, they don't, they don't like it.
>
> Zelda: They're pretty—they're pretty—they're pretty—they're pretty racist when it comes to this. Like, "I would only want you to marry an Asian." Most likely—
>
> Mary: Any kind of Asian?
>
> Zelda: Any kind of Asian. . . .
>
> Sephi: My parents don't want me marrying anyone.
>
> Zelda: I don't want—personally, I don't want to get married, but if I ever got married—if I ever got married, I would marry someone of my own kind. . . .
>
> Mary: Why is that important to marry someone like you?
>
> Zelda: I don't know; we share the same ideals—

Chibi-Kim: Mutual connections.

Zelda: Cultural, yeah, cultural ideals.

Mary: Well, what kind of cultural ideal do you have that's Filipino?

Zelda: You know, we have the, well, the majority of us are Catholic, and we have—

Mary: But Latinos are Catholic.

Sephi: Yeah.

Zelda: Yeah, but they're, like, not, I don't know, I don't know. There's just—

Sephi: Filipinos are the beaners of Asia.

Mary: They're what?

Sephi: They're the beaners of Asia.

Mary: The "beaners"?

Chibi-Kim: The beaners of Asia.

Mary: What does that mean?

Chibi-Kim: You know, you know, that's, like, a term for Mexicans, you know, "beaners." . . .

Mary: No, I didn't know that. So they call you "chinky," you call them "beaners."

Zelda: Yeah, we call—

Chibi-Kim: And whites "crackers."

Mary: Crackers. That's what I am, I'm a cracker. That's an old one.

Sephi: Redneck.

Zelda: They call us, they call us, they call us beaners because, like, because we, like, we have a Hispanicized culture. We were colonized by the Spanish.

Chibi-Kim: When Spain came to us.

Zelda: Yeah, and so our culture's, like, mixed, and our country's, like, a melting pot.

Sephi: My last name is [surname].

Zelda: Yeah, she has a Spanish last name.

Mary: Yep.

Zelda: Like, a majority, a lot of us have a Spanish last name.

There is much to be said about this excerpt, but here I draw only two points to the fore. First, when I ask the girls about interracial dating, Zelda speaks about marriage and what she and her parents think of it. This reframes the discussion in terms of marriage and the "family line" rather than as dating and a more youth-oriented, perhaps even frivolous, sexual practice. Thus, the question of sexuality is taken up in the conversation as a complex weave of heteronormative family and racial practice. While the girls deflect the racist undertones to their parents (e.g., dealing with the question by replying that *they* are pretty racist), they themselves take up the issue of race and sexuality by connecting it directly to family and marriage.

Second, dissimilarly to the other girls I met, these Filipinas bring up colonialism and the connections it forced. They make sense of these colonial histories in the ways that their high school's particular spatiality brings them together with Mexicans. They negate the religious commonalities with Mexicans, instead hinting that religion is more of a racial difference—at least before I interrupted Zelda's hesitation to find a common identity as Catholic with Mexicans at school. Food here again plays a role in defining a cultural practice, and Spanish surnames likewise define a family's colonial legacy. The girls therefore find similarities as "Hispanicized cultures" but mark the severe limits to this common ground. Sexuality and the question of intermarriage and its colonial legacies instigate the very clear distinctions of racial differences in the girls' narratives. Racial and national differences articulate through spatiality: inheritances of colonialism that travel with families and, simultaneously and continuously, distinguish otherness in the everyday spaces of girls' lives.

One last case closes this section. The first excerpt is from my interview with Mayra, who, like the Armenian girls previously, explains that her mother's immigrant status prohibits her from understanding the practices of her American-raised teenager. I think it is important to show that this frustration was not just characteristic of Armenian girls but that Mexican girls like Mayra also experienced it.

> Mayra: If I tell my mom [that I'm going out], "Oh, Mom, you know, some, you know, one of my guy friends is going to pick us up, and from there we're going to go to my friend's house." You know, I'd rather just tell her, "Oh, my friend's mom is going to pick us up." You know? And it's different because for my brother, you know, they don't really care because he's a guy, but for us [girls], it would be more like, "Oh, what, a guy's picking you up?" You know? . . . So yeah, sometimes I do have to tell her, you know, you know, lies, and be, like, oh, I'm going somewhere else instead of, you know [where I'm actually going]. But that's only because if she were to—
> Mary: But that's not, like, bad stuff [you're lying about].
> Mayra: No, but it's because she doesn't understand. I mean, you have to [understand] she—she was born and raised in Mexico. . . . She doesn't understand the pressures of how it is here; she doesn't understand that, you know. That if, you know, friends within each other, we take care of each other. She doesn't understand stuff like that. So yeah, I do have to lie to her sometimes.

Unlike her Armenian classmates, however, Mayra's home, family, and neighborhood settings frame her social and racial practices through very different spaces. Here we see again her frustrations at being labeled "whitewashed," a concept that is introduced in Chapter 4 in the exploration of social-racial segregation on campus. While her friends thought hanging out with a white friend at school "whitewashed" her, here this becomes an intimate family accusation.

Mayra: I was, you know—growing up I was taught, oh, look like a gangbanger is what's "in." Well, now I know better because, I mean, one of my cousins, he died because he was so tough, and he was a gangbanger, and, you know, he died because of that. And I saw that as, that's so stupid. Like, that was an eye opener for me. Like, wow, you know, he died defending some stupid name. That doesn't mean anything.

Mary: How'd he die?

Mayra: There was a, kind of like the riot at school, between two gangs, and out of all the people that were there, he was the only one who got shot and killed. And—

Mary: How old were you when that happened?

Mayra: That was, like, two years ago. And I mean, even, like, growing up, 'cause back then, there was a lot more gangsters in this area. And I can tell either they moved to, like, Bakersfield, but back in the day there was so many, you know? And then where I grew, where I grew up, which was, like, in the ghetto part of Hollywood, that was the thing to be, I mean, you weren't anything else. There—I mean, I didn't even know there was, like, there were people who dressed preppy until I got to [my current high school]. Because over there it was just straight, you know, gangbangers, gangs. I mean, you're raised, you know, that's what you're going to be, you know, you're going to represent your sister's or your brother's, you know, group and stuff.

Mary: Did your mom say anything to you when your cousin died about it?

Mayra: She was just like, he's so stupid; look at what he died for. And, I mean, there was talk about it within the family, you know. And I mean this one cousin that's, he's really, like, bad, they talk about him too, but they love him because he has a great personality. So they don't really talk about him, you know, messing up or anything.

Mary: So do you have a close family, extended family? Do you have other family here . . . on your mom's side?

Mayra: My mom's side of the family, they have a lot of problems, which cause problems between the children. I mean, right now, I have a cousin who's waiting to, like, beat me up. Actually, it's, like, three cousins. But they're older, they're, like, I mean, one of my cousins, she's, like, thirty; she must be, like, thirty-five. So, two of them, they're, like, thirty-five, you know, talking smack about me. I mean, put it like this: I was wearing a skirt that was below my knees when I came to church, and because I looked conceited and I looked whitewashed, they don't like me anymore. And this is all over what I was wearing to go to church.

Mary: So they think that you were acting white.

Mayra: Basically, "Oh, she's trying to be white; what's wrong with her?" You know? So, three of my cousins stop talking to me because of that, and it was all over an outfit. You know, because I was trying to be whitewashed.

Mary: Did they ask you about it?

Mayra: No, they just—they started talking about it amongst themselves, and I ended up finding out. And, I mean, it's really stupid.

Mary: They're so much older; you think they'd be mature.

Mayra: But, I mean, because they're the ones growing up we saw, you know, them dropping out of high school. None of my cousins from one of my aunts, you know, none of them graduated from high school.

Mary: So if you do well in school, that's being white?

Mayra: Oh, to, like, some of [the] cousins that's being, like, . . . "what a schoolgirl." You get made fun of, you know? But, you know, to my mom, I guess, she was, like, proud of me, I guess, but she just never told me. She never let me know; she never acted like—because I would work really hard to get those A's. I mean, to some people they may come easy, but to me they were hard, hard work.

Mary: You know what? If anyone tells you it comes easy, they're lying.

Mayra: I hope they are because it makes me feel stupid.

Mary: No, it's hard.

Mayra: And so, I have to pretend, you know, to be this person, and that's the way I was before. I mean, I mean, in all of middle school, for two years, sixth and seventh grade, I stayed inside the classroom with teachers because I was student body treasurer, I was . . . gifted, I was, . . . my tests were, like, you know, ninetieth percentile. And so it's kind of, like, I really didn't have [trouble] . . . with them, until eighth grade when all the problems started. That's when my dad left, you know, for the first time. Because he had been there throughout my childhood; he had always been there. But since he left, I really don't know what it was, but ever since he left, it was just, everything was just different. And so, I just started eighth grade, yeah, I started having things in common with all these, you know, people that are messed up, like, "Wow, your parents split up too? Wow, mine did too," you know. And then it just begins to, you know, [you] start hanging out; you have more things in common. And ever since eighth grade, that's [it], you know. And I stopped—I stopped caring about school anymore because I said, "Why care if she's not going to be proud of me ever?" She's always going to be comparing me to other people. Always.

The processes of racial-ethnic scrutiny are evident in numerous places in this narrative. First, Mayra examines her own self-styling by questioning the gang look as she grew older, especially when she moved to the Valley from Hollywood (which is in Los Angeles south of the Hollywood Hills). This spatial flux and changing context, along with a growing awareness of the futility of gang violence, prompted Mayra to shift from a so-called ghetto, gang-infused "what's 'in'" look. Second, Mayra feels heavily scrutinized by her family, from her mother always "comparing me to other people" to her cousins policing her clothing. As she describes her cousins seemingly trivial yet cruel taunts, her story points to the ways that racial pressures are intensely familial, and familial relations are intensely racial. The threat of their violence, given one cousin "who's waiting to beat me up," brings home the daily iterations of racial norms and the possibilities of failing to live up to them. The inability of Mayra to make her mother proud is united with the practices of proper Mexican-LA girlhood—which are pulled by different people in divergent directions. To make her mom proud, she must continue to do well in school despite the increasing pressure to underperform by cousins and peers who judge her academic achievements as white. Yet she claims that her mom cannot ever be satisfied by her achievements; even when she was doing well in school, her mom failed to be proud of her. "She's always going to be comparing me to other people. Always." I do not know exactly who these other people are, but Mayra's feelings of inadequacy in comparison to these other people results in *her* practices changing. She had failing grades when we met.

According to Mayra, her family pulled her in opposite directions: to be a gang girl and not whitewashed or a schoolgirl to please her mother. The lesson to take from this excerpt is that Mayra is herself pulled in opposite directions over her own self-identification—that is, what it means to be Mexican in Los Angeles. Pulling away from gang life, doing well in school, and wearing non-hoochie clothes marks her as whitewashed and less than Mexican. Sharing family grief over a cousin's violent death pulls her closer to her Mexicanness (and raises issues of her own experiences with school riots) and illustrates the spatial proximity of neighborhood and family allegiances. In Mayra's stories, a less than ideal family life itself is definitive of "Mexican": the sharing about family dissolution through which she makes friends at her new school, strife with cousins in the old neighborhood, and distinguishing from her mother's old country Mexican conservativeness. In the end, all of these pulling influences leave Mayra experiencing a lot of disappointment: in herself, her cousins, and her mother. This disappointment, I argue, is the failure of a racial-ethnic identification to be able to buttress so much of the emotional-psychic weight of subjectivity. It is insufficient to summarize one's subjectivity, despite Mayra trying so hard for it to do so, by any category of social difference.

Conclusion

The other is always impersonal and contextual, and so, in a sense, is the self. The inherently social-spatial qualities of relations with others, impacted by the unconscious psychic investments by both subjects and their others, means that subjects' stated intentions are never so simply to be taken at face value. They should be analyzed for the psychic processes that enable them and constrain their possibility and scope. The social spatiality at the high school constantly forms through subjects' practices of such differences, and differences themselves are fundamentally informed by the spaces that mutually define them.

The mechanisms of racial, gender-sexual, and generational identification, I have suggested, exist as psychic stumbling blocks for the girls' hopes of racial conciliation. The trajectory of my arguments about the trenchant attachment to social differences and the ambivalence of identification also carries with it deep implications for multicultural norms and programming in U.S. education and, indeed, for the norms of antiracist and feminist scholarship and politics. Some may even find this a deeply conservative argument. Does it lead to the conclusion that any attempts to effect a nonracialized society are impossible? Why bother to work for nonviolent futures, then? Does difference equal the eventuality of conflict? In the hopes of at least bringing these questions to the table, I insist that acknowledging the antinomy at the heart of each subject and its long spatial constitution are arguments that need to be made in the quest of finding more effective methods at addressing youth violence and racism, not to mention the emphasis in girlhood studies on autonomous subjectivity. With segregation increasing in U.S. urban schools, certainly new frameworks are necessary.

Girls may not only yearn for peace but also take great pleasure in conflict and racism via their investments in racial identifications determined on fundamental difference. Of course, within their families, the girls also take pleasure in distinguishing themselves through conflict with their parents, even if they also illustrate through their practices and narratives that they are as committed to social identifications such as nationality and race as their parents are. As subjects, they do not necessarily admit or consciously realize the psychic rewards of conflict, and the productive practices of identification that ensue through the conflicts they discuss are certainly not a part of daily selfhood. They are a part of subjectivity, however.

6

What Girls Want at School

Surveillance, Care, and a Predictable Space

As my interview time with each girl or group of girls drew to a close, I asked them what questions I may have neglected that they thought would be important to address in my research. Although many of them said, "I think we covered everything," one other issue came up repeatedly: education.

> Mary: So what do you think are important things in your lives that . . . you want to talk about?
> Amy: Education.
> Mary: Education.

> Lola: Probably I would ask about school because that's, like, education. . . . It's the biggest part of our lives.

> Rachelle: School is, like, our only real priority in life at this point. So I guess the only thing we can do [is cope with our school's problems]. If I told my parents, I'm like, yeah, you know, this is what happened today, la la la. They're like, "Yeah, just stick with it because . . . you're going to graduate in [just] a couple of years."

My conversations with the girls ranged far from the topics of school relations and the riot and included their own and their friends' sexual practices and experience, popular culture (especially music), dreams for travel or college, and living in Los Angeles. Since we always started our meetings with the school riot, it was common to end on alternative topics such as these. So I was often surprised to have the girls return insistently to the topic of school with my summary question. Perhaps this statement says more about me than them, but even in my previous research with girls in South Carolina, an open final question did not elicit concerns about education. Clearly these Angelino girls had many things to say about their particular school and what they saw as its many, many failures and shortcomings. Some of them had ideas for improvements, but many, like Rachelle, were resigned to the futility of protest and just wanted to ride out the time they had left in high school.

Overwhelmingly, the girls' specific comments pointed to their disappointment at their school's response to the riot. They were angry and disgusted by what they saw as its misguided and useless attempts to quell racial-ethnic conflict. This chapter first deals with these many moments in interviews when the girls discuss the school administration's feeble replies to the riot. Their primary outrage is the administration's failure to reach out to students to discuss the violence and racial discord. Second, I examine the girls' own ideas about what could help their school rebound from racial discord, particularly their interest in having a more controlled and surveilled campus. Central to this was their proposal that administrators and teachers exert a firm hand over student chaos. While the girls admitted that lax security and rules enforcement benefited them in some ways, they also indicated that they yearn for a structured, strict campus that would ensure their bodily safety and academic advancement. Finally, the chapter draws together the girls' opinions about their teachers and classes to provide an overall argument about their desires for education and adult relationships at school. "Teachers do not care about us" means that students feel that their efforts to be good or attentive students are wasted energies. They often explain their poor grades as the fault of uncaring or unqualified teachers, such as faulty classroom management, racial preferences for others, or just plain lack of concern by the teachers.

These examples and the overall chapter content indicate that the girls' voices are strongly reflexive. They very carefully and closely consider the conditions of their failing school and, for many, their own behavior at school. According to Dawn Currie, Deirdre Kelly, and Shauna Pomerantz, this kind of reflexivity "signals the ability to critically reflect upon processes through which girls are positioned in the social world." They continue, "As feminists, we equate critical reflexivity with empowerment because it *might* enable girls to challenge discourses that help sustain women's subordination to men" (2006: 420, my emphasis). Yet, contra to Currie and colleagues' faithful optimism in the potentials of a feminist voice, I argue in this chapter that, overwhelmingly, the girls avoid a politicized approach to their school's problems. My reading concentrates on the "might" of Currie and colleagues, and I consider why the girls in this case do not unequivocally—or perhaps even partially—translate their critical reflexivity into an active agency beyond their verbal complaints. They do not protest at school, unify to seek change, or plan responses to the school riot themselves. Their resistance to the school's administration and structure is limited to speaking to me and each other about the "school's stupidity" and, in the case of teachers, adult apathy. Understanding these voices is an important rejoinder to feminist investments in the politicized, feminist girl subject, and it also helps to situate possible responses to the woeful deficiencies of American multiculturalism and urban education. At the heart of this is addressing how girls depoliticize their own commitments to racial harmony.

The School Administration Did Not Deal Effectively with the Riot

Jane, the speaker in the following excerpt, is Armenian.

> Mary: What did the administration or the principals do after it [the riot] happened?
>
> Jane: They didn't really do much. Like, they came on the PA [public address system], and they just, like, said a few words about respecting each other. And, like, the Armenians—people who don't speak English in that school, they wouldn't understand it, you know? Because the Armenian translator that they have, and I don't know about the Hispanic because I don't speak [Spanish], you know, but the Armenian translator, like, I didn't understand anything she said whatsoever. At all.
>
> Mary: You mean her Armenian wasn't any good?
>
> Jane: Wasn't any good at all.
>
> Mary: That's all that they did—they had an announcement? There was no other sort of activity?
>
> Jane: That's all they did, and I was shocked, you know, because we keep hearing [about the riot] on the news and stuff. And why wouldn't they at least, like, have, like, a—get everybody into, like, a group, like an auditorium, you know, and talk to them? I mean, I'm not sure if talking would help, but at least it's, like, doing something, you know? . . .
>
> Mary: Do the teachers talk about it at all in classes?
>
> Jane: They did. And all they said was that the people who started it were stupid. That's all they said.

Mayra, the speaker in the following excerpt, is Hispanic.

Mayra: They really, they don't have any—any conversations with us. I mean, like, to just sit down, like I'm sitting down with you, and just telling you everything. And I would [be willing to sit with the administration], but then they'll be like, "Oh, tell me who they are, exactly." So, I can't do that. You know, with you I know I can tell you, "Oh, there's this, this, this going on." Because you're not going to force me to tell you, "Oh, well, who is it exactly?" You know?

Mary: So even after [the fight] . . . , the administration at the school didn't actually say, "I want to hear from students about what's happening on campus?"

Mayra: No, I mean, they got the—some of the gang members which they thought were the big ones [i.e., the main culprits]. But they don't know; they're not inside. I mean, they're not part of the group. So they don't know exactly who it is. So they got whoever looked—looked the part of being one of the main guys. And they got some of the Armenians, which looked like the main ones. And they sat them together, and they made them talk it out. The thing is, yeah, they may have talked it out. [But] it didn't change any[thing]. . . . It really didn't.

In this section, I focus on the girls' voices of discontent with their school's response to the riot by situating both voice and self as limited by the girls' largely unacknowledged affirmations of their own subjectification in school spaces. The girls rely on their own supposed powerlessness to evidence their resistance to school policy and administration. (Ironically, as I show in the next section, the girls depict the school as a completely disempowered place for youth *and* as a place that is ruled by youth, given the administrators' and the teachers' fears of students and just plain neglect.) In other words, the girls claim that the school does not care what they think about the violence, and then they use that claim to show their disgust and skepticism. These emotions stand in for girls' resistance to what they think of as the ineptitude of the school administration and its misguided enforcement of control over student bodies in other respects. Yet their strong opinions and voices hint at the other commitments they have to being highly structured at school. They criticize the school's administrators for their lack of response and yearn for a strong, controlling hand on campus. They also articulate a desire for a deeper analysis and reaction to be given by the school, for the school to "address" the problem in a critical way. Unfortunately, these overwrought administrators, according to Mayra, focus on the few main instigators of the fight, or those they stereotype as the probable leaders. They neglect the larger problems of segregation, distrust, and racism.

In both Jane's and Mayra's statements, there is a clear indication of their displeasure at the school's failure to use the riot as an opportunity to involve students in a response to violence. Jane "was shocked" that there was *only* a PA announcement, one that utterly lacked fluency for the non-English Armenian speakers at school. In the "least" she expected the school to organize a student body assembly to address the severity of the riot and the ongoing racial tensions on campus. She saw the absence of any event at school as a sharp juxtaposition to the media's attention to the fight and, of course, to the students' own ongoing conversations, anxieties, and energies. The severity of the violence, she indicates, necessitated a much stronger reaction by the school. (Also note that Jane relies on an idealized multicultural gathering as a proper response by the school; more on this later.)

Mayra's depiction of the school's response validates Jane's, and she is more forthright in saying that she would welcome the opportunity to discuss the racial tension on campus with administrators. Mayra has friends in Latino gangs, although she does not affiliate with any, and her "insider" viewpoint, she says, gives her the perspective to know better than the school administration what is "really" happening with the boys who fight. She refuses to provide names, and ratting on friends is what she anticipates the school would ask of her, if she shows any interest in addressing the broader topic of racial discord and violence. Mayra thus labels the school as too focused on individuals, when the issue should be addressed at a broader level. The administration rounded up the usual suspects of gang members who, as Mayra puts it, "looked the part" of being capable of violence and fighting. Such racial profiling, Mayra indicates, does not work; the "big ones" do not always fit the easy stereotype. A small conversation between supposed gangsters does not begin to address the overwhelming issue of racial tension and segregation on campus. "Talking it out" among a few boys does not change anything, Mayra indicates.

The girls also said that teachers did not take the riot as an opportunity for small-group discussions in class. Jane says that teachers indicated only the stupidity of the fighters, which is, of course, remarkably simple and similar to the girls' language about "stupid boys." With teachers, however, Jane expects more than such a reduced lesson. No girl gave me any indication that any teacher in a formal classroom or an informal conversational setting approached the issue or made a pedagogical opportunity of the violence. I return to the girls' stories about teachers in a separate section, but here it is important to note the lack of a critical education about multiracial violence at the school, despite the school's and the district's programmatic investment in multiculturalism.

Of course, the girls' own embrace of the possibilities of multiculturalism comes through in their evaluations of the school administration's response. In the previous excerpts, Jane and Mayra both called for a community discussion of the riot: Jane's auditorium gathering and Mayra's "sitting down" and talking. Jane admits that the idea may not "help, but at least it's, like, doing something, you know?" The something that she could imagine is, I think, limited by the banal lessons that uncritical multiculturalism has extended in her education in urban Los Angeles. The idea that youth could glean healing words from the school's administrators or communally discuss the outbreak of racial violence is a simplistic idea that racial difference and conflict can be overcome with an hour of conversation in a packed auditorium. The talking cure, if you will, in both Mayra's and Jane's imaginations, would be severely limited to the airing of grievances—if indeed the talk could commence from groups that are so segregated in everyday life. Why they would be compelled to sit down together and then "get along" is the missing logic in the girls' calls for *talk*. The multicultural fantasy that this possibility could result in less conflict is buttressed by the disavowal that racism and sexism structures subjectivity and its spatialities. It narrowly defines racial conflict as a school space, rather than a conflict that extends far beyond the space and time of the students' marred interactions.

So what *did* the school do after the riot? The girls mentioned increased emphasis by the school on enforcing what they see as petty rules. Most importantly, they all talked about a program of "tardy sweeps" that channeled late students into the lunchroom instead of allowing them to go to class. The next grouping of excerpts shows how many of the girls were concerned about these sweeps. They especially raise the girls' ire and frustration and indicate to them the school's lack of concern for students' education and urban lives. The policy operates by sweeping all latecomers into one room—the cafeteria—rather than allowing students to go to their classes. Thus, the girls say that being just a few minutes late means that they miss an entire class and fall behind in their work. They characterize the tardy sweeps along with other increased policing of the dress code and cell phone, iPod, or CD player usage as a banal and off-point reaction to the riot. On the other hand, some saw the sweeps as a legitimate way to skip class. Dawdling meant that they would be swept into the cafeteria and would get to avoid class.

The following excerpt is from a group interview with Latinas Alison, Gaby, Julie, Rachelle, Sarah, and Susie (however, I am unable to identify from the recording which girl is speaking).

Speaker 1: But, I mean, the way the school runs things, they're worried about someone walking down the hall with their hood on, their CD player on—

Speaker 2: —when there's drugs being sold in the bathroom. You have people bringing guns and knives, and they're worried about someone that's walking down the street showing her stomach or maybe, like, her skirt is too short or something like that.

Speaker 3: I think they do that so they—

Speaker 4: It's understandable—

Speaker 3: —can have at least some kind of power because if they didn't tell you how you should be dressing or if they didn't tell you how to, like, not to listen to your music, then they really have no control. Because they can't stop—obviously they can't stop us from fighting, so I don't know, I think they think if we're not listening to our CD player or not doing certain things, then they're like, "Oh, we got you there; we can get you." I think they just . . . have to at least have one thing; they have to have, like, some kind of control.

Mary: What would you say to the school administrators if you could? I mean, what would you say to them about your school?

[*talking over each other*]

Speaker 5: Actually do their job.

Speaker 6: They don't ask us; they should be asking us instead of discussing it among themselves.

Speaker 7: We're the ones that know what's going on.

Speaker 8: Exactly.

Mary: . . . They haven't asked students?

[*talking over each other*]

Speaker 9: They completely, like, went off on us.

Speaker 10: They threatened us.

Speaker 11: Yeah, they threat—now we have these whole idiotic, like, routine everyday [sweeps,] . . . even in the mornings, like, coming to school. We're like, "Oh, we were stuck in traffic." "Well, that's your fault." It's ridiculous.

Speaker 12: So we miss the class.

Speaker 13: We miss the class—the whole period.

Mary: This is the sweep thing?

All: Yeah.

Speaker 14: This is the bad idea.

Speaker 15: It's horrible idea; I'm failing most of my classes here. Well, not really, but.

Speaker 16: And some people, instead of going to class, they just go there.

Speaker 17: Pretty much [there's] a lot of ditching.

Speaker 18: Yeah, it's the legal way to ditching actually. A lot of people go in there just to stay in there. And [they] don't do their work.

Elizabeth, the speaker in the following excerpt, is Anglo.

Elizabeth: As far as the administration, they haven't really made much effort. The multicultural fair is just tradition. And so other than that, they don't really do anything. They don't make an effort as far as I can see. . . .

Mary: What do you think they are doing? What are they doing instead?

Elizabeth: Trying to focus on little things. Just to distract themselves. I mean, tardy walkouts or something that they spend almost—they spend the entire day doing. If kids are one minute late, then they miss the entire period. And I don't think that's exactly—I don't think that's a good idea because I tend to be late, even though I'm down the street. I live with two other women, and we're late sometimes.

Blindy and Nane, the speakers in the next excerpt, are Hispanic.

Blindy: Nobody really cares [about enforcing rules on campus].

Nane: They say no chains; we still bring our [wallet] chains.

Blindy: They don't care. They—they banned—supposedly, it's like, we have a dress code and everything, and we can't bring electronics [to school] or anything. . . . They don't really enforce it, but when the whole riot thing came . . . [the principal started] keeping a watch on us. That's when they really enforced everything.

Nane: About the dress code, yeah, they don't [enforce it]. They say, "Oh, you can't wear this and this," but they don't do anything about it. You see girls showing their butts with, like, no underwear even. They don't do anything about it. They just say it, but they don't do anything, so people don't—don't listen.

The girls in these excerpts succinctly summarize the school's ludicrous emphasis on policing petty offenses in the face of more violence, even given what they say are the more serious situations of guns, knives, and drugs on campus. The girls' tone reflects their incredulity of this policing. Yet they are savvy to recognize that the policing of the dress code (often through the girls' clothing) and the student use of technology are attempts by the school's administrators to exert some sort of control onto the students: "They have to have, like, some kind of control." The girls realize that the school's hold on students is tenuous, and any attempt to blanket campus with authority and rules enforcement is better than letting the students gain an upper hand. At the same time, of course, the girls demean these attempts and suggest that, instead, the administrators need to "actually do their job." The girls do not see the petty policing as the core function of the administration after the riot. Elizabeth similarly sees the administration's "efforts," like the tardy sweep, as a distraction away from the riot toward "little things."

These tactics also draw direct attention to the ways, as Nicola Ansell (2009b: 23) puts it, schools "engage and shape children's bodies." In her work on Lesotho's education sector, she argues that AIDS prevention (focused on the vulnerability of children's bodies) and mitigation (focused on bodies already affected) strategies in schools operate as surveillance of the body. Both strategies "cast on children the responsibility to minimise risk to society, and seek to normalise children's bodies such that they are once again amenable to education of the mind" (22). Central to the operation of these strategies is a shift from overt to covert regulation of the student body. Covert regulation thus shifts the responsibility of education, AIDS prevention, and disease mitigation onto children themselves. Ansell's motivation is to question how national and international education policy and practice regulate "bodies that are young, poor and black" in the service of Western pressures to conform to hegemonic Western society (e.g., through funding and pressure to accept Western models of schooling) (33). The new surveillance strategies of the LA school administration, according to Ansell's useful logic, illustrate that the school is just as concerned (perhaps more so) with regulating and disciplining bodies as it is with the education of its students (26). Tardy sweeps prevent learning, but they educate girls—and youth in general—to accommodate to constant surveillance, herding, and social control by the state.

Like Jane and Mayra, the girls in the previous excerpts want to be consulted, not simply corralled or ignored. They have valuable knowledge, they contend, about the nature of the school's racial problems, but the rules enforcement and the "threats" by administrators are "idiotic" diversions away from student insight. Instead, the administration is making the entire school a target of control rather than focusing on the heart of the problems. Lola, a Hispanic girl, and Sammie, an Armenian girl, also refer to these "idiots":

Mary: So what else—anything else that we haven't covered?

Lola: I don't know, like, just school, board meetings, because I don't like them.

Mary: The school board. Yeah, see, I never would have thought to ask you what you think about the school board.

Lola: I hate them; they're just so, ah, they're idiots.

Mary: Right, why?

Lola: I don't know, they always, like, make up these stupid rules that would not help at all.

Sammie: Yeah.

Lola: Like, a month ago they were, like, trying to eliminate our nutrition—

Sammie: Because they were like, oh, they [fighters] talk about the nutrition, like the fights during the nutrition.

Lola: Yeah, that's when all this starts—

Sammie: Like, they plan the fights.

Lola: Yeah, I think that's so stupid.

Mary: So get rid of nutrition to get rid of the fights?

Sammie: They're like, get rid of nutrition because that's when they talk about what's going to happen during lunch.

Lola: That's when they plan. . . .

Mary: Do you have any other kind of rules at school that you think are stupid?

Sammie: Oh.

Lola: The tardy sweep!

Sammie: Oh, yeah. That's so dumb.

Lola: Oh my god, that's the stupidest thing ever.

Sammie: People are actually like, hey, you want to get caught in the tardy sweep and hang out?

Lola: Yeah, I've done it. I've done it. If I don't want to go to class, me and my friends just go, oh, let's go [to] tardy sweep. We don't do anything there; we just catch up on homework. . . . You go back inside class, and you don't need a note or anything. The teacher asks, "Oh, why were you absent?" You say tardy sweep; they're like, okay, fine. Like, nothing happens.

These girls sharply mark the futility of the sweeps as a response to campus violence. They see the sweeps as a wasted—and very large, I might add—effort to corral students out of unsupervised mingling spaces and into controlled spaces; they recognize that such efforts are mismanaged and misdirected. These "stupid" rules "would not help at all"; prohibiting interaction during certain moments of the day does very little to ease the racial tensions that exist in *all* school and urban spaces. The school administration considers the common school campus spaces as unruly, which is a misreading of the other spaces on campus that are just as deeply imbued with racial-ethnic meaning and conflict. Furthermore, the girls give examples in which they use the tardy sweeps to avoid class or act as study breaks, with no repercussions whatsoever. There is simply no emphasis placed on getting students to class. Rather, the efforts of a great many staff are channeled toward policing the movements of bodies on campus to show a strict routine of punctuality and avoid feared interactions among youth. This policing, of course, does nothing to restrict interactions before or after school, between classes, or during food breaks. The school administration neglects to see the students as resources in their quest to affect violence. It is unfortunate to recognize that this much passion could be channeled into pedagogic activity, rather than just "herded" through tardy sweeps into the cafeteria.

Yet this emphasis on corralling youth predictably falls into the all-too-usual pattern of policing youth and punishing the slightest transgressions. As Aaron Kupchik (2010) explains, schools in the United States turn toward such petty surveillance as a way to address violence: "The result is overkill and a set of practices that ignores the real problems in an attempt to punish rather than correct misbehavior" (6). Enforcing the code of conduct to a fault, which exacerbates students' learning problems and, in this case, segregation, distracts from the real issue at hand, and students learn that schools do not care about the "real" issues facing them. The students become "cattle," as one girl put it in the following group interview with Latinas.

Mary: How many [of you] have ever talked to an administrator?
Speaker 1: I mean, the only students they know are the ones that get in trouble. They always get along with the [bad kids]. You just see them "Hi." "Hi." . . .
Mary: I'm curious, what would you tell them?
Speaker 2: The main thing is the tardy sweep.
Mary: It's what?
Speaker 2: It's affecting our grades.
Speaker 3: Yeah, our grades. . . .
Speaker 4: What sucks about it is that they treat you like such cattle. Like, they're just, like, herding you into this auditorium, and then, like, I don't know, it's so rude. Like, they're like, "No, don't sit over there. You don't deserve to sit down on a chair; go sit down against the wall." It's horrible.
Speaker 5: They treat you really bad, and all you're doing is coming in late.

Thus, the girls feel victimized by the violence, while the "bad" kids, in their minds, are the few who get to have closer relationships with the school authorities. They end up being treated rudely for what they see as a minor offense, just because the school is desperately trying to control campus spaces in the wake of the riot that probably involved about 20–25 percent of the student body. Kupchik describes this sort of discipline practice as "non-empathetic, impatient" and simply "masculine" (2010: 51).

Let me be clear that I am of two minds in this section. The first is despairing of the school's circumscribed response to the riot. I agree with the girls that opportunities to address the violence were lost in feeble attempts to police space and newly enforce previously underemphasized rules. The structure of the school curriculum certainly prohibits the chance to take up particular, focused issues as replies to particular events, but campus leadership could have allowed for some, even brief, classroom interventions to allow students to consider, academically, the situations that lead to violence. With background knowledge about violence and critical adjudication, such classroom events could propel wider campus discussions and debate. There is every reason to believe that girls were interested in the ideas of masculinity and violence, given the material I present in Chapter 4. Even organizing informal discussion groups around feminist pedagogies and theories of violence could have stimulated girls to think beyond their summations of "stupid boys."

The second mind departs from my agreement with the girls' evaluations toward giving attention to the ways that the girls put forth their opinions on the school's response. Therefore, just to be clear, I agree with them and support their voices of frustration, but I still want to think more complexly about what lessons to take away from this example. In the end, validating the girls' voices omits important questions about how to reconcile girls' racism, sexual investments in racial and gender difference, and family commitments to racial-ethnic uniqueness in multicultural Los Angeles. And remember, Chapter 2 also critiques the girls' limited ideas of solutions to racial violence, which should be juxtaposed with their criticisms of the school here. What is involved in girls' desire for the school to be interested and attentive to their voices?

The girls are quite uniform in their desire to be heard by adult administrators; they desire attention to be paid to their youth knowledge of what "really" happens at school and where some roots of conflict might lie. They are speaking against their invisibility on campus. But the invisibility is also an indication of the inability to be seen and heard by an institution that is set up to disempower youth, to be sure. The girls' comparisons of youth to cattle illustrate this aptly. Yet, the issue of this desire extends beyond the structural power relations that position them via this adultist logic. Their desire, articulated in social terms but analyzed according to psychoanalytic logic, is not only a *social* need to contribute to the creation of school spatiality but also a psychic desire to be considered as full a subject as one experiences oneself to be (Dean 2000). The girls are not merely "young people," or even more discursively degrading, "young girls." They push against the notion that they have no contributions to make toward the event, whether it is to explain it or think about future strategies to change campus interactions. I think that this desire is evidenced throughout this project, as the girls yearn to "come together" in multicultural understanding and for others to accept them into segregated spaces from which they are, by racial definition, excluded.

Yet this desire to be full subjects stands in stark contrast with the girls' own capabilities to see others as full subjects, as I have also argued in previous chapters. They expect treatment at school that they themselves cannot extend to peers. This marks an extreme contradiction in the girls' subjectivities: to be seen, valued, and respected but at the same time to not be capable or interested in doing the same. This contradiction is not simply their failure; it is a condition of subjectivity. One's desire is always more urgent, immediate, and spatially evident than one's other, who can never occupy a position of full subjecthood in the self's own eye. I think this desire indicates a limit to the ways that the agential voice can be relied on for changing the politics of youth within a specific context of urban segregation and racist schooling.

At the same time, remaining focused on this voice of the self—and taking it for granted as evidence that the desire to be visible extends to a capacity to see others despite racial, sexual, and gender difference—retains the limits of the discursive relationship of self-other. In other words, scholars must push past the self's relationship to others as a facile and surficial *possibility*, rather than addressing the dynamic motivations that centralize that relationship and frame the limits on possibility. To paraphrase Tim Dean, the best way to inhabit one's desire is to realize that the other's desire is also barred from fulfillment (2000: 205). The quest to fulfill one's desire in this case takes the girls down a road of believing that others fail to see them and actively segregate against the passive self, but a conversation about hurt feelings can change these practices. My argument is that these yearnings delineate a simplistic space-time of interaction and neglect the many complex spatialities and temporalities that contribute to identification and practice. Such efforts are bound to be inadequate by confining violence to a set date and place.

Girlhood scholars—and girls—think, to use Dean's phrasing, that "an oppressive regulatory regime has arranged the world to one's disadvantage" (2000: 205). I believe that sexism and racism do "arrange the world to one's disadvantage," to be sure, but that should not solely frame the theory of girl subjectivity and an agency that follows. Agential voices then assume a position of being subjected to a conspiracy of power that paradoxically constricts agential acts and practices. Saying one is oppressed, in other words, does not do anything to affect that oppression. Moving away from an agential voice, a voice that relies on an egoistic assumption that one's self is a possible answer to any social problem, provides a possible opportunity to find routes to change that might exist through other strategies.[1]

In the next sections, I develop my argument further by considering the contradictions of girls' narratives about the spatial and subjective control of and by students on campus. Underlying these narratives, I suggest, is girls' desire to be controlled by adult protectors and have a regulated, policed, and "safe" school.

---

1. Simply put, Dean advocates a Lacanian argument that highlights the loss inherent in subjectivity's inception and ongoing desire. This would mean considering the bar that prevents any subject from fulfilling some notion of social wholeness; wholeness is a ruse that psychoanalysis illuminates as a fantasy of the ego/I.

Students Are in Control of Campus; School Is Dangerous and Out of Control

Denise: I think students are uprising against the faculty, and pretty much they're calling the shots. Faculty tries to manage them, but they're not really successful. . . . And it's sad because I think it's kind of hopeless. I think students, they're so outraged with each other.

Chibi-Kim: If teachers would be more, like, like, be around the campus, they would be, like, on the lookout for the bad things that are going on. Then the kids [would start] small things first to, like, make them [i.e., these bad things] better, you know?

Mary: So does that happen? Are there people walking around at lunch?

Zelda: No.

Chibi-Kim: No.

Mary: Why not?

Zelda: Well, I don't see anything.

Chibi-Kim: Well, they just stand there. They see it, [but] they don't do anything.

Mary: Why do you think they should do anything?

Zelda: Well, there are actually, like, cops at our school.

Sephi: One of the cops got beat up by this Puerto Rican dude. Yeah, no one stopped him.

Mayra: We talk on the phone all the time in class. . . . We have no rules. If we want, we can do whatever we want. That's the way everyone [is]. . . .

Mary: And do the teachers just give up?

Mayra: Yeah. They do. They just give up; they just say, "Oh, well, leave the classroom." So once you do, you walk around. So what would you rather do? Get kicked out of class and go walk around or stay in class and have to listen?

Sammie: Yeah, like my fifth period, it's just like, kids are always yelling and yelling and yelling, and the teachers kind of, like, don't know how to handle it, you know? It's like, one of my teachers in third period, she just, like, sends everybody to the dean, you know, if they were disrupting, like, disrupting [class]. So, yeah, so it's like, I don't know, I think it's just like, they should be more strict about it, or, like, if somebody—if, like, one year a kid's acting really bad, they should take him out of the [honors] program because it's supposed to be a program for people that want to go faster.

These six girls paint a fairly grim picture of school, from classrooms to the quad. Students are out of control with each other and in control of school space because the teachers and the administrators are unable to affect student behavior. Or, the girls say, the teachers are unwilling to intervene, uninterested in making a difference or simply outnumbered. The result, Denise says, is that students "are calling the shots" and, according to Mayra, that "we can do whatever we want." "We" here is taken for granted by Mayra and sits uncomfortably next to the anxieties of the other girls. Sammie is worried about her academic program being held up by others' bad behavior, and Denise is worried about the simmering "outrage" among racial groups (she reduces the outrage between "each other," which singularizes two groups rather than broadens the outrage as more generally between students). Chibi-Kim, Sephi, and Zelda are less generous than Denise and paint a picture of a few lurking faculty who merely watch violence and "don't do anything." Even the cops are hapless against the "Puerto Rican dude" who brazenly attacked one of them, says Sephi.

Even the cops get beat up. What Sephi's comment reveals is a deep fear that the symbols of control on campus are too few, too weak, and too disinterested to make a difference. Zelda's reference to a police presence as a possible remedy to the teachers' indifference was castrated quickly by Sephi's example of a "dude" able to negate that presence. Lurking in all of these excerpts is also a despair that the teachers just cannot stem the pressure and strength of the students who outnumber them. Sammie's "yelling and yelling and yelling" gives the impression of massive overpowering in volume; Denise's "hopeless" assessment results from the inability to counter "outrage"; and Mayra capitulates to a sort of nihilistic wandering of campus, since both the campus and the classroom lack structure.

Chibi-Kim argues that if teachers would be "on the lookout for the bad things," then youth would interpellate this care and surveillance and would likewise do "small things" to "make them better." So Chibi-Kim places responsibility for changed violent behavior at the feet of the teachers, rather than the students. She absconds from any responsibility or notice that the change in daily interactions must come from the students. Therefore, while students claim to want a different school spatiality of race relations, beliefs like Chibi-Kim's illustrate the limits to those claims.

Coupled with this is an ongoing fear that any space at school could turn into a student-led uprising. The previous excerpts reflect the girls' increased awareness of the small acts of disobedience in classrooms and their desire for more controlled spaces. Yet, that control, they claim, must discharge from the teachers, posed as the authorities of those spaces. They posit a very hierarchical structure of possibility, from classrooms to casual interactive spaces on campus at other times. This idea of spatial control sits contradictorily beside their claims that the teachers cannot have control of these spaces, and even the intensified rules of policing at school is a ruse and ineffective. The hopes of the girls remain with the adults as capable agents in regaining the upper hand against unruly students (Chibi-Kim's hope for an initially small adjustment; Sammie's hope for calm and productive classrooms). The girls' sadness lies in their belief that the teachers have "given up." The flip side is a lack of hope placed in students themselves. They give precious little indication that they have hope that youth would be the source of changed relations themselves. Status quo racism and segregation are the result, in other words, when *teachers* do not force change. Here is another example of the girls having strong voices lamenting violence and its aftermaths but shrugging to the work of change itself. Perhaps they know, without being able to articulate it, that this sort of change is so fundamental that they cannot fathom a way out.

Mayra casually shrugs at the ease of getting out of class after behaving badly, but her conversation with me yielded more insight into her tone of disinterest and resignation. She indicates a kind of triumph at being able to get out of class (by being "kicked out"), but she delves more closely into her resignation and its source beyond school space.

> Mayra: It's scary to come to school; it really is, but you just, you don't let people know that. And I'm sure many people feel the same way I do.
>
> Mary: What does your mom say? . . . Does she know about this?
>
> Mayra: Yeah.
>
> Mary: What does she say about this?
>
> Mayra: I mean, she says, "Be careful," but . . . some parents are like, "Oh, we're going to move our kids out of the school," and, sure they did, but those are the parents of the good kids. I mean, if you're a good kid, most likely you have a really nice home, and your mom cares about you, and she's going to be like, "Oh, let's move, right now." You know? "That's it, you're not going to [this school] anymore." The thing is that most of the kids who are the ones who are messing up, they don't have a nice home.
>
> Mary: Right.
>
> Mayra: So they don't have anybody there to help, so they're still going to be there. . . . And maybe—I think that if she would have controlled me a bit more, which is good because she lets me do a lot of stuff, but if she were to act—if she were to care more, I think I wouldn't be the way I am right now.
>
> Mary: What do you mean, the way you are?
>
> Mayra: Because I don't like the way—I don't like who I am right now. I really don't. . . . Because, I mean, like, okay, before I was—I'm still [tracked] as gifted. Before I was honors; god forbid that, like, I get a

C on a report card because that would just be the end of the world. And now, it's like, I failed four classes . . . and I think it's because she would always compare me. . . . It was either "Oh, you're too fat; look at her, she's really pretty" or just "Oh, look at her daughter got AP [advanced placement] classes; how come you don't have AP classes?" . . . I mean, that's the only reason why I took the AP class because I said okay, if my mom is—I'm just looking for her to say, "I'm proud of you." Because she's never, honestly, she's never told me that.

Mayra connects campus safety to her care about grades, and more explicitly she ties an unsafe campus to her uncaring mother. She says that if the school abdicates on its responsibilities to keep her safe, then her mother should make up the difference. She wants *someone* to show an interest in her and her education; otherwise she has no reason to do so herself.

Mayra weaves her self-worth and her mother's love into her body and its supposed inability to measure up to classed and racialized standards of thin beauty; into her failing grades as she enters this high school and gets lost in a bad crowd (see Chapter 4); and into the comparison to other, more worthy daughters. Mayra told me at another point that she did not think her mother loved her, and that message shows up here, as well. If her mother did love her, surely, Mayra indicates, she would not put her in danger's way by sending her off to school every day. Having a "nice home" would fix her, which is another coded reference to class and what Mayra sees as its privileges—including more parental love and protection. Of course, the truth lies somewhere in here, since privilege allows parents with more financial means to move to avoid a troubled school. But Mayra does not temper her disappointment with an honest assessment of how difficult that would be for her family, who must get by on just her mother's income. Her desire for a loving mother involves a desire to belong to a racial-class norm in which love and care are presumably available naturally. Again, this desire is also tied to Mayra's self-evaluation as not lovable because of her "fat" body and what lurks in that reflection: an ugly self, an unlovable self, whose own mother cannot even love her.

Finally, in addition to bringing the home into the equation of school safety, Mayra's narrative provides another way that the school spatiality of danger is not contained by campus boundaries. Note that her solution, however, is restricted to campus space.

Mayra: I see a lot [of] older guys that are Armenian [just off school property]. I mean if you stand by the corner at school, where the gangsters hang out in the corner, they're out there.

Mary: They're not kids from school?

Mayra: They pass by there like crazy; I mean, they pull out their guns. It gets—it gets really dangerous to walk through that corner.

Mary: After school.

Mayra: Yeah, I mean, it's—the Armenians are getting all their brothers and cousins, anybody who they can involve into this and pulling them into fights with little fifteen-year-olds. . . . I honestly don't feel the school does anything.

Mary: What do you think they could do?

Mayra: The schools in LA,[2] they have metal detectors.

Mary: You know, when I came today, I just walked in; nobody said anything to me.

Mayra: I—wait, they're not going to listen to this, right? At school?

Mary: Oh no. No, no.

Mayra: Okay, I've walked out of school. . . . It's the easiest thing: ditching class is [the] easiest thing ever; selling drugs is [the] easiest thing ever. Doing them, I mean, today, just today, I saw some kid, you know, people that I hang out with, they said, "Hey, let's bust a light" [smoke crystal meth].

Mary: Yeah.

Mayra: On the spot, right there, . . . like nobody's business.

Mary: So you think the school should actually have a stronger fist?

Mayra: They really, really should. Because at my sister's school, I mean, they even, you know, for girls, when they—you know how they wear their nails; they need a note that their parents said that they can have that. I mean, everything at her school's so structured.

By marking this threat just outside the school boundaries—on the sidewalk in front of the school—Mayra claims that the school's racial tensions extend beyond the immediate spatiality of the actual conflict. The school's attempts to influence students with campaigns of rule enforcement and tardy sweeps also neglect a much wider phenomenon of interaction and threat. The school administration is obviously impotent to deal with the influx of muscle after school, but there are police cruisers that routinely drive by at the end of the day. This corner has a stoplight where pedestrians must cross (else they must go several blocks out of the way), so there are hundreds of students passing by within minutes of the final bell.

Mayra juxtaposes these older, armed men with "little fifteen-year-olds," who are presumably Latinos targeted for "pulling" into fights. Thus, she situates

2. When the girls distinguish Los Angeles in this way, they mean those parts of the city south of the San Fernando Valley, like Hollywood and South Los Angeles (formerly known as south central).

the heavily armed and stronger Armenian "men" as taking advantage of the "little" Latinos, who are set up as possible victims in her story. She is frightened and rightly so, but her careful attempts to show that this problem extends beyond the school itself does not influence her ideas to address it. Her solution to the problem includes metal detectors, which would be used only when entering the school grounds. This solution would not address the problem on the streets around the school (or home life, for that matter). Open drug sales and use and truancy are some of the "easiest" things to do, and of course, metal detectors would also not address these problems.

Her second example of affecting school safety is yet another case of the bodies of female students being surveilled, as with the previous examples of enforcement of a dress code (see Hyams 2000). She values the "structure" of her sister's school, but problematically she places this value with the control of those girls. Having a note for nails does not address guns on the sidewalk surrounding campus. This case of the control of feminine sexuality came up several times, as with Nane in the previous section talking about girls violating the dress code by "showing their butts." While the girls mark the violent potentials of unstructured and uncontrolled campus space, these examples illustrate how they desire the control of other girls' bodies. These types of control indicate to them that the school "cares" about them as girls; ironically, the girls think that by policing feminine bodies and practices of sexual embodiment, the school is showing them care (see Best 2000, especially chap. 7). Rather, the reverse is true: the girls have taken up the misogynist surveillance of feminine bodies—theirs and others—and then evaluate other girls for failing to self-police. These other girls are "out of control" of their bodies and need a strong administrative hand to set them right. Of course, this works against all girls by equating appearance and behavior (gendered, classed, racialized, and sexualized) with worth. Again, the girls note that the change in behavior should come from rules and adults.

In Mayra's narratives, the wish for stronger control is obviously paradoxical to her comments about using the lack of control to her benefit, such as getting out of class rather than having to sit through it. That voice of resistance against the unstructured classroom and teachers who have "given up" masks a desire to be surveilled and watched; these are equated with being cared for and valued. At the same time that she says she benefits and wants the careless-carefree space to be able to get out of class, her narrative is insistent about her need to be in a structured space (i.e., structure as a *caring* space), at home, at school, and in urban space. Kupchik (2010) is again instructive here, as he explains that students acting out often do so to mask their fears at being unable to keep up in class; rather, they do not want to experience the shame of being outed as "stupid."

A final example to close out this section comes from the three Filipinas, who share similar language but indicate a bit more criticism of school surveillance:

Mary: Do you feel unsafe at school?

Zelda: When the cops are not around, yeah.

Mary: What do you think would—could happen?

Zelda: Like, they might draw a knife and start stabbing—

Chibi-Kim: Start a fight. Start a fight again.

Zelda: Yeah.

Mary: Are there knives at school?

Zelda: Well, I mean some of them—

Chibi-Kim: Some people—

Zelda: They can, like, hide it. . . . At the middle school, it's better because in our middle school, we had surveillance cameras, and we had a search dog sniffing for weapons, and we had, like—

Chibi-Kim: It was more strict in our middle school.

Zelda: Stricter in middle school.

Chibi-Kim: But, high school is so, like, all over the place. . . .

Mary: You'd think it would be more strict in high school. You'd think it would be more strict.

Zelda: Yeah, I would think more strict.

Mary: But it's not.

Zelda: It's not; it's the total opposite.

Chibi-Kim: They don't care.

Sephi: I suggested metal detectors for our school, and many people told me to shut up.

Mary: So what do you think about having surveillance? . . .

Zelda: In a way it's kind of like—

Chibi-Kim: Invading our privacy—

Zelda: Yeah, kind of like invading your privacy, but in an—but at the same time it makes you feel safe.

Mary: So you would rather sacrifice the privacy to feel safe?

Zelda: Yeah.

Mary: Yeah?

Zelda: I would, I would.

Sephi: You're never safe as long as there's a terrorist.

Although Zelda says she feels safe only when a cop is around, recall that earlier Sephi remarked that even the cops can be beaten up by students. In this excerpt, the girls' fear after the riot centers more on *random* violence, like a random "stabbing" in which they might be caught as an innocent victim. Thus,

Sephi and Zelda are willing to accept metal detectors as a trade-off with giving up "privacy." Such surveillance could only make her "feel" safe; she does not say that it would actually make her safer (see Nayak 2003b). In fact, Sephi concludes that one can never be entirely safe, given the possibility of random violence—not to mention that "you're never safe as long as there's a terrorist."

This striking language draws out the relevance of the redefined politicization of the racialized body after the 9/11 attacks in the United States (Maira 2009). To be sure, terrorism is a racialized word, drawing on the violent image of the other who wants to destroy your way of life. As Ash Amin (2010: 12) tells us, the politics of the deviant body is framed by an assumption that the world is "increasingly unstable and dangerous." The national discourses about terrorism here seep into the girls' narratives about school to prove just how unsafe the world is, so you can never fully prepare for or expect violence. Amin regards this new political development as urging "constant alertness and preparedness in the face of mounting hazard and risk, under the leadership of a 'security state' . . . Being in a state of permanent alert . . . demands naming, tracking and disarming the threatening body well before the act, even if this means suspending protocols of proof, legal conduct, civil liberties and human rights" (12).

In the wake of the fight, many said that they want more police on the school campus and more surveillance technologies, such as metal detectors, to make campus safer for them. I find that this call for surveillance is an intensely conservative move for youth to make in a city known for racist policing. The fact that these girls are not white indicates a strange collusion, against their racial interests, with the racist state. The lens for analyzing the girls' insistence that their school needs more surveillance, not less, is a stark comparison to their paranoid experiences of themselves being surveilled (as seen in Chapter 4). While they harshly critiqued others' views of their racialized bodies as potentially criminal, for instance in consumption spaces, they call for surveillance of brown bodies on the school campus. This desire may look like a local or feminine strategy to create a safe campus given masculine violence at school, but when placed within an urban, racialized surveillance regime, the girls are working against their own self-interests. They had no understanding that calling for more surveillance was in direct conflation with their own painful experiences of being surveilled. Further, their calls for the explicit policing of female bodies sits painfully with their experiences of being policed, evaluated, and excluded by other girls when they cross segregated territories (also in Chapter 4).

Caring Teachers

Perhaps the most repeated way that the girls evidenced the lack of structure and care they receive at school is through their complaints about teachers.

Over and over they use the phrase, "they don't care" and insist that teacher apathy impacted their own behavior, grades, and affect. In the excerpts that follow, the girls also reduce teachers' motivations as educators solely to getting a paycheck. These comments are meant to deal a blow to teachers as caregivers, which is a normative account of what teachers' skills and efforts are meant to provide to students. The girls have taken up this norm of the "caring teacher" (which is a saturated media and popular representation of the urban educator in underfunded, minority high schools) and presumably the accompanying hope it places in a teacher being able to turn a youth's life around. The girls strongly wish for a guiding hand, a careful mentor, and a caring adult—an education that can steer them to upward mobility. Yet their narratives also indicate the many times some of them skip class, are "lazy," or give up on school. I argue in this section that it is somewhat easy for them to displace the blame onto those greedy teachers who just want to make money from captive student time at school. They look elsewhere for academic hope and find teachers an appropriate target.

In this final section, I again organize the interview excerpts together to illustrate their overlapping message. Jane, the speaker in the following excerpt, is Armenian.

> I don't actually [think the teachers are good]. I don't. Because they don't—first of all, they don't care about you. They don't care, like, they don't know you. If you asked, like, sometimes some teachers, if you asked them, like, "Okay, what's my name?" after one week, you know, or after a month, let's say. You know, they wouldn't know you; like, for example, my biology teacher. And I understand, like, they have a lot of kids, they have a lot of classes to deal with, you know. But you still need to know who your [students are]—in order to, like, teach them well—you need to know the person.

Daija and Keisha, the speakers in the following dialogue, are African Americans.

> Daija: They [teachers] need to make stuff harder. . . . I'm not used to great education [here].
> Mary: It's not good enough?
> Keisha: A lot of teachers, some teachers—
> Both: They don't care.
> Keisha: They just get their money and go.
> Daija: They just want to get [paid]. . . . But they don't teach.

The following is from a group interview with the Latinas:

Speaker 1: They [teachers] have such a high opinion about themselves. . . .

Speaker 2: I think they somewhat, I think, just don't care.

Speaker 3: Yeah, they're pretty apathetic towards it.

Lola (interviewed together with Sammie) is Hispanic.

Lola: I'm pretty, like, I don't know, I'm a good student, I guess, but I don't really like the education in [my school] because, basically, the teachers. Like, I have all these honors and AP classes, and we don't really do anything in there. We just sit, and then they assign the homework, and then we do it. They don't really teach anything. [Later in interview] We're all [students] in agreement that the teachers that we have right now aren't really that great.

Mary: Right.

Lola: I'm serious. . . . They don't really care. They just—I'm serious, I'm not, I'm not even exaggerating or anything—it's like, every single class that I have, we don't do anything. It's basically just a place to sit and talk because they—like, my fourth period, it's [math], my teacher, she writes the assignment on the board, and then she just goes and sits at her desk, and you can do whatever you want. And basically it's really been, like, killing my grades because I'm not—I need a push, like, to do my best. I'm pretty lazy, so. I need somebody to push me. So, I don't know. My grades have kind of been going down because the teachers—because they don't put any pressure on you.

Mayra, quoted in the following excerpt, is a Latina.

I mean, my PE [physical education] teacher, he's very, very, very strict with me. I mean, that's the only class that I'll be like, "Okay, okay." He—he acts like he cares about us. And he—he's not just going to give up because he says that's his job, and he's going to do the best at it. And so, when you see that, a teacher gives up on you, like my math teacher, he's just like, "Get out of class." Alright. I don't really care about him anymore. . . . You lose respect for them because you see they don't care; they don't care about their job.

The three friends in the following excerpt are Filipina.

Zelda: If the teachers would do their job—some teachers just stand there and look at something [e.g., a fight] going on.

Mary: Do you think they're scared?

Zelda: Huh?

Mary: Do you think the teachers are scared?

Zelda: No.

Sephi: They only care about their money.

Chibi-Kim: I think they only care about their money.

Zelda: Yeah, they just care about doing their job.

Sephi: They think they care about our education, but they don't.

I do not want to insinuate, to the contrary of the girls, that the teachers are, in fact, effective, skilled educators. I do not know the teachers. Rather, my aim is to consider the girls' narratives *about* teachers, not to prove whether the girls are right or wrong in what they say. (Although they do give some amazing accounts of teacher apathy, some also value certain teachers, as Mayra's interview shows.) I want to draw out several points that culminate in an argument about the bounded space of education that the girls assume operates at their school.

First, I am interested in how the girls' narratives indicate their investments in normative educational discourses and what these indicate about the limits of girls' reflexivity and agency. In these examples, several girls make a direct correlation between their teachers' attitudes about teaching and their own behavior in class (see Lopez 2003). The repeated phrasing of "care" in the excerpts means that the girls have a limited view of how teachers' affect to them should proceed. On the one hand, the girls seem to discount teachers' professional status by bringing up pay and money as a way to criticize them. The fact that they earn a paycheck means to the girls that they must be limited in their motivations, and when the girls interpret teachers as being apathetic, money becomes a simple target for the impersonal "uncare." On the other hand, the girls think that their teachers should be more than professional; that is, they should exceed the nature of being hired help. Their teachers should "care" about them, love them perhaps, and indicate their dedication to the girls' academic and personal advancement. These views reflect the norms of the caring teacher that the girls have come to expect. The girls also might be reacting to the "masculine" petty policing (Kupchik 2010: 51) of their transgressions (such as the tardy sweeps). The recourse to feminine care is a nondirect response to this masculinism and lack of empathy in the usual treatment of youth bodies and circumstances.

Second, the girls also claim that teachers do very little actual teaching in the classroom. They present a picture of assignments impersonally distributed and then a virtual study period following, which the girls say results in them being able to "do whatever they want." As Lola claims, this practice is "killing my grades" because "I need a push to do my best." Mayra, Keisha, and Daija (see the next excerpt) share this evaluation and need to be challenged. They thus articulate a need for a certain type of education, a clear reflexivity about their needs and goals for their individual strengths and weaknesses. This education is bound up, I argue, with their desire for personal attention and caregiving in the classroom. Again, the girls rely on an assumption that teaching should ideally be a nurturing relationship between two people (teacher and student), highly structured, and reflective of a teacher's natural interest in their students' personal needs and desires.

The girls clearly show a strong opinion about their school and again illustrate how much they think about education and its importance in their lives. The problem with this reflexivity is that their examples indicate the narrow spatiality of their conscious judgment of urban education. They focus in very closely, literally to their own campus and the people located there. This localized analysis of school problems and relationships mean that the girls themselves have taken up the normative assumption that particular individuals are responsible for "good" education. Therefore, I am not only pushing girls' narratives to make a claim about the limits of feminist scholarship that narrows onto girlhood's reflexive voice but also indicating that the U.S. urban girl subject has also "internalized" this sort of individualist ideal. This individual—in this case, the teacher—is meant to have an agency embodied by responsibility. The girls discount the teachers for cruelly abdicating on that liberalist responsibility and leaving them to fend for themselves.

Daija and Keisha, both African American, note the geographic differences between schooling and point out the class and wealth disparities that determine which schools provide better education in the Valley. Daija and Keisha are unique in their broader viewpoint on the urban educational system of Los Angeles.

> Daija: I'm just used to more challenging stuff, like, because mostly all my life I've been going to schools that challenge me. . . . I guess [this school is] just in the [different] part of the Valley over here, because I went, like, to school in the rich area and stuff. And I came here and I'm like, what is this? . . . 'Cause it's not, yeah, it's not exciting. You barely want to be there. . . .
>
> Mary: So you wish it was harder because then you would do better, be motivated to go?
>
> Daija: Yeah.
>
> Keisha: Yeah.
>
> Mary: Do you feel the same way?
>
> Keisha: Really. I don't even want to go to this school no more.

The next excerpt highlights the racial tensions that these two girls experience in their math classroom. They attribute this friction to an Armenian teacher's preference for Armenian students.

> Daija: They should hire some new teachers. I got an Armenian teacher for math, and today [I said,] "I don't know how to do this [math problem]." . . . I was like, "Excuse me. [I need help.]" He was like, "I know, you don't get it." I was like, "That means you're supposed to help me." He was like, "Yeah, whatever."
>
> Mary: Wow.
>
> Daija: I do not like him. I was good at math, like, until I came here, and I got him. . . . He don't teach us nothing.
>
> Mary: Does he act that way with all the students?
>
> Daija: No. I'm the only black person in there.
>
> Mary: Right.
>
> Daija: Wait. Am I? Yeah, I am.
>
> Mary: What do the other students say when that kind of thing happens? Do they acknowledge it? What do they say?
>
> Daija: Like, they notice that he treats, like, treats the Armenian students and stuff in his class better than he treats [others]. There's Mexicans. . . . Like, he treats the Armenian students better than he treat us. . . . He would talk in Armenian. . . . I'm like, talk English.
>
> Mary: He talks Armenian in class?
>
> Keisha: You're not supposed to do that.
>
> Daija: And I was like, "That's rude." He was like, "What's rude?" I was like, "You're not talking English." He was like, "Don't tell me what's rude." I was like, whoa.

In their final assessment, Daija and Keisha told me that they would rather attend school in South Los Angeles because there are many more African Americans in that part of the city. They also explained to me that because South Los Angeles is primarily Latino and black, the Latinos treat them with more respect there. In the Valley, they explain, "Mexicans" oversexualize and racialize them. Latinas, they say, expect that they will sleep with their boyfriends, and the Latinos taunt them with fake "black names" (see Chapter 3).

For these reasons, plus their experience in the school with what they think are racist teachers, the girls would rather go to more poorly performing schools in primarily black neighborhoods. More so than even the "rich" schools, they value racial solidarity over the quality of education (compare Fordham 1996). I believe they have developed more of a racial consciousness because they are African American in an urban context rife with racism against African Americans (see Thomas 2005b). In the short run, racial solidarity and consciousness motivate them to want to attend high school in black South LA neighborhoods, which would benefit them by reducing the impacts of racism they face every day while in high school. Of course, in the long run, this choice would mean that they would have even poorer educational training and fewer options for advanced education. (Both girls say they would like to attend college, but neither girl has the grades or the family support and income to make achieving this goal likely.) Their local strategy to reduce racial anxiety and the racism targeting them is a spatial strategy that neglects to consider their placement within a larger context than just life in the San Fernando Valley.

A Final Note

The girls' spoken shock and disappointment in their school's (lack of) response to racial violence at school, coupled with their failure to take a political stance through action at school, are not just indications of the girls' acquiescence to be in a controlled space. They also illustrate the profound disfunction of urban educational spaces like this one that fail to educate youth about the conditions of social difference, despite attempts to foster multiculturalism at school—or, more to the point, *because* of those banal attempts. I may critique the girls' normative calls for education space in this chapter; however, I also demand that the girls' requests for a good—or even sufficient—urban education not be considered an extraordinary or heroic call but a right for all city kids (Dwyer and Wyn 2001).

Unfortunately, given the material in this chapter, I think the girls themselves are wrong about what they think would frame a sufficient education at their school—namely, teacher and administrative care, increased surveillance, and spatial control (Kupchik 2010; see also Pastor, McCormick, and Fine 2007). The narratives illustrate the girls' foundational hope and belief in a localized spatiality of educational capacity through better communication with each other (also seen in Chapter 2). Of course, as I argue throughout this book, such a view negates their fundamental distrust of those others who share and also produce these spaces. The juxtaposition of the various spaces of identification crash such hopes of racial conciliation and openness against the limits of subjectivity.

7
Conclusion

B anal multiculturalism saturates American urban education. Youth are inundated with its messages of respect, diversity, and "getting along." This book has shown the effectiveness of these banal messages and ways that girls hold on to them with feeling, commitment, and the desire for peaceful school relationships. Yet banal multiculturalism has given rise to problematic identities that allow youth to espouse humanistic beliefs of similarity while remaining committed and invested in racial, sexual, and gender difference. The girls indicated the racial antagonism they felt through the resentment of others' privileges, their naturalizations of racial segregation, the pain of interracial friendships, and the familial ties that bind them to racialized and sexualized categories of ethnicity, language, and nation. Multiculturalism has given the girls I interviewed an all-too-easy language of "we are all the same," despite their strong narratives detailing just how differently they see others' bodies, behaviors, and actions. This contradiction results in a radical gap among their humanism, racism, and heterosexism. Hegemonic whiteness, gender and sexual binaries, and middle-class consumption frame these evaluative processes of difference and subjectivity, a point I have maintained in this book. These powerful norms have a real impact on the girls' senses of self; their gendered and racialized fantasies for sexual life; and their evaluations of race, ethnicity, and language—of themselves and others.

I have argued that this contradiction of multicultural girlhood identity—that radical gap—can be explored and theorized beyond the rubrics of humanism and agency through psychoanalytic theories of subjectivity. Girls cannot simply resist the categories that provide their senses of self and contour their subjectivity, and of course, I have questioned whether we can rely on the assumption that girls would simply want to do so anyway. At the same time, analyzing the spaces of girls' lives has shown the inconsistency of identity and agency and the complexity of the psychic life of power (Cheng 2009; Butler 1997b) beyond the confines of discrete stories, hurt feelings and friendships, parents and dating, or schools and disaffection. By considering the spaces of girlhood in vibrant contrast, conflict with others, whether at school or at the mall, becomes harder to explain away with banal multicultural fixes.

The solution to school violence, if there is one, must take this complexity seriously. The ways that girls, or any youth for that matter, learn about linguistic, national, ethnic, gender-sexual, and racial difference is just as contingent on home, urban, and national spaces as in the moment that they boil in conflict within a particular school. There are no discrete contexts; rather, such spaces meld and influence dynamically (see Weis and Fine 2000). The issue that this book provokes is how to explain that moment of violence and its instigations, in a broader time-space than a focus on just the race riot at the school allows. The spaces away from the campus are just as important to include in an understanding of school segregation and racist violence. Therefore, thinking about racial conflict only at school does very little to theorize the gender-sexual, racial, national, and ethnic identifications that girls form throughout their lifetimes over multiple spaces. To insist that ambivalence, unacknowledged paradox, and mixed messages live at the heart of subjectivity is to extend a radical challenge to the common norms and assumptions about diversity and getting along that frame many high school contexts in urban America today. As such, drawing out their complexity might help to provide a broader understanding of the difficulty of prescriptions seeking to quell youth violence in multiracial schools.

Youth as a time of subjectivity also implies a displacement of "getting along" to the future. Knowing what limits exist for getting along today is centrally invested with a hope for better tomorrows. Certainly this quest is important and vital, but the issue here is understanding how this hope is wrapped into a notion of youth as tomorrow's subjects. Youth are especially relegated to be subjects-in-the-making, and their potentials and problems are often shifted onto futurisms that focus on what could be done for tomorrow. On the other hand, banal multiculturalism in American schools too often relies on the instantaneous micropolitics and microspaces of place-bound conflict and identity rather than considering the extensive time-spaces of subjectivity. Getting along is not just about doing so in the here and now and figuring out the spark that triggered the race riot in the moment; it is also exploring how the "there" and "then" fundamentally shape behaviors and identities and affect the possibilities for solutions to racist violence, ethnocentrism, and heterosexism. Critical scholars exploring national multiculturalism in the United Kingdom, Australia, the United States, and Canada have astutely examined its reliance on nostalgia, empire, whiteness, and gender-sexuality (e.g., Ahmed 2010; Fortier 2008; hooks and Mesa-Bains 2006; Goonewardena and Kipfer 2005; Povinelli 2002; Hage 2000). The present multiculturalisms of nations are therefore theorized as temporally and spatially suspect; in other words, multiculturalism in its banality masks a sinister investment in inequality and supremacy (see Amin 2010). This fine-grained critique of multiculturalism's workings must play a role in understanding the embodiment and psychology of the multicultural subjectivities of youth. They might be young, but their subjectivities live through spaces of long years. Attending to the potentials of girlhood agency—of youthful yearnings to get along—therefore places an immense affective burden on youth.

In this final chapter, I expand the following themes to consider the possible ways forward from the arguments of this book: girlhood agency, subjectivity, and opacity; the futurism embedded in the notion of progressive multicultural girlhood identities; and the question of getting along to interrogate the conflicts that it displaces. The spatial and temporal complexity and subjective contradictions involved in multicultural identity make it impossible to take a spoken agency for racial harmony—or a feminine commitment to peace and harmony—for granted. Social differences and identifications rely on their conscious and unconscious interarticulation for their production. We cannot assume that progressive identities are simply potential sources for future multicultural "getting along" or answers to today's problems. To confront racial violence in urban schools without attention to the sexual and gender investments spurring it would result in a further failure to address its remarkable complexities.

Girlhood Subjectivity beyond Agency

Existing fields of girlhood study, as with multiculturalism, emphasize agency and humanistic investments in better futures. "Girl power" is buttressed by an assumption of girls' manifest interest and agency in combating sexism and racism. The conservative racial and sexual practices of American girlhood in feminist and social science scholarship have been grossly neglected, I believe, in this foregrounding of girls' agency and supposed interest in feminist futures. Girls are neither essentially ethical (compare Mahmood 2005) nor agential heroes, and they should not be held fully responsible for the trenchant spaces of segregation, hegemonic whiteness, and heterosexism that shape their everyday geographies.

In this section, I tackle the assumptions surrounding girlhood agency in an attempt to relieve girls of its burden. I have also been uneasy about offering an analysis of girls' narratives along simple lines of girlhood agency, despite girls' strong voices and clear articulations of disappointment, because the agential effects of these narratives are not so easy to characterize. A voice calling for change, I contend, does not necessarily have a straightforwardly resistant source, function, or effect. A sole emphasis on that reflexive voice does not take into account the context of how the voice functions within a more complex and constrained spatial subjectivity. As Judith Butler insists, "The means by which subject constitution occurs is not the same as the narrative form the reconstruction of that constitution attempts to provide" (2005: 69). What we say is not the whole story of our subjectivity.

Girl literatures have been perhaps too quick to rely on the spoken voice—the self—rather than to situate and contextualize the speaking subject within a field of constraint, including the spaces that shape behavior and reflexivity and the unconscious commitments subjects have for ambivalent spaces and socialities such as class, race, age, and sex-gender (Gonick 2003). They provide a problematic conceptualization of the girl subject that relies on a too-close relationship between gender-feminine *identity* and girls' *agency*. This conceptualization stems, I think, from analyses of girls' voices that do not theorize the distinction between the feminine speaker and social-psychic subjection.

Feminist scholars exploring Western girlhood often frame their research by deliberating on the divergent discourses of femininity available to teenage girls (e.g., Aapola, Gonick, and Harris 2005). I think it is safe to depict the overall approach to girlhood as a consideration of how these discourses hamper girls' abilities to define themselves in positive—nonsexist and nonharmful—ways. The goal of feminist research and advocacy for girls follows this formula of subject-creation: illustrate girls' capabilities to resist, document the ways they already do so, and seek to change the discourses of gender that confine girls' self-expression and political potential. In other words, scholars maintain that changing or resignifying the terms of feminine identity can proceed to a heightened or more accomplished agency for girls (e.g., Cahill et al. 2004; Miranda 2003; Baumgardner and Richards 2000; Leblanc 1999). The argument is that more discourses of femininity would allow girls to resist negative images and maligned femininity and choose empowering or empowered ones instead. In large part, feminist politics itself is founded on the idea that self-reflexivity and consciousness raising can work to change the devaluations of femininity in society.

Thus, scholars closely inspect the discourses that circulate and that are taken up, or resisted, by teenage girls. Discourse, in other words, is often the starting point for an examination of girlhood. Moreover, discourse is likely depicted by girlhood literatures as representing a dichotomy of gendered meanings. For example, Marnina Gonick (2006) summarizes the contemporary period as bifurcated between "girl power" and "reviving Ophelia." Gonick contends that both rely on an individualistic notion that girls can choose their own feminine identity, although, of course, both offer ambivalent choices in that neither can signify the remote possibility of a break from the power/victim-gendered dichotomy (e.g., 19). Other scholars bring their own labels for the dichotomies of girlhood to their studies, such as Anita Harris' (2004) split between "can-do" and "at-risk" girls and the commonly found division of "good" and "bad" girls (Charlton 2007; Gonick 2003; Magline and Perry 1996; Tolman and Higgins 1996; see also Valentine 1996). All agree that girlhood faces a severe contradiction given the dichotomous discourses that posit the restricted possibilities of femininity. Yet, fashioned from Butler's work on gender performativity, many scholars (e.g., Bettie 2003) indicate that agency follows the contradictions already present in discourse. As Shauna Pomerantz, Dawn Currie, and Deirdre Kelly put it, agency is "playing discourses against each other in an attempt to offset how hegemonic masculinity and emphasized femininity are produced" (2004: 549). Others, such as Gonick (2003), suggest that bringing "out" the inner desires or fantasies of other girlness that already exist in subjects, given the ambivalent discourses and identities of girls, is an opportunity to foster feminist resistance to sexism and misogyny. A central assumption about these approaches is that a girl subject can "speak [her]self into existence" (Currie, Kelly, and Pomerantz 2006: 434). Whether or not she does so effectively is seen to depend on her class, race, familial, regional, and educational positioning and privilege (Harris 2004; Bettie 2003). As I indicate in Chapter 1, race is often deemed a "problem" for nonwhite girls. Scholars frequently provide race in a list of important categories to consider and then omit an analysis of its effects—which is especially true when white girls are the topic of research. Subjectivity is defined through its ability to be agential and even voluntaristic to a point, but constitutive impediments might have the upper hand in the last assessment of girls' actual abilities to speak and therefore achieve agency.

However, this framework fails to push a definition of subjectivity beyond just taking girls' words for it. Girls are usually assumed to want to recode devalued femininity because they say so, and the scholarship on girls pulls these "voices" of girls to the fore amid their other narratives and practices. Femininity's reliance on whiteness is rarely interrogated in this body of work. Girls (e.g., geeks, skaters, and punks) who criticize other girls for being too feminine or playing the muse to boys' sexual desires, for example, are held as exemplars of shifting practices away from the circulation of femininity to masculinity's core sexist gravity (e.g., Leblanc 1999; Currie, Kelly, and Pomerantz

2006). Often, however, the self-proclaimed "alternative girls" resist femininity's limits by degrading other (usually girlie) girls as being dominated by boys and boys' priorities. This tactic was used by the girls in my research study, like Nane (see Chapter 3), who differentiated herself from "the usual girls walking around showing their ass, or their stomach, their breasts, with a lot of makeup that they look like fake Barbie dolls." Feminists value these voices of resistance, rather than also lamenting the girls' misogyny shown in their depicting other girls as dupes to sexism.

Further, these analyses neglect the unconscious desire that may propel girls to want social visibility and value, despite also feeling strongly critical of those girls who gain mainstream social status and popularity. Girls' voices of resistance also proceed through their desires to be socially and personally valuable and experience the supposed pleasure that they think those "other" girls have (in Lacanian terms, their *jouissance*). In other words, criticisms of sexy, pretty, or popular girlie girls assume that those girls are having fun, and there is often a desire to have it, too; the vociferous critiques indicate some desire within the criticism. There is desire in narratives such as Jane's in Chapter 5, when she fantasizes about the "let loose" (and white) family life for the girl on *Full House* who is allowed to date. These desires proceed along false assumptions, of course, that the other has a pleasure that the self can capture—when, in fact, the other is just as incomplete and fantastical as the self. The voice of girls, therefore, must be examined for its enabling psychic and social contexts and for those often unconscious pressures that prevent the self from living up to its words.

Focusing feminist analysis on girls' voices of agency assumes that these voices operate and function as self-consciously evident—rather than as effects of a subjectivity that *masks as much as it articulates*. Girls are somehow seen to be able to pick and choose among discourses that already exist, rather than discourse being theorized as perpetuated through the girls' practices—unconscious or not. We must theorize how the voice comes to be and function so that when we analyze what it says, there is a context of power relations, subjectivity, and space in play. Relying on the powerful voices of girl agency assumes a neutral field or discrete space in which girls live and maneuver. This voice is not possibly negated in another moment or spatiality of utterance, so that the voice/self is seen to be consistent rather than spatially variant or contingent. Put another way, voice and behavior vary by spatial contexts, in that they provide contingent power relationships that impact, shape, and contribute to social practice. The spaces of girls' voices in much of the literature seem vacant of power relations, pressure, or the interacting spatial relations that frame social viability. I hope this book has forcefully made this point: the narratives throughout should be spatialized so that the vibrant paradox that many subjects live is remembered.

In the end, this neglect of space and subjectivity naturalizes girls' agency as always possibly *active and progressive* in a feminist potential (see Driscoll 2002). A feminist interest in achieving powerful girls restricts an analysis of hegemonic whiteness in feminine identification, heteronormative couplings of female and male, and an emphasis on youth as always potentially politicized, even as girl power often proceeds through consumptive icons and media and what Angela McRobbie calls "hedonistic female phallicism" (2009: 5). I would like to see more scholarship considering girls' attachments to power relations that might reward them (psychically) even though socially they are punitive. Spatially, a strong girl voice or "resistant" practice may be rewarded in one context but not another, pointing to an uneven spatiality of relationships of difference and subjectivity (Thomas 2004). Strong girlhood voices are, by definition, restricted by the many valuations of racial difference, sexualized femininity, and multiple spaces of power that imbue and enable them. My methodology may be a disquieting approach for some fans of the girlhood genre, which often places much more faith and emphasis on girls' progressive narratives to the detriment of theorizing other themes in their "voices." I do not disavow American girls' hopes for nonracist worlds, but I have placed their hopeful words within a broader spatial context than merely the moment and place of speaking. There are many and competing narratives, geographies, and messages to consider among girls and within each girl. My central claim is that we must analyze this full range to present different theories of girlhood subjectivity and agency.

The impacts of this argument do not extend solely to American audiences. The gross globalization of girl power stretches a reliance on youth agency and a hope in recognition's identity politics (like multiculturalism) to disparate spaces and places. Youth everywhere share the burdens of an idealized agential girlhood and neoliberalism's agential effects on youth (Harris 2004; see also Jeffrey and McDowell 2004). Easy prescriptions for buttressing the power of children and young people criminally neglect the contexts and spatialities of injustice and maltreatment in which they live (Holt and Holloway 2006; Katz 2004). Youth cannot "feel" empowered to reshape the global economy; trenchant social, familial, and psychic investments in patriarchy; American hegemony and militarism; poverty and lack of infrastructure; and a lack of jobs. Girls cannot, contra to the hopes of the United Nations or the World Health Organization, solve the HIV epidemic by unilaterally taking responsibility for sexual practice and safety. Discourses and representations of girl power merely set girls up to fail; they burden girls to solve their own—not to mention the world's—problems by suggesting that girls can be "encouraged" to be self-sustaining and "empowered" by their femininity in straightforward and uncomplicated ways. They displace radical potential to a hope that future worlds can be celebratory of femininity. This not only burdens girls and women to be outside of power but also relies on a postfeminism that assumes that gender power floats by for the grabbing—and that all or most girls and women will want to grab when it floats by aspatially (see McRobbie 2009).

The Time of the Girl

The political investment in girlhood agency stems in great part from a problematic reliance on a temporality that posits a supposedly definite, progressive futurism (see Holt 2007; Katz 2008; Aitken, Ragnhild, and Kjorholt 2007). This futurism is taken as a foundational fact of feminist politics and scholarship on girlhood, as well as a global institutional displacement of change, care, and responsibility. Girlhood contains normative ideals of change and hope, but isn't this idealism based on sexism rife with undercurrents predicting femininity's nonviolence? It naturalizes gender binaries and then asks girls to live up to these gender representations. Its aspatiality means that girls are deemed to have this potential at all times—particularly in the future—and in all places. Gender remains situated as the core aspect of girls' subjectivities for self-harnessing social change; gender's core within an intersectional approach eliminates the deep challenges of social and spatial differentiation and identification. Girls are primarily gendered—self-evidently so; they are eager for social change and ready to work toward these futuristic spaces. This book places a hold on these assumptions and demands a rethinking of the racialized and sexualized narratives of space, place, and girlhood.

I partially take the tenor of this argument from Lee Edelman's (2004) *No Future: Queer Theory and the Death Drive*. Edelman allows a critical stance concerning the optimism placed on imagining "future generations" through a queer critique of the normative political reliance on the Child. The figure of the Child, he argues, is buttressed by a fantasy that the future could be defined by wholeness rather than lack. He rejects the recourse to "futurism" as it takes the form of an insistence of hope or an ideal social order. Rather, Edelman suggests that negativity, which he conceptualizes through the death drive, can be as productive a base for political claims. *No Future* thus provides the theoretical lens through which to consider the subject's own ambivalent engagement with futurism alongside aggressive social practices of racism (perhaps "negativity," in Edelman's language). Edelman's thesis calls for a queer politics, one that simultaneously rejects normative reproductive heterosexuality and its investment in the Child as it also insists on the impossibility of a stable recourse to identity as a possible accomplishment of wholeness. The Child, of course, also represents the political hope that wholeness is just ahead of us.

In contrast to Edelman's scathing account of the Child's figural position stands Harris's (2004) *Future Girl: Young Women in the Twenty-First Century*. Both scholars consider the temporality embedded in an episteme, yet Harris takes a drastically different approach than Edelman. While she asks how the teenage girl has come to be figured as an epitome of agency in neoliberal times—what she calls "future girl"—Harris remains committed to an understanding of girlhood as a distinct possibility for a new future, one resistant to the discourses that currently frame girlhood in the West. To be fair, she directly confronts the production of the teenage girl as the embodiment of "vanguard" subjectivities and questions the subsequent pressures placed on girls' lives given their increased social visibility and economic-political responsibilities. The ultimate goal of *Future Girl* is to imagine how girls can avoid the social and spatial definitions of stereotypical girlhood (and the individualist emphasis in "late modernity" on "responsibility"; see Harris's introduction) to carve alternative spaces for themselves.

Harris rightly and excellently questions a social, political, economic, and scholarly reliance on heroism. However, her commitment remains fixed on girls' *capacity* to be "good" and resistant subjects. The hope placed in girlhood's response to the pressures extended to girls requires Harris to be invested in the girl subject's gendered identity. This substantialization of identity, as Edelmen puts it, installs optimism in signification, or in his Lacanian terms, in the Symbolic (2004: 4–5). Such a move neglects the troubling aspects of subjectivity and the psyche's effects on the material embodiment of girls, not to mention on the materiality of the social more generally. No subject can operate solely in the register of social meaning—in alterity. The social is not cleavable into simple motives or spaces. The reliance on alternative or resistant feminine capabilities assumes that the contingency of space and subjectivity is not as impactful or confused as it is—contrary to my arguments throughout this book.

The futurism that Harris invokes is reliant on a space of *future possibility*— that is, a time-space defined by political intent and agency per se. Harris's final chapter, for example, is an attempt to map out "how a range of young women carve out unregulated spaces for themselves at a [neoliberal] time when they are so scrutinized" (2004: 152). There is a definition of space here that is required for girl agency to be possible, and that definition is, in the face of the arguments I have presented, problematic. Simply put, there is no such thing as an "unregulated space" in terms of either the individual subject and the processes of her psychic and self-imposed social regulation or the social-political constitution of relations made material through spaces of difference and power.

The girls' interests lie in "getting along," yet they do not necessarily enact the call. The hope for peace is futuristic, since the present is already painful and segregationist. The recourse to thinking about possible solutions is a way for the girls to displace their own culpability in today's racial geographies, in the here and now. They do so furthermore by blaming boys. There is clear evidence in their narratives of a desire for recognition and integration, and as such, it would be fairly easy to hone in on those words to demonstrate an inherent possibility for carving out spaces for interaction and respect for multiculturalism. The arguments of this book illustrate the deeply problematic assumptions guiding this aspatial and temporal view of girlhood, subjectivity, and education.

Let me be clear that I am not motivated by an antifeminist pessimism ("we're doomed"), and I am not suggesting that political agency and resistance are not possibilities for those of us wishing to advocate for changed gender, sexual, and racial relations for youth and girls in particular. What I am pursuing is a critique of the baseline working assumptions that gird the advocacies of girlhood scholars. My goal is to work through different strategies of resistant politics rather than relying on girls' own ethical responsibilities as agential selves and the coordinating assumption that there are "spaces" of opportunity that girls can create or open up—without contingency. I find both of these deeply troubling, and ultimately, they identify a stance that sets girlhood on a path of failed potential. The investment in the political Girl relies on a failed theory of spatiality and a gendered identity overdetermined with feminist intent (see Driscoll 2002). Banal multicultural girlhoods neglect the subjective, historical, and spatial legacies of race, ethnicity, language, and capitalism and maintain a misogynist, white supremacist idiom of autonomy, individual embodiment, and self-command (Ahmed 2010; hooks and Mesa-Bains 2006; Winnubst 2006).

Edelman's queering of futurism might sit too uncomfortably with the dominant feminist commitment to social justice for girls. His is an open-ended politics with no reassurances, built on negativity, which is definitional of some queer politics (Winnubst 2010). Yet it also exposes, as Edelman writes, "the obliquity of our relations to what we experience in and as social reality, alerting us to the fantasies structurally necessary in order to sustain it and engaging those fantasies through the figural logics, the linguistic structures, that shape them" (2004: 6–7). In the final analysis, it is emphatically not my point to sustain a critique that girls are nowhere resistant, nowhere pushing against oppressive discourses, or that their voices of resistance are merely symptoms. Simplifying the subject as one who is fully social and capable cannot begin to do justice to the complications of spatial subjectivity and the politics that follow its formulation (Rose 1997; Pratt 2000). Encouraging youth to be subjects "on their own terms" sustains a fantasy of feminist futurism and agential girlhood, when to my mind a more appropriate feminist politics would be to work with conflict, not against it. Refusing an identity of resistant girlhood would certainly be a radical move for normative feminism so deeply invested in the potential of girls (see the excellent Driscoll 2002). Yet such a move would work to deflate the overdetermined figure of the Girl that over time and space has come to be as much a feminist production as a dominantly cultural one.

Toward an Opaque Politics of Girlhood

In a quest to think politically and spatially about the girls' hopeful murmurs, their desires for new worlds, and the glimmers I saw of their reaching out in an effort to get along, I briefly turn to Butler's (2005) *Giving an Account of Oneself.* I do so to consider possible lessons about the constraints of subjectivity—not as problems but as opportunities. In this text, Butler considers the subject's opacity and continues her project to theorize subjectivity as a continual process of social and psychic relations with others. (On the scope and unfolding of this project, see Kaye Mitchell 2008.) To Butler, there is an enabling and limiting field of constraint (2005:19) for subjectivity, which marks both the livability of the subject and the subject's inability to emerge beyond the power and social relations that shape intelligibility. In other words, a regime (she uses Foucault's term) of intelligibility constrains what a subject can understand, do, be, and express. Psychoanalysis comes into the project to explain how the unconscious deals with that constraint on the subject's emergence. Suffering is one indication that the social and psychic "inassimilability" to these regimes is ongoing, "produced, enforced and managed over time, that get[s] lived out, or that set[s] a limit to what can be lived out" (Bell 2010: 134).

Basically, Butler's subject is formed through ambivalent relations to norms and power: "the 'I' has no story of its own that is not also the story of a relation—or set of relations—to a set of norms. . . . The 'I' is always to some extent dispossessed by the social conditions of its emergence" (Butler 2005: 8). Butler looks to this dispossession as "the condition for moral inquiry" (8). She writes, "Suspending the demand for self-identity or, more particularly, for complete coherence seems to me to counter a certain ethical violence, which demands that we manifest and maintain self-identity at all times and require that others do the same" (42). In the question of "Who are you?" there is, she argues, "a desire for recognition, [but] this desire will be under an obligation to keep itself alive as desire and not to resolve itself" (43). That is, though the question of "Who are you?" can and should be asked, *the answer should never be assumed as possibly transparent or self-evident.* The question should be a process of openness, not an indication that identity descriptively answers itself. (On the otherness of childhood, see O. Jones 2008.)

To Butler, the "I" as an experience of subjectivity is fundamentally embodied, but that body is not fundamentally personal or, of course, solely ontological. "There is a history to my body of which I can have no recollection" (2005: 38). This history is both social and psychic to her, and to me, it is also spatial. The temporality and spatiality of the body are not merely a matter of empirical study—they're not just about embedded relations of power but also about psychic process and primary relations. She writes, "If we are formed in the context of relations that become partially irrecoverable to us, then that opacity seems built into our formation and follows from our status as beings who are formed in relations of dependency" (20). The unconscious imposes limits "on the narrative reconstruction of a life" (20)—and of a body (39). To Butler, the unconscious is "instituted and maintained depending on how the domains of rationality and intelligibility are circumscribed and instituted" (quoted in Bell 2010: 132; Butler does not hold that there is a structural unconscious uninfluenced by social and personal relations and norms).

Thus, to Butler, recognition is not an ontology that assesses "social relations of power [as] always a *post hoc* effect," as Lois McNay (2008: 9) posits. Recognition in Butler's view must emphatically not become a normative or recuperative politics. Butler proposes an opaque politics of recognition, which is never to be transparent in demand or answer to subjects. Instead recognition is a kind of psychic and social desire—a desire completely unfulfillable but still ethically productive. Recognizing embodied opacity gives one "an ability to affirm what is contingent and incoherent in oneself [that] may allow one to affirm others who may or may not 'mirror' one's own constitution" (2005: 41).

While actively recognizing race, many of the girls' narratives bring to the fore the conflicting forces of seeking racial recognition and resisting racial reduction by others (even as they may reduce others in turn). In a context of complex processes of subjectivity, there is an ambivalence of racial identification: one is both *more* than one's race and always socially and spatially *accountable* for the materiality of one's body.[1] Therefore, my use of recognition is meant to mark the *failures* of identity politics. The girls' hopes to be recognized as authentically racialized, peace loving, racially mobile, or sexual and racial vanguards neglect the powerful racial, gender-sexual, and class relations that shape ideal norms for behavior in particular spaces. Any call or desire for recognition (along the lines of "I just want to be seen as who I am") overlooks the social-spatial relations that already influence a subject's *need* to be seen as such.

Many of the examples in this book also illustrate that these calls draw on an idealized whiteness; whiteness as "open" space, sexual freedom, and class privilege. Whiteness becomes vacated of power relations and occupies

---

1. Just to be absolutely clear, I do not want my use of recognition here to indicate a position that validates the politics of recognition. I am swayed by McNay's (2008) *Against Recognition*, which cautions theorists not to rely on prescriptions for agency and resistance in terms of identity. Rather, McNay urges us to remember the power relations (hers follow Bourdieu) that shape the terms of calls for recognition.

a central focal point for some of the girls' hopes of peace at school and in a proposed postracial Los Angeles. Whiteness and heterosexual gender binaries solidify their hold as normative spatial ideals in particular ways through everyday life and subjectivity. Their constraining context, according to Butler, must be accounted for in any analysis of their hopeful voices; we must work to understand the context that idealizes racial mobility through whiteness, class privilege, and gendered-heterosexual bodies. The paradoxes and ambivalences in girls' narratives are not personally, psychically, and politically reconciled by the girls themselves. I also do not think we should assume they *should* be. Following Butler, the paradoxes and ambivalences indicate to me a *starting* point for conceptualizing subjectivity and embodiment, not a *tripping* point for hopeful politics of antiracism and girlhood agency.

Banal Conflict: The Spaces of Multicultural Education

Violence and racial segregation—and the overwhelming, compounded problems with public urban schools—are not issues that can withstand reduced recipes for intervention. The cyclical violence and the entrenchment of severe racial-ethnic social segregation in cities and urban schools in Los Angeles (and in too many other places) illustrate the walls that failed solutions hit year after year. However, there is usually a normative ideal—based in fantasies of communicative American democracy—that straightforward communication about conflict is possible so that one can talk consciously about one's differences, account for them, and presumably work through them. (I borrow this terminology on democracy from Dean 2009.) This illusion of full reflexivity proscribes problems from the start. Win-win conflict resolution is an overwhelming model of multicultural education, assuming that everyone can sit equally at the table with the proper infrastructure, attitude, and process. It similarly assumes that every subject can be heard and seen (i.e., a subject who is transparent), in contrast to the opaque subject. There is a subjective limit to how any person can comprehend others' experiences, pain, and identities, given the psychic pleasures one gains through others' suffering (see, e.g., Skeggs 1997; Lane 1998). And the subject's constant recentering of the self (as a victim of racist suffering, for example, and not also a force in racial segregation and strife) presents a tough block to talking "respectfully" about segregation, race, and why violent outbreaks occur when and where they do. The latent importance of heterosexuality and normativity to racial segregation did not surface, to my knowledge, in any conversations seeking to quell the riot's impact and repetition.

The girls certainly have a stake in the belief that face-to-face talk and win-win resolution is possible, and seemingly so did the school administration in the riot's aftermath. However, as my analysis of the girls' narratives illustrates, such straightforward self-understanding about the differences that frame senses of self and identities is neither categorically simple nor coherent. While rivalries or competing positions are taken for granted, such as between different racial-ethnic groups, neighborhoods, and economic classes, it is less likely that rival positions are assumed to come from the same person. We wish away the irrational and focus on only what we want to see: the so-called rational positions that are proscribed from the start by our own framing references—how we learn to see the world through categorical and falsely tidy identity/difference (Mouffe 2000).

To the contrary, my argument has been that subjects themselves are not even fully aware of the ways that their identities work on and through them through the processes of identification and spatial subjectivity. After all, othering is a primary way that one becomes a self (Cheng 2009). Public persona and reflexivity depend on a personal-psychic process that is not wholly self-evident and often results in profound contradiction. These contradictions must be accounted for in the ways that identities exist and circulate. We must consider their object and power relations, affects, spaces, and contexts. This argument extends, vitally, to the *subject*, not students, communities, or neighborhoods, as most would have it. By neglecting spatial subjectivity, however, the basic assumptions about what identity is and how it works is flawed.

Worse yet, multicultural American girlhood remains pitted against itself and is encouraged to ignore its own ambivalences in the face of intense pressure to be girls and subjects who "get along." This process maintains status quo whiteness and class elitism in American education while furthering the entrenchment of feminine heterosexual norms. The effects are all too real on teenage girls, who must negotiate mixed messages about gender and sexuality, race and belonging, family pressures, peer and formal schooling, and public education. The ongoing results are contradictory and conflicted geographies, from the agential to the unheroic, from the conscious to the muddled.

Perhaps we must dispel with the notion that "getting along" is the right affect from which to build the proper nonviolent goal: a real state of being. It insinuates a material public space where that is possible, rather than the spaces of subjection and subjective complexity that I have tried to evidence throughout this book. Furthermore, in post-9/11 America, assuming a public sphere not tainted by the institutions of a police state, and a possibly reflexive citizenry that a deliberative democratic public relies on, seems almost nostalgic itself. Citizens and migrants go "missing" (Maira 2009) and face new insecurities through intense everyday, local policing (Coleman 2009); extreme school discipline and zero tolerance policies punish youth before transgressions are even enacted (Kupchik 2010); and some youth (as seen in Chapter 6) glibly recommend further surveillance of their bodies and activities in service to a state that places scant investment in their education and intellect (see Alonso et al. 2009).

While some may say that they are interested in conflict resolution, their daily geographies often evidence otherwise. As Gill Valentine (2008) shows, the creation of sites for spatial engagement and positive encounters does not necessarily translate into changed attitudes. Rather, "in the context of negative encounters minority individuals are perceived to represent members of a wider social group, but in positive encounters minority individuals tend to be read only as individuals" (332). Perhaps more importantly, the objectification of the other remains steadfast, since even if the individual is noted as being (momentarily) positive, that other remains an object to analyze and through which to analyze the self's reaction. This objectivity and naturalization of race and identity are spatial processes, and the spaces of subjectivity "can tell us something about the ways in which [racialized] geographies are a response to existing spatial paradigms" (McKittrick 2006: 14; see also the urban geography of Dikeç 2007).

Ash Amin proposes that contact itself be a basis for engagement, rather than "an ethos of community," with "a vocabulary of rights of presence, bridging difference, getting along" (2002: 972). He also strongly warns against the notion that public space can "inculcat[e] interethnic understanding" (696). Here "getting along" remains the goal still, even though Amin's "pessimism" given the "consistency of race" that surfaces in his later writing (2010: 13). He realizes the "long and arduous" task that would be required to "build a humanist or other type of non-racial counter-legacy that starts to become second nature in institutional and vernacular practice" (13). He continues, "I see these efforts, however, as part of a politics of neutralizing, rather than transcending race, without assuming the need for humanity to rise above itself in order to tackle racism" (14). To Amin, "the crucial question, however, is whether ethical humanism can discursively and practically unsettle the elaborate machinery of fear, suspicion and discipline that is being put in place by the new biopolitics of emergency. . . . It too uses the language of human being and becoming in order to select between the good and the bad, building powerful moral and affective impetus behind the choice to discipline particular human subjects (Brown 2006; Žižek 2008)" (16). Amy reflected this outcome (see Chapter 2) when she told me, "But there's other people who, just, they're not about school; they're not about life; they don't think this." Her affective hopes for getting along contain within them that moral impetus that Amin marks as racial discipline.

Banal multiculturalism in urban American schools is mired in a biopolitics of identity and recognition based on the simultaneously flawed logic that, via humanism, we're really all the same "inside"—that somehow race can be paradoxically transcended through the surficial and phenotypical performance of it day in and out. It gets stuck on the impetus's potential with no force to counter the discipline of subjects. Saying that racial-ethnic difference matters in all sorts of ways over years of compounded messaging, from school food fairs to extracurricular ethnic activities, situates embodied difference as central to the racial education of youth. They are taught, in the words of bell hooks, that multiculturalism "says let's all have our own little cultures and fight for visibility." In doing so, it "invites liberal individualism," and through public policy, it maintains white supremacy (hooks and Mesa-Bains 2006: 82).

At the same time as saturating educational spaces with this powerful banality of identity as naturalized not disciplinary, expressive not biopolitical, and individual not social and psychic, multiculturalism also teaches youth that conflicts around the junction of space, race, sexuality, and language are inappropriate. Within this muddled terrain, it makes absolute sense that violence erupts and masculinism occupies its elevated position on campus and that hegemonic whiteness and heterosexism reinscribe subjectivity through consumption and gender. The mixed and mutually produced messages of peace and violence, race and racism, and respect and misogyny create spaces of absolute confusion. Youth are told to be different but not too different, to get along but to work hard to maintain their individuality. This central reliance on identity helps to create the spatial paradox of subjectivity and the subjective spaces of urban education. The quest in much of multicultural girlhood has been to advocate for new identities to propel girls into the future with strong tools of tolerance, respect for self and others, sexual agency, ethnic and racial pride, and multicultural consumption. Identity ties subjects to a fantasy that wholeness is out "there," conflict can be mitigated by transparency and communication, and getting together can lead to getting along.

It is from these spaces of conflict that a reconsideration of feminist and antiracist motivations must tentatively start; I have argued that there is no denying them. Conflict could instead replace identity as the central organizer of youth contact and affect. While instituting conflict (and emphatically not violence) would be productive of new challenges, starting with the opportunities that conflict presents means that facile contracts with multiculturalism must be suspended. Schools, policy, and subjects cannot agree to agree on the face of it yet live and feel deep segregation, distrust, and discord. That compliance with multiculturalism mutes the anger that youth have about the inadequacies of their education and urban spaces and teaches them that they should be grateful for being brown in a white supremacist society. That anger becomes a tool in the biopolitical "machinery" as it is subsumed so that individual psychologies are targets for condemning conflict and, yes, violence.

The anger and stress in the girls' narratives are clear in this book. They worry that their parents, particularly their mothers, do not love them; they are paranoid and also aware of the constant surveillance of their bodies and behavior by even those whom they "love"; they fear that they will not incite the passions of violent boys; and they know their educations are insufficient for the demands of today's economy and society. Some even worried that they were not giving me what I was looking for, that somehow their answers were inadequate. Perhaps they worry that their selves are inadequate; after all, the psychoanalytic subject as lack propels desire (Dean 2000).

These are all examples of the psychic life of power—the ways that spatial legacies of age, racism, misogyny, and empire all stick to us, in us, and thus live on. Cheng suggests that the "acceptance and attention to this 'stuckness' may do more important political work for the future than the rhetoric of willful progress" (2009: 91). Learning that there is no resolution of difference and that conflict is possibly productive of new social and spatial formations is one path to a critical education beyond banal multiculturalism. These formations may not always have been politically progressive, but one thing is certain: the psychic and spatial life of power must be considered, for there is, I have argued, no simple overturning of it. The task is to work toward an understanding that anger, fear, and conflict are forces of togetherness, even though they are opaque, troubled, and troubling. The binding and desirous ties of togetherness may not indicate an interest or straightforward agential capacity to "get along" in every time and space. But if solidarity is wrested away from the banal norms of getting along, then perhaps conflict itself can be reimagined as solidary.

References

Aapola, Sinikka, Marnina Gonick, and Anita Harris. 2005. *Young femininity: Girlhood, power and social change*. New York: Palgrave Macmillan.

Ahmed, Sara. 1999. Home and away: Narratives of migration and estrangement. *International Journal of Cultural Studies* 2:329–347.

———. 2000. *Strange encounters: Embodied others in post-coloniality*. London: Routledge.

———. 2002. The contingency of pain. *Parallax* 8 (1): 17–34.

———. 2010. *The promise of happiness*. Durham: Duke University Press.

Aitken, Stuart C. 2001a. *Geographies of young people: The morally contested spaces of identity*. New York: Routledge.

———. 2001b. Schoolyard shootings: Racism, sexism, and the moral panics over teen violence. *Antipode* 33 (4): 593–600.

Aitken, Stuart, and Randi Marchant. 2003. Memories and miscreants: Teenage tales of terror. *Children's Geographies* 1 (1): 151.

Aitken, Stuart C., Lund Ragnhild, and Anne Trine Kjorholt. 2007. Why children? Why now? *Children's Geographies* 5 (1–2): 3–14.

Alder, Christine, and Anne Worrall, eds. 2004. *Girls' violence: Myths and realities*. Albany: SUNY Press.

Alonso, Gaston, Noel Anderson, Celina Su, and Jeanne Theoharis. 2009. *Our schools suck: Students talk back to a segregated nation on the failures of urban education*. New York: New York University Press.

Amin, Ash. 2002. Ethnicity and the multicultural city: Living with diversity. *Environment and Planning A* 34 (6): 959–980.

———. 2010. The remainders of race. *Theory, Culture and Society* 27 (1): 1–23.

Amin, Ash, and Nigel Thrift. 2007. Cultural-economy and cities. *Progress in Human Geography* 31 (2): 143–161.

Ansell, Nicola. 2009a. Childhood and the politics of scale: Descaling children's geographies? *Progress in Human Geography* 33 (2): 190–209.

———. 2009b. Embodied learning: Responding to AIDS in Lesotho's education sector. *Children's Geographies* 7 (1): 21–36.

Baumgardner, Jennifer, and Amy Richards. 2000. *Manifesta: Young women, feminism, and the future*. New York: Farrar, Straus, and Giroux.

Bell, Vikki. 2010. New scenes of vulnerability, agency and plurality: An interview with Judith Butler. *Theory, Culture and Society* 27 (1): 130–152.

Best, Amy. 2000. *Prom night: Youth, schools and popular culture*. New York: Routledge.

Bettie, Julie. 2003. *Women without class: Girls, race, and identity*. Berkeley: University of California Press.

Boghossian, Naush, and Lisa M. Sodders. 2005. School hate crimes spike (up 400% in decade). *LA Daily News*, June 20, 2005.

Bondi, Liz. 2005. Making connections and thinking through emotions: Between geography and psychotherapy. *Transactions of the Institute of British Geographers* 30:433–448.

Bone, Stanley, and John Oldham. 1994. Paranoia: Historical considerations. In *Paranoia: New psychoanalytic perspectives*, ed. J. Oldham and S. Bone, 3–15. Madison, CT: International Universities Press.

Bonilla-Silva, Eduardo. 2003. *Racism without racists: Color-blind racism and the persistence of racial inequality in the United States*. New York: Rowman and Littlefield.

Brown, Wendy. 1995. *States of injury: Power and freedom in late modernity*. Princeton, NJ: Princeton University Press.

———. 1996. Injury, identity, politics. In *Mapping multiculturalism*, ed. A. Gordon and C. Newfield, 149–166. Minneapolis: University of Minnesota Press.

———. 2001. The impossibility of women's studies. *Differences: A Journal of Feminist Cultural Studies* 9 (3): 79–101.

———. 2006. *Regulating aversion: Tolerance in the age of identity and empire*. Princeton, NJ: Princeton University Press.

Burman, Michele. 2004. Turbulent talk: Girls' making sense of violence. In *Girls' violence: Myths and realities*, ed. C. Alder and A. Worrall, 81–103. Albany: SUNY Press.

Butler, Judith. 1993. *Bodies that matter: On the discursive limits of "sex."* London: Routledge.

———. 1997a. *Excitable speech: A politics of the performative*. London: Routledge.

———. 1997b. *The psychic life of power: Theories in subjection*. Stanford, CA: Stanford University Press.

———. 2001. Giving an account of oneself. *Diacritics* 31 (4): 22–40.

———. 2002. Bodies and power, revisited. *Radical Philosophy* 114:13–19.

———. 2004a. *Precarious life: The powers of mourning and violence*. New York: Verso.

———. 2004b. *Undoing gender*. New York: Routledge.

———. 2005. *Giving an account of oneself*. New York: Fordham University Press.

Cahill, Caitlin. 2007a. The personal is political: Developing new subjectivities through participatory action research. *Gender, Place and Culture: A Journal of Feminist Geography* 14:267–292.

———. 2007b. Negotiating grit and glamour: Young women of color and the gentrification of the Lower East Side. *City and Society* 19 (2): 202–231.

Cahill, Caitlin, Erica Arenas, Jennifer Contreras, Jiang Na, Indra Rios-Moore, and Tiffany Threatts. 2004. Speaking back: Voices of young urban womyn of color using participatory action research to challenge and complicate representations of young women. In *All about the girl: Culture, power, and identity*, ed. A. Harris, 231–242. New York: Routedge.

Carr, Brian. 2004. Paranoid interpretation, desire's nonobject, and Nella Larsen's *Passing. PMLA* 119 (2): 282–295.

Caruth, Cathy. 2001. An interview with Jean Laplanche. *Postmodern Culture* 11 (2).

Charlton, Emma. 2007. Review essay: "Bad" girls versus "good" girls: Contradiction in the constitution of contemporary girlhood. *Discourse: Studies in the Cultural Politics of Education* 28 (1): 121–131.

Cheng, Anne Anlin. 2001. *The melancholy of race: Psychoanalysis, assimilation, and hidden grief*. Oxford: Oxford University Press.

———. 2009. Psychoanalysis without symptoms. *Differences: A Journal of Feminist Cultural Studies* 20 (1): 87–101.

Chesney-Lind, Meda, and Katherine Irwin. 2004. From badness to meanness: Popular constructions of contemporary girlhood. In *All about the girl: Culture, power, and identity*, ed. A. Harris, 45–56. New York: Routledge.

Chin, Elizabeth. 2001. *Purchasing power: Black kids and American consumer culture*. Minneapolis: University of Minnesota Press.

Coale, Samual Chase. 2004. *Paradigms of paranoia: The culture of conspiracy in contemporary American fiction*. Tuscaloosa: University of Alabama Press.

Coe, Cati. 2005. *Dilemmas of culture in African schools: Youth, nationalism, and the transformation of knowledge*. Chicago: University of Chicago Press.

Coleman, Mathew. 2009. What counts as the politics and practice of security, and where? Devolution and immigrant insecurity after 9/11. *Annals of the Association of American Geographers* 99 (5): 904–913.

Crapanzano, Vincent. 1998. "Lacking now is only the leading idea, that is: We, the rays, have no thoughts": Interlocutory collapse in Daniel Paul Schreber's "Memoirs of my nervous illness." *Critical Inquiry* 24 (3): 737–767.

Currie, Dawn. 1999. *Girl talk: Adolescent magazines and their readers*. Toronto: University of Toronto Press.

Currie, Dawn, Deirdre Kelly, and Shauna Pomerantz. 2006. "The geeks shall inherit the earth": Girls' agency, subjectivity and empowerment. *Journal of Youth Studies* 9 (4): 419–436.

Dávila, Arlene. 2008. *Latino spin: Public image and the whitewashing of race*. New York: New York University Press.

Dean, Jodi. 2009. *Democracy and other neoliberal fantasies: Communicative capitalism and left politics*. Durham, NC: Duke University Press.

Dean, Tim. 2000. *Beyond sexuality*. Chicago: University of Chicago Press.

Delaney, David. 1998. *Race, place and the law, 1836–1948*. Austin: University of Texas Press.

Deutsch, Nancy. 2008. *Pride in the projects: Teens building identities in urban contexts*. New York: New York University Press.

Deutsch, Nancy, and Eleni Theodorou. 2010. Aspiring, consuming, becoming: Youth identity in a culture of consumption. *Youth and Society* 42 (4): 229–254.

Dikeç, Mustafa. 2007. *Badlands of the republic: Space, politics, and urban policy*. Malden, MA: Blackwell.

DiPiero, Thomas. 2002. *White men aren't*. Durham, NC: Duke University Press.

Dolby, Nadine. 2000. Changing selves: Multicultural education and the challenge of new identities. *Teachers College Record* 102 (5): 898–912.

Driscoll, Catherine. 2002. *Girls: Feminine adolescence in popular culture and cultural theory*. New York: Columbia University Press.

Dwyer, Owen, and John Paul Jones III. 2000. White socio-spatial epistemology. *Social and Cultural Geography* 1 (2): 209–222.

Dwyer, Peter, and Johanna Wyn. 2001. *Youth, education and risk: Facing the future*. New York: Routledge.

Dyson, Jane. 2010. Friendship in practice: Girls' work in the Indian Himalayas. *American Ethnologist* 37 (3): 482–498.

Edelman, Lee. 2004. *No future: Queer theory and the death drive*. Durham, NC: Duke University Press.

Ehrenreich, Barbara. 2009. *Bright-sided: How the relentless promotion of positive thinking has undermined America*. New York: Metropolitan Books.

Elwood, Sarah, and Deborah Martin. 2000. "Placing" interviews: Location and scales of power in qualitative research. *Professional Geographer* 52 (4): 649–657.

Eng, David. 2001. *Racial castration: Managing masculinity in Asian America*. Durham, NC: Duke University Press.

Epstein, Debbie, and Richard Johnson. 1998. *Schooling sexualities*. Buckingham, UK: Open University Press.

Evans, Bethan. 2006. "I'd feel ashamed": Girls' bodies and sports participation. *Gender, Place and Culture: A Journal of Feminist Geography* 13:547–561.

———. 2008. Geographies of youth/young people. *Geography Compass* 2 (5): 1659–1680.

Farrell, John. 1996. *Freud's paranoid quest: Psychoanalysis and modern suspicion*. New York: New York University Press.

Ferguson, Roderick. 2005. Of our normative strivings: African American studies and the histories of sexuality. *Social Text* 23 (3–4): 85–100.

Fish, Stanley. 1997. Boutique multiculturalism, or why liberals are incapable of thinking about hate speech. *Critical Inquiry* 23 (2): 378–395.

Fong, Vanessa. 2004. *Only hope: Coming of age under China's one-child policy*. Stanford, CA: Stanford University Press.

Fordham, Signithia. 1996. *Blacked out: Dilemmas of race, identity, and success at Capital High*. Chicago: University of Chicago Press.

Fortier, Anne-Marie. 2008. *Multicultural horizons: Diversity and the limits of the civil nation*. New York: Routledge.

Freud, Sigmund. 1957. Mourning and melancholia. In *The standard edition of the complete psychological works of Sigmund Freud*, vol. 14, ed. J. Strachey, 237–258. London: Hogarth Press.

———. 1958. Psycho-analytic notes on an autobiographical account of a case of paranoia (dementia paranoides). In *The standard edition of the complete psychological works of Sigmund Freud*, vol. 12, ed. J. Strachey, 1–82. London: Hogarth Press.

———. 1959. *Group psychology and the analysis of the ego.* New York: Norton.

———. 1961a. *Civilization and its discontents.* New York: Norton.

———. 1961b. *The ego and the id.* New York: Norton.

———. 1966. *Introductory lectures on psychoanalysis.* New York: Norton.

Gagen, Elizabeth A. 2006. Measuring the soul: Psychological technologies and the production of physical health in Progressive Era America. *Environment and Planning D: Society and Space* 24 (6): 827–849.

Gill, Rosalind. 2008. Culture and subjectivity in neoliberal and postfeminist times. *Subjectivity* 25:432–445.

Gillborn, David. 2005. Education policy as an act of white supremacy: Whiteness, critical race theory and education reform. *Journal of Education Policy* 20 (4): 485–505.

Giroux, Henry. 1992. Post-colonial ruptures and democratic possibilities: Multiculturalism as anti-racist pedagogy. *Cultural Critique* 21:5–39.

Gonick, Marnina. 2003. *Between femininities: Ambivalence, identity, and the education of girls.* Albany: SUNY Press.

———. 2006. Between "girl power" and "reviving Ophelia": Constituting the neoliberal girl subject. *NWSA Journal* 18 (2): 1–23.

Gonick, Marnina, Emma Renold, Jessica Ringrose, and Lisa Weems. 2009. Rethinking agency and resistance: What comes after girl power? *Girlhood Studies* 2 (2): 1–9.

Goonewardena, Kanishka, and Stefan Kipfer. 2005. Spaces of difference: Reflections from Toronto on multiculturalism, bourgeois urbanism, and the possibility of radical urban politics. *International Journal of Urban and Regional Research* 29 (3): 670–678.

Hage, Ghassan. 2000. *White nation: Fantasies of white supremacy in a multicultural society.* New York: Routledge.

Harris, Anita. 2004. *Future girl: Young women in the twenty-first century.* New York: Routledge.

Hey, Valerie. 2009. The girl in the mirror: The psychic economy of class in the discourse of girlhood studies. *Girlhood Studies* 2 (2): 10–32.

Holloway, Sarah, Phil Hubbard, Heike Jons, and Helena Pimlott-Wilson. 2010. Geographies of education and the significance of children, youth and families. *Progress in Human Geography* 34 (5): 583–600.

Holloway, Sarah, and Gill Valentine, eds. 2000. *Children's geographies: Playing, living, learning.* London: Routledge.

Holt, Louise. 2007. Children's sociospatial (re)production of disability within primary school playgrounds. *Environment and Planning D: Society and Space* 25:783–802.

Holt, Louise, and Sarah Holloway. 2006. Theorising other childhoods in a globalised world. *Children's Geographies* 4 (2): 135–142.

Honig, Bonnie. 2001. *Democracy and the foreigner.* Princeton, NJ: Princeton University Press.

hooks, bell. 1994. *Teaching to transgress: Education as the practice of freedom.* London: Routledge.

hooks, bell, and Amalia Mesa-Bains. 2006. *Homegrown: Engaged cultural criticism.* Cambridge, MA: South End Press.

Hurd, Clayton A. 2008. Cinco de Mayo, normative whiteness, and the marginalization of Mexican-descent students. *Anthropology and Education Quarterly* 39 (3): 293–313.

Hurtig, Janise. 2008. *Coming of age in times of crisis: Youth, schooling, and patriarchy in a Venezuelan town.* New York: Palgrave Macmillan.

Hyams, Melissa. 2000. "Pay attention in class . . . [and] don't get pregnant": A discourse of academic success among adolescent Latinas. *Environment and Planning A* 32 (4): 635–654.

———. 2002. "Over there" and "back then": An odyssey in national subjectivity. *Environment and Planning D: Society and Space* 20 (4): 459–476.

———. 2003. Adolescent Latina bodyspaces: Making homegirls, homebodies and homeplaces. *Antipode* 35 (3): 536–558.

Jeffrey, Craig. 2010. Geographies of children and youth I: Eroding maps of life. *Progress in Human Geography* 34 (4): 496–505.

Jeffrey, Craig, Patricia Jeffery, and Roger Jeffery. 2008. *Degrees without freedom? Education, masculinities, and unemployment in North India.* Stanford, CA: Stanford University Press.

Jeffrey, Craig, and Linda McDowell. 2004. Youth in a comparative perspective: Global change, local lives. *Youth and Society* 36 (2): 131–142.

Jones, Nikki. 2010. *Between good and ghetto: African American girls and inner-city violence.* New Brunswick, NJ: Rutgers University Press.

Jones, Owain. 2008. "True geography [] quickly forgotten, giving away to an adult-imagined universe": Approaching the otherness of childhood. *Children's Geographies* 6 (2): 195–212.

Katz, Cindi. 2004. *Growing up global: Economic restructuring and children's everyday lives.* Minneapolis: University of Minnesota Press.

———. 2008. Childhood as spectacle: Relays of anxiety and the reconfiguration of the child. *Cultural Geographies* 15 (1): 5–17.

Kingsbury, Paul. 2007. The extimacy of space. *Social and Cultural Geography* 8 (2): 235–258.

———. 2010. Locating the melody of the drives. *Professional Geographer* 62 (4): 519–533.

Kobayashi, Audrey. 2003. GPC ten years on: Is self-reflexivity enough? *Gender, Place, and Culture* 10 (4): 345–349.

Kupchik, Aaron. 2010. *Homeroom security: School discipline in an age of fear.* New York: New York University Press.

Ladson-Billings, Gloria. 2003. New directions in multicultural education: Complexities, boundaries and critical race theory. In *Handbook of research on multicultural education,* ed. J. A. Banks and C. M. Banks, 50–64. San Francisco: Jossey-Bass.

Lane, Christopher. 1998. The psychoanalysis of race: An introduction. In *The psychoanalysis of race,* ed. C. Lane, 1–40. New York: Columbia University Press.

Laplanche, Jean. 1996. Psychoanalysis as anti-hermeneutics. *Radical Philosophy* 79:7–12.

———. 1999. *Essays on otherness.* London: Routledge.

Laplanche, Jean, and J.-B. Pontalis. 1973. *The language of psychoanalysis.* Trans. D. Nicholson-Smith. New York: Norton.

Leblanc, Lauraine. 1999. *Pretty in punk: Girls' gender resistance in a boys' subculture.* New York: Routledge.

Lee, Stacey J. 2005. *Up against whiteness: Race, school, and immigrant youth.* New York: Teachers College Press.

Leledakis, Kanakis. 1995. *Society and psyche: Social theory and the unconscious dimension of the social.* Oxford: Berg Publishers.

Lewis, Amanda. 2003. *Race in the schoolyard: Negotiating the color line in classrooms and communities.* New Brunswick, NJ: Rutgers University Press.

Lopez, Nancy. 2003. *Hopeful girls, troubled boys: Race and gender disparity in urban education.* New York: Routledge.

Lugones, Maria, and Price Joshua. 1995. Dominant culture: El deseo por un alma pobre (the desire for an impoverished soul). In *Multiculturalism from the margins: Non-dominant voices on difference and diversity,* ed. D. Harris, 103–127. Westport, CT: Bergin and Garvey.

Lustig, Deborah Freedman. 1997. Of Kwanzaa, Cinco de Mayo, and whispering: The need for intercultural education. *Anthropology and Education Quarterly* 28 (4): 574–592.

Mac an Ghaill, Mairtin. 1999. *Contemporary racisms and ethnicities: Social and cultural transformations.* Buckingham, UK: Open University Press.

Magline, Nan Bauer, and Donna Perry, eds. 1996. *"Bad girls"/"good girls": Women, sex, and power in the nineties.* New Brunswick, NJ: Rutgers University Press.

Mahmood, Saba. 2005. *Politics of piety: The Islamic revival and the feminist subject.* Princeton, NJ: Princeton University Press.

Maira, Sunaina. 2009. *Missing: Youth, citizenship, and empire after 9/11.* Durham, NC: Duke University Press.

McKittrick, Katherine. 2006. *Demonic grounds: Black women and the cartographies of struggle.* Minneapolis: University of Minnesota Press.

McNay, Lois. 2008. *Against recognition.* Cambridge: Polity Press.

McRobbie, Angela. 2009. *The aftermath of feminism: Gender, culture and social change.* Los Angeles: Sage Publications.

Mendoza-Denton, Norma. 2008. *Homegirls: Language and cultural practice among Latina youth gangs.* Malden, MA: Blackwell.

Miller, Jody. 2001. *One of the guys: Girls, gangs, and gender.* New York: Oxford University Press.

———. 2008. *Getting played: African American girls, urban inequality, and gendered violence.* New York: New York University Press.

Miranda, Marie "Keta." 2003. *Homegirls in the public sphere.* Austin: University of Texas Press.

Mitchell, Katharyne. 2003. Educating the national citizen in neoliberal times: From the multicultural self to the strategic cosmopolitan. *Transactions of the Institute of British Geographers* 28:387–403.

———. 2004. Geographies of identity: Multiculturalism unplugged. *Progress in Human Geography* 28 (5): 641–651.

Mitchell, Katharyne, Sallie Marston, and Cindi Katz. 2004. Life's work: An introduction, review and critique. In *Life's work: Geographies of social reproduction,* ed. K. Mitchell, S. Marston and C. Katz, 1–26. Oxford: Blackwell Publishing.

Mitchell, Kaye. 2008. Unintelligible subjects: Making sense of gender, sexuality and subjectivity after Butler. *Subjectivity* 25:413–431.

Modern Girl around the World Research Group. 2008. *The modern girl around the world: Consumption, modernity, and globalization.* Durham, NC: Duke University Press.

Morris-Roberts, Kathryn. 2004a. Colluding in "compulsory heterosexuality"? Doing research with young women at school. In *All about the girl: Culture, power, and identity*, ed. A. Harris, 219–229. New York: Routledge.

———. 2004b. Girls' friendships, "distinctive individuality" and socio-spatial practices of (dis)identification. *Children's Geographies* 2 (2): 237–255.

Mouffe, Chantal. 2000. *The democratic paradox*. New York: Verso.

Nagar, Richa, and Susan Geiger. 2007. Reflexivity and positionality in feminist fieldwork revisited. In *Politics and practice in economic geography*, ed. A. Tickell, E. Sheppard, J. Peck, and T. Barnes, 267–278. London: Sage.

Nayak, Anoop. 2003a. *Race, place and globalization: Youth cultures in a changing world*. New York: Berg.

———. 2003b. "Through children's eyes": Childhood, place and the fear of crime. *Geoforum* 34 (3): 303–315.

Oldham, John, and Stanley Bone, eds. 1994. *Paranoia: New psychoanalytic perspectives*. Madison, CT: International Universities Press.

Pastor, Jennifer, Jennifer McCormick, and Michelle Fine. 2007. Makin' homes: An urban girl thing. In *Urban girls revisited: Building strengths*, ed. B. R. Leadbeater and N. Way, 75–96. New York: New York University Press.

Perry, Pamela. 2002. *Shades of white: White kids and racial identities in high school*. Durham, NC: Duke University Press.

Pile, Steve. 2008. Where is the subject? Geographical imaginations and spatializing subjectivity. *Subjectivity* 23:206–218.

———. 2010. Intimate distance: The unconscious dimensions of the rapport between researcher and researched. *Professional Geographer* 62 (4): 483–495.

Pollock, Mica. 2004. *Colormute: Race talk dilemmas in an American school*. Princeton, NJ: Princeton University Press.

Pomerantz, Shauna, Dawn Currie, and Deirdre Kelly. 2004. Sk8er girls: Skateboarders, girlhood and feminism in motion. *Women's Studies International Forum* 27:547–557.

Povinelli, Elizabeth. 2002. *The cunning of recognition: Indigenous alterities and the making of Australian multiculturalism*. Durham, NC: Duke University Press.

Pratt, Geraldine. 2000. Research performances. *Environment and Planning D: Society and Space* 18 (5): 639–651.

———. 2002. Collaborating across our differences. *Gender, Place, and Culture* 9 (2): 195–200.

Proudfoot, Jesse. 2010. Interviewing enjoyment, or the limits of discourse. *Professional Geographer* 62 (4): 507–518.

Pulido, Laura. 2006. *Black, brown, yellow, and left: Radical activism in Los Angeles*. Berkeley: University of California Press.

Riley, Chris, and Nancy Ettlinger. 2011. Interpreting racial formation and multiculturalism in a high school: Towards a constructive deployment of two approaches to critical race theory. *Antipode* 43, doi:10.1111/j.1467-8330.2010.00825.x.

Roberts, Rosemarie, Lee Bell, and Brett Murphy. 2008. Flipping the script: Analyzing youth talk about race and racism. *Anthropology and Education Quarterly* 39 (3): 334–354.

Rose, Gillian. 1997. Situating knowledges: Positionality, reflexivities and other tactics. *Progress in Human Geography* 21 (3): 305–320.

Ruddick, Sue. 2003. The politics of aging: Globalization and the restructuring of youth and childhood. *Antipode* 33 (2): 334–362.

Salecl, Renata. 2009. Society of choice. *Differences: A Journal of Feminist Cultural Studies* 20 (1): 157–180.

Sears, Stephanie. 2010. *Imagining black womanhood: The negotiation of power and identity within the girls empowerment project*. Albany: SUNY Press.

Sedinger, Tracey. 2002. Nation and identification: Psychoanalysis, race, and sexual difference. *Cultural Critique* 50:40–73.

Sharma, Nitasha Tamar. 2010. *Hip hop desis: South Asian Americans, blackness, and a global race consciousness*. Durham, NC: Duke University Press.

Sibley, David. 1995. *Geographies of exclusion: Society and difference in the West*. London: Routledge.

Skeggs, Beverly. 1997. *Formations of class and gender: Becoming respectable*. London: Sage.

Somerville, Siobhan. 2000. *Queering the color line: Race and the invention of homosexuality in American culture*. Durham, NC: Duke University Press.

Spivak, Gayatri Chakravorty. 1999. *A critique of postcolonial reason: Toward a history of the vanishing present*. Cambridge, MA: Harvard University Press.

Stack, Allyson. 2005. Culture, cognition and Jean Laplanche's enigmatic signifier. *Theory, Culture and Society* 22 (3): 63–80.

Stambach, Amy. 2000. *Lessons from Mount Kilimanjaro: Schooling, community, and gender in East Africa*. New York: Routledge.

———. 2010. *Faith in schools: Religion, education, and American evangelicals in East Africa*. Stanford, CA: Stanford University Press.

Stearns, Elizabeth. 2004. Interracial friendliness and the social organization of schools. *Youth and Society* 35 (4): 395–419.

Stoler, Ann Laura. 1995. *Race and the education of desire*. Durham, NC: Duke University Press.

Tatum, Beverly Daniel. 1997. *"Why are all the black kids sitting together in the cafeteria?" and other conversations about race*. New York: Basic Books.

Thien, Deborah. 2005. Intimate distances: Considering the question of "us." In *Emotional Geographies*, ed. J. Davidson, L. Bondi, and M. Smith, 191–204. Aldershot, UK: Ashgate.

Thomas, Mary E. 2004. Pleasure and propriety: Teen girls and the practice of straight space. *Environment and Planning D: Society and Space* 22 (5): 773–789.

———. 2005a. "I think it's just natural": The spatiality of racial segregation at a US high school. *Environment and Planning A* 37 (7): 1233–1248.

———. 2005b. Girls, consumption space, and the contradictions of hanging out in the city. *Social and Cultural Geography* 6 (4): 587–605.

———. 2007. The implications of psychoanalysis for qualitative methodology: The case of interviews and narrative data analysis. *Professional Geographer* 59 (4): 537–546.

———. 2010. Introduction: Psychoanalytic methodologies in geography. *Professional Geographer* 62 (4): 478–482.

———. 2011. Sexuality. In *A companion to human geography*, ed. J. Agnew and J. Duncan, 475–485. Oxford: Blackwell.

Thorne, Barrie. 1993. *Gender play: Girls and boys in school*. New Brunswick, NJ: Rutgers University Press.

Tolman, Deborah, and Tracy Higgins. 1996. How being a good girl can be bad for girls. In *"Bad girls"/"good girls": Women, sex, and power in the nineties*, ed. N. B. Maglin and D. Perry, 205–225. New Brunswick, NJ: Rutgers University Press.

Torres, Carlos Alberto. 1998. Democracy, education, and multiculturalism: Dilemmas of citizenship in a global world. *Comparative Education Review* 42 (4): 421–447.

Tuhkanen, Mikko. 2001. Of blackface and paranoid knowledge: Richard Wright, Jacques Lacan, and the ambivalence of black minstrelsy. *Diacritics* 31 (2): 9–34.

Valentine, Gill. 1996. Angels and devils: Moral landscapes of childhood. *Environment and Planning D: Society and Space* 14:581–599.

———. 2008. Living with difference: Reflections on geographies of encounter. *Progress in Human Geography* 32 (3): 323–337.

Walkerdine, Valerie, Helen Lucey, and June Melody. 2001. *Growing up girl: Psychosocial explorations of gender and class*. New York: New York University Press.

Weis, Lois, and Michelle Fine. 2000. *Construction sites: Excavating race, class and gender among urban youth*. New York: Teachers College Press.

Wiegman, Robyn. 1999. Whiteness studies and the paradox of particularity. *Boundary 2* 26 (3): 115–150.

Willis, Paul. 1990. *Common culture: Symbolic work at play in the everyday cultures of the young*. Milton Keynes, UK: Open University Press.

Winnubst, Shannon. 2006. *Queering freedom*. Bloomington: Indiana University Press.

———. 2010. Review essay. No future: Queer theory and the death drive. *Environment and Planning D: Society and Space* 28 (1): 178–183.

Yeğenoğlu, Meyda. 1998. *Colonial fantasies: Towards a feminist reading of Orientalism*. Cambridge: Cambridge University Press.

Zaslow, Emilie. 2009. *Feminism, Inc.: Coming of age in girl power media culture*. New York: Palgrave Macmillan.

Žižek, Slavoj. 1997. Multiculturalism, or, the cultural logic of multinational capitalism. *New Left Review* 225:28–51.

———. 2008. *Violence*. London: Profile Books.

Index